HOW LANGUAGE WORKS IN POLITICS

The impact of vague legislation on policy

Matthew Williams

BRISTOL
UNIVERSITY
PRESS

First published in Great Britain in 2018 by

Bristol University Press
University of Bristol
1-9 Old Park Hill
Bristol
BS2 8BB
UK
t: +44 (0)117 954 5940
www.bristoluniversitypress.co.uk

North America office:
Policy Press
c/o The University of Chicago Press
1427 East 60th Street
Chicago, IL 60637, USA
t: +1 773 702 7700
f: +1 773-702-9756
e: sales@press.uchicago.edu
www.press.uchicago.edu

British Library Cataloguing in Publication Data
A catalogue record for this book is available from the British Library

Library of Congress Cataloging-in-Publication Data
A catalog record for this book has been requested

978-1-5292-0020-1 hardback
978-1-5292-0021-8 ePdf
978-1-5292-0023-2 ePub
978-1-5292-0024-9 Mobi

Cover design by blu inc.graphics ltd.
Printed and bound in Great Britain by CPI Group (UK) Ltd, Croydon, CR0 4YY
Bristol University Press uses environmentally responsible print partners

MIX
Paper from responsible sources
FSC® C013604

For Teddy

Contents

List of figures and tables

Figures

Tables

Preface

I have long been fascinated (even mildly obsessed) by politics. However, this is not for highfalutin reasons. Politics, to me, is a sometimes-grubby soap opera. Like a box set, I cannot, dare not, tear my eyes away from the drama. In my doctoral research, I became fixated on what I saw as a foundational battle in this drama – the battle for supremacy over language. In any country purporting to be democratic, it is language that is the ultimate medium of conflict. Violence and intimidation can, it is true, be used democratically, but only when abetted by rules of law. As such, years of tense bargaining and swirling multilayered ambitions are captured and promulgated through humble words.

When considering representative democracy, a principal requirement is therefore that language represents reality to some extent. It is common to define representativeness as the *re*-presentation of interested parties by competent proxies at negotiations over scarce resources. However, those proxies must also conclude negotiations with a construction of words that represents something meaningful, and legitimate. Words, their grammatical arrangement and their range of possible meanings are at the foundations of political dispute. Even storing these words for future generations is fastidiously regulated. As recently as March 2017, it was finally accepted that Acts of Parliament need not be recorded on durable vellum, after half a millennium of so storing them. Acts will continue to be stored, of course, but on a modern synthetic medium, rather than calf-skin.

My particular route into this battle over language was via the study of judges in British politics. Scorn was poured by some in the media and government on judges as unwelcome interlopers in public policy. Criticism was especially stern when judges ruled against the government and in favour of asylum seekers and immigrants. I wanted to work out why judges were interloping. A rudimentary hypothesis emerged when I examined what precisely it is that judges do, and have tried to do since as far back as Solomon. Adjudication – the only truly pre-democratic mode of governing to have survived the 20th century – is at essence an independent-minded arbitration over what is true, and, where possible, what is just. Truth and justice have, for centuries, been recorded in publicly accessible messages passed between government and governed. My contention was that judges will arbitrate more creatively if these messages from government to governed are less meaningful. This contention underpins the book.

Political language is less determinate today than it was, with various significant policy consequences.

There are rich theories that have long considered the interplay of reality with our perceptions and presentations of it. My aim was to take advantage of modern computing to measure such uses of language comprehensively. This book is hence a work of history, but with a 21st-century twist of lime. In these pages, I present machine-reading results from practically every primary public law enacted by Parliament since 1900. That amounts to some 41.5 million words communicated to British citizens over more than a century. There are also similarly detailed analyses of immigration cases, homelessness provision, anti-discrimination laws and national constitutions. These entirely new analyses reveal manifold difficulties faced by politicians in finding a form of words that is, on its face, meaningful. Considering recent hand-wringing at democratic decline and rising populism, these pages reveal a particular pathology of 21st-century statecraft. This pathology was revealed to me through a striking irony. By programming a computer to read everything the Mother of Parliaments has said since 1900, I was forced to use language with absolute precision. Yet, I uncovered a pattern of increased indeterminacy in political communication. As we continue into the Information Revolution, it was certainly a surprise to me that while clarity is valued in private-sector information management, in the public sector, we are seeing an increased reliance on loose language and individual interpretative discretion.

There are some alarming implications. If politicians continue to under-represent truth and justice in their uses of language, citizens may not trust the authority of any public utterance. In an age of post-truth, #fakenews and disdain for expertise, much may be consequent on communicative indiscipline. However, my aim is not to chide. Political parties in advanced democracies are generally well aware that they struggle to connect with voters and speak to them plainly. In the contexts of transnational capital flows, ecological threats and global terrorism, it is difficult to construct meaningful statements of how a country, on its own, should perceive its own reality. It is contextual uncertainty that overwhelms textual clarity, therefore. Furthermore, politicians are not rewarded for 'straight talk' under these circumstances. A truth-telling Cassandra, ironically, is hard to believe because their messages appear so austere and pessimistic. However, the opposite situation, of Pollyanna-politicians painting in rosy hues, does breed cynicism when reality bites.

This book is empirical history. It describes what has been, not what ought to become. There is nonetheless an unavoidable lesson to draw

– that any citizen keen to enhance democratic performance needs to consider how language is used by the powerful to represent reality and justice. Besides what institutions say, it matters how they say it, and how the rules of politics are set up to encourage politicians to speak plainly to citizens. Obsessive observers of politics, such as myself, may revel (and even modestly profit) from dramatic unpredictability. However, to solve knotty social problems, we need a form of words that is accessible and functional. Text needs, at least in part, to dominate context.

Producing this book would have been unthinkable without the support, kindness and constructive cajoling of others. Especially heartfelt thanks go to my DPhil supervisor – Professor David Robertson. David sadly died in 2017, but I am constantly reminded of his wonderful tutorials. He is sorely missed and certainly not forgotten.

I am also in the debts of my DPhil examiners – Peter Edge, Christopher Hood, Nick Owen and Stewart Wood. I had the exhilarating yet terrifying experience of sitting an early viva in 10 Downing Street thanks to Stewart Wood. In addition, I am very grateful, in particular, to Christopher Hood and Nick Owen for supporting my career with letters of recommendation and teaching jobs. In a similar vein, I should very much like to thank those who have supported me in various ways as a junior academic, especially Bill Child, Elias Dinas, Ruth Dixon, David Doyle, Alex Lumbers, Paul Martin, Caroline Mawson, Karolina Milewicz, Alan Renwick, Petra Schleiter, Noa Schonmann, Marc Stears, Zofia Stemplowska, James Tilley, Stuart White, Stephen Whitefield and Radek Zubek. In addition to which, the Political Studies Association and the convenors of its Parliaments Group have been exceptionally kind in allowing me to present early drafts. Thanks to you Marc Geddes, Louise Thompson and Alexandra Meakin, in particular. Also, thanks are due and gladly given to Rebecca Tomlinson of Bristol University Press for inviting me to submit a book proposal and supporting me at every step thereafter. I am likewise grateful for the kind and constructive comments of anonymous reviewers, and the help of copyeditors, proofreaders and indexers.

Finally, I wish to thank my loving family, especially the amazing (and patient) Claire and my son, Teddy. Writing is not an activity that I feel confident in, but family provided both the motivation and support needed to keep on. When it comes to constructing a shared and meaningful language, predicated on respect, understanding and love, my family have always shown me the way.

Jesus College, Oxford
December 2017

Part One: Language and politics in the UK

ONE

Introduction: how language works in politics

> there is one thing more, about which the Society has been most sollicitous; and that is, the manner of their Discourse: which, unless they had been very watchful … had been soon eaten out, by the luxury and redundance of speech. The ill effects of this superfluity of talking, have already overwhelm'd most other Arts and Professions; insomuch, that when I consider the means of happy living, and the causes of their corruption, I can hardly forbear recanting what I said before; and concluding, that eloquence ought to be banish'd out of all civil Societies, as a thing fatal to Peace and good Manners.
>
> *Sprat 1722 [1667]: 111*[1]

Bishop Sprat, just quoted, laid praise on the young Royal Society for its plain use of language. He went so far as to say that 'eloquence ought to be banish'd out of all civil Societies'. By eloquence, he meant language that sounds intelligent but fails to communicate any clear messages. The problem with eloquence is that only the individuals using the language fully understand what has been said. It is an exclusive form of communication. It is communication that works for those with the power and prestige to avoid searching analysis of what they have actually said. Put baldly, eloquence is language that does not work as a general medium of communication. It works instead as a means of bamboozling an audience, or intimidating them into silent approval.

[1] With thanks to Daniel Curtis, editor of *Cherwell*, for drawing my attention to this quote.

This book asks as its principal question: how does language work in politics? In addition, and by extension, what impact does language have on the effectiveness of policy? The particular language interrogated in these pages is parliamentary legislation. This language is not prone to eloquence in the manner described by Sprat, but legislation can and does contain parts of speech that similarly fail to communicate clear meaning. The principal answers offered in these pages are: first, that legislative language has undergone major changes in form and function since 1900; and, second, that it increasingly takes a form that does not work at communicating clear policy instructions, with the implication of this second point being that indeterminate language in legislation undermines effective policy delivery. The book offers the first computer-assisted analysis of all 41.5 million words of parliamentary legislation enacted from 1900 to 2015. Findings show that changes in the language of legislation have had significant policy and social impacts. Particular findings include the observation that conjunctions in immigration law make the government more likely to lose court battles. It will also be shown that loose adjectives such as 'vulnerable' in homelessness law have led to thousands of individuals being denied housing assistance. There is even evidence in these pages that high numbers of adjectives in a national constitution are correlated with poor economic performance, as well as corruption. Other chapters look at how indeterminacy can be attenuated with, among other things, human rights law. These laws provide a sort of policy dictionary capable of inserting meaning into otherwise meaningless legislation. However, even these instruments have not filled the gaps in Britain's legislative language. This language of the sovereign Parliament is therefore a variable that affects policy outcomes, and the effects of language are, in part, independent of the forces that created it. When meaning cannot be carried by legislation, it does not strictly work as a form of discourse. Instead, it creates partial meaning and waits to be adapted by individuals responding to events.

From logic to analogic

Fans of crisp radio quality have welcomed 'the digital switchover'. Simple binary strings of data replaced rich-textured, yet distortion-prone, analogue radio. However, the language of politics has been making the opposite move. In the past, legislation was dominated by simple 'if *A*, then *B*' logical propositions. However, the language of legislation increasingly requires more reasoning by analogy to be meaningful. Analogic reasoning is the construction of meaning through comparison of real-world cases. A rule constructed by analogic reasoning is achieved in a process familiar to common law judges: of ensuring that like cases are treated alike. The problem is that analogic reasoning is, like its radio counterpart, prone to distortion. The language used to allow for the comparison of cases will typically be indeterminate. It is language that is both incomplete and subject to qualification. Unlike 'If *A*, then *B*' binary connections, it is instructions framed in the manner of: 'if *A*, in accordance with *B*-like factors, then *C* pertains, provided that *D* or *E* are satisfied'. Legislation increasingly does not, therefore, offer a determinate rule of law. This has implications for the implementation of policy, as well as the accountability of policy executives. It is these effects of indeterminate legislative language that are the principal subjects of this book.

However, what politics underlie indeterminate law? Specific propositions are detailed in the following paragraphs, as well as in later chapters. As an introductory summary, the politics of indeterminacy are a function of demands for and supplies of public policies moving out of kilter, the causes of which were at first historical, then ideological. With the end of the Second World War, Britain enjoyed moral and global superiority, but material enfeeblement. Domestic expectations for lavish public services were aroused by the Beveridge Report and subsequent state expansions into health care and social insurance. Yet, the British government lurched from crisis to crisis when attempting to manage transnational economic forces, without sufficient means.

In this context, indeterminate law offered both intrinsic and functional utilities. Intrinsically, indeterminate law is politically cheaper, in the sense of requiring less detailed *ex ante* deliberation, and admitting less *ex post* accountability. The meaning of indeterminate words can be fixed on a later date by ministers without incessant resort to Parliament for approval. Hence, functionally, indeterminate law appears to be better suited to squaring the circles of having so many demands with seriously constrained and uncertain material and political supplies. In addition, crucially, indeterminacy was facilitated by the Westminster Model. Britain's Parliament, with its unimpeachable sovereignty, is stewarded in its sovereign acts by governments that can utilise whips, standing orders and dissolution to cajole. In any country with procedural and substantive constraints on producing legislation, such degrees of indeterminacy would be significantly more difficult to extract from a legislature.

As mentioned, indeterminacy is a function of both demand and supply. It is not simply the case that the British public do not know what they want, or what is possible to achieve. Put technically, goal ambiguity in public policy is not a sufficient explanation for indeterminate legal language (Rainey and Jung 2015). Also at work has been the deliberate withholding of clarity for ideological reasons. In particular, Thatcherite disapproval of rationalist philosophies, and the lauding of pragmatism, spurred even greater resort to indeterminate expressions of sovereign will in the 1980s. Furthermore, it was not only Thatcherite politicians who disapproved of shared consciousness, expressed in plainly worded agreements. Unions, civic organisations, political parties of various hue and even religions became, after the 1960s, inured to individualist axioms. Coordinated interpretations of reality were replaced by authoritarian interpretations, and individual expressionism. Put differently, all perspectives are deemed valuable, but only those backed by material and political power will get anywhere.

At root, the politics of indeterminacy are more led by structure than agency, in that while individuals have at times chosen to be unclear, this was largely in response to the perceived requirements of context. Hence, the changing demography of Parliament is likely to have had an impact, with turnover to neophyte MPs and the increased diversity of members. However, for the most part, lawmakers are bounded in their rationality. It seems unlikely that they were acting malevolently or irrationally. Instead, politicians are bounded, in particular, by time, scarce resources, media interest, electoral cycles and globalisation. So, it is not that politicians were unclear as to what should be done, but that they were more unclear on how, and with what resources. Hence, indeterminacy derives more from supply-side constraints than demand-side ambivalence. This explains the significant inter-party consistency in moves towards indeterminacy, albeit that there are some interesting patterns revealed in Chapter Three, with Conservatives more inclined to craft indeterminate powers and Labour preferring indeterminate duties.

At root, sovereignty depends on a degree of clarity. Absolute power cannot work absolutely if it is only partially communicated. Legal texts need, therefore, to guide interpretations of context, subtext and intertextuality. That legal texts have increasingly failed to so guide is fitting with Britain's penchants for pragmatic and ideologically unburdened government. However, as will be argued and demonstrated, widespread indeterminacy in law creates ineffective and anti-pragmatic governance. Besides the effects on policy, there are wider implications for democratic theory as Parliament has increasingly failed to make its voice heard. Sovereignty has partly returned to its pre-democratic default of executive dominance, broad unaccountable discretion and heightened secrecy. The social consequences are similarly alarming. Might is right as the weakest lose disproportionately in battles over the meanings of words. It is little wonder that the legal profession has grown enormously in size, servicing, for the most part, those citizens with the material means to assert their preferred interpretations of indeterminate law.

Before proceeding further, an illustration is needed. The following excerpt from section 189 of the *Housing Act 1996* exemplifies modern legislative language. This extract describes the concept of priority in homelessness law:

> (1) The following have a priority need for accommodation –
>
> (a) a pregnant woman or a person with whom she resides or might reasonably be expected to reside;
>
> (b) a person with whom dependent children reside or might reasonably be expected to reside;
>
> (c) a person who is vulnerable as a result of old age, mental illness or handicap or physical disability or other special reason, or with whom such a person resides or might reasonably be expected to reside;
>
> (d) a person who is homeless or threatened with homelessness as a result of an emergency such as flood, fire or other disaster.
>
> (2) The Secretary of State may by order –
>
> (a) specify further descriptions of persons as having a priority need for accommodation, and (b) amend or repeal any part of subsection (1).

The meaning of these subsections is indeterminate. First, adverbs and adjectives pepper the text. The Secretary of State, being the subject of these sentences, must determine their meaning. Words such as 'reasonably', 'vulnerable' and 'special' have little meaning until considered relative to a yardstick. No yardstick is provided in the legislation itself, and so must therefore be, in part, asserted by the Secretary of State and, in part, extrapolated from context. Second, with regard to the object of these sentences (a housing applicant), conditional conjunctions keep the meaning of priority pliable. The conjunction 'or', for instance, is used 11 times. 'Or' therefore accounts for nearly 10% of all words in the excerpt, and it allows the text to be adapted to varied circumstances, and individuals. Specifically, 'or' conjoins disparate conditions, such as 'physical disability or other special reason'. Third, the use of auxiliary modal verbs enables broad interpretations, with 'might' and 'may' being used instead of 'will' or 'shall'. Finally, enabling verbs in these subsections allow the Secretary of State (and National Assembly for Wales) to 'amend or repeal any part' of the subsection.

So, what has Parliament actually said here? The underlying philosophy is reasonably clear: housing allocations are to be prioritised to those most in need. However, specific details on how this philosophy is to be executed have been omitted. This language contrasts to the clarity of a precursor law from 1900, the *Housing of the Working Classes Act*:

> 1. Where any council, other than a rural district council, have adopted Part Three of the *Housing of the Working Classes Act, 1890* (in this Act referred to as 'the principal Act'), they may, for supplying the needs of their district, establish or acquire lodging houses for the working classes under that Part outside their district.
>
> 2. Adoption of Part Three of the Act by rural district council …
> (2) In giving or withholding their consent under this section, the county council shall have regard –
> (a) to the area for which it is proposed to adopt the said Part; and
> (b) to the necessity for accommodation for the housing of the working classes in that area; and
> (c) to the probability of such accommodation being provided without the adoption of the said Part; and
> (d) to the liability which will be incurred by the rates, and to the question whether it is, under all the circumstances, prudent for the district council to adopt the said Part.

This language – as with all language – still depends on context and individual discretion to be meaningful. However, there is significantly less latitude granted to policy executives. A narrow range of possible interpretations has been established by Parliament. Put simply, it establishes more obligation than discretion. This can be inferred from the language. There are fewer adjectives and adverbs in the 1900 Act, with 'prudent' a lone counter-example.[2] Other potentially indeterminate parts of speech are couched as nouns, with 'the probability' and 'the liability'. These nouns are marginally more objective than would be their adjectival equivalents: 'probable' and 'liable'. The differences between 'probable' and 'probability' may be marginal, but are arguably significant. The former suggests a hunch, whereas the latter denotes a more precise evaluation. There are also fewer conjunctions in the 1900 Act. Furthermore, the whole section is rooted to the determinate modal verb 'shall', rather than 'may'. If we boil it down to something akin to a line of computer code it reads: 'the county council shall have regard … to the area … the necessity … the probability … and the liability'. This compares starkly to the 1986 Act and its adaptable encoding:

> The following have a priority need … a pregnant woman or … or might … a person who is vulnerable … or … or … or … or … or might … a person who is homeless or … or … The Secretary of State may … specify … amend or repeal.

What we see in the 1996 Act is language that requires significant post-enactment interpretation to be meaningful. This interpretation will be dominated by the government and its agents. Especial importance will be placed on how powerful policy executives analyse changeable circumstances. The 1900 Act, by contrast, offers greater clarity. Its language would also have required interpretation, but the range of plausible interpretations is narrower. However, as will be demonstrated in Chapter Two, language in legislation increasingly relies on indeterminate parts of speech. In the words of Lester and Piore (2004: 264): 'language evolves from clarity to ambiguity – in precisely the opposite direction of evolution that one finds in analytical problem-solving. Language development evolves, in other words, toward the creation of interpretative space'.

The digital to analogue metaphor used earlier is a simplification, but it highlights in essence a shift in legislative language and the 'creation of interpretative space'. Democracy is founded on the solidity of a social contract agreed to by citizens and state. Indeterminate language forms an asymmetric contract to the state's benefit. Individual state agents will decide what the language means in response to circumstances.

[2] Technically, 'rural' and 'county' are also adjectives, but here they impose no interpretative difficulties.

Of course, cherry-picked comparisons of two Acts of Parliament are no basis for inference. Therefore, this book offers unusually detailed analysis of 6,635 statutes, 148,275 sections and 41,579,744 words[3] enacted by Parliament between 1900 and 2015. Every single word of legislation has been analysed, with the omission of just 25 Acts of Parliament that have no available digital copies.[4] These 25 laws amount to just one third of 1% of the entire legislative output in the 115-year scope of this book. It is the most comprehensive analysis to date of UK legislative language. Capacity for such analysis comes from machine-reading technologies, similar to those used in modern search engines. Specifically, I have applied the natural language processing (NLP) capabilities of the Natural Language Toolkit (NLTK) software to read and analyse the data set.[5] All data are freely available to download at the website associated with this book.[6] Readers are also invited on this site to analyse any text in English, using the same program that produced the snapshot shown in Table 1.1.

Six times the number of words were enacted during 2011–15 as compared to 1900–04. Besides this obvious and well-documented increase in legislative output, contemporary Acts are also more reliant on parts of speech that have indeterminate meaning. This change

Table 1.1: Comparisons of all legislation enacted during 1900–04 and 2011–15

	Variables	1900–04	2011–15
Statutes	Total number of statutes	211	132
	Total number of sections	1,945	5,392
	Mean number of sections per statute	9	43
Words	Total number of words	296,306	1,820,614
	Mean statute length in words	1,404	13,793
	Mean preamble length in words	18	54
Parts of speech (per section)	Mean number of adjectives and adverbs	3	12
	Mean number of conjunctions	9	13
	Mean use of 'may' or 'might' modal verbs	1	3
	Mean use of 'shall' or 'will' modal verbs	3	0
	Mean use of 'make' or 'amend' enabling verbs	0	1

Note: Excludes all financial legislation and scheduled material.

[3] This figure excludes all scheduled material, which was not analysed. The figure also excludes the 231,310 words in all preambles, which were analysed separately.

[4] These omitted Acts are listed in the Appendix.

[5] This software runs on the Python programming language.

[6] See: http://matthewlippoldwilliams.com

in determinacy has not been subject to sufficient scrutiny, and begs several questions that will be addressed here. Besides a synoptic view of 41.5 million words, I will describe how important individual words can and have been. The adjective 'vulnerable', cited earlier in the 1996 Act, has made it noticeably more difficult for homeless applicants in England to find a place to stay. A word like that has no *prima facie* meaning, and was not sufficiently defined in legislation. Its meaning has developed through use. It was interpretation by repeated analogic reasoning – by comparing and contrasting more or less 'vulnerable' applicants. The policy was therefore adaptable to shifting conceptions of vulnerability, but its meaning was subject to wide discretion, as well as the vicissitudes of context.

This introductory chapter begins by further elaborating the questions, arguments and aims of the book. This is followed by a review of the literature and an explanation of this book's contribution. After which, the research designs used are described, as is the progression of the argument through the book's chapters. The final section offers concluding remarks.

Questions, arguments and aims

There are four core questions addressed in this book: first, 'How has Parliament's use of language changed?'; second, 'Why has Parliament's use of language changed?'; third, 'What impact have the changes had on policy?'; and, fourth, 'What can and has been done to address indeterminate legislation in the UK, and in other countries?'. This book is, in essence, a modern history of British institutions. Here, 'institutions' refers to the 'rules of the political game' (Hall and Taylor 1996). As with any rules, institutions curtail individuals' autonomy, and constrain will. Institutions therefore rely on norms of decision-making, or proscribe action, rather than allowing for unrestrained choice (March and Olsen 1989: esp ch 3 on 'Interpretation and the institutionalization of meaning'). Language is the principal tool by which institutions transmit instructions. A lack of plainness in legislation points to institutional failure as being an inability to communicate will effectively. This is an overlooked aspect of institutional failure, with significant consequences for policy, and society. It is with regard to the effects of indeterminate legislation that the book's analysis is dominated. Three chapters assess the impact of specific variations in the subjects, objects and verbs of legislation. These chapters interrogate evidence from, respectively, central government powers to manage immigration, local government duties to tackle homelessness and supranational rights against discrimination. The findings are detailed to the extent of predicting how far conjunctions affect the implementation of immigration policy, and the degree to which an adjective in homelessness law precipitated unintended and grave consequences.

For the four questions outlined earlier are the following principal arguments. The first is descriptive: that the language of UK legislation became significantly more indeterminate between 1900 and 2015, with accelerated change after the war. Increased indeterminacy in legislation was caused by rising policy ambition, with diminished capacity and will to guarantee outcomes. As telegraphed earlier, there was a growing disequilibrium between demands for and the available supply of public power. With relatively few barriers to policymaking in Britain, there was a profusion of new laws to address the public clamour for action. Indeterminacy was symptomatic of uncertainty, as well as occasional ambivalence as to what law is able to achieve (Bauman 1991). This demand and supply disequilibrium accelerated markedly post-war, especially after the 1960s. There was, around that time, and subsequently, reduced capacity to guarantee policy outcomes given the contexts of globalisation and the UK's relative economic decline. Policymakers were incentivised to draft laws that ensured flexible decision-making, with wide discretion to change policy where circumstances demanded it. Interpretative space in the language of law meant that *ad hoc* solutions could be created to cater for multiple foreseen and unforeseen eventualities.

Such elasticity in the rule of law had intuitive advantages for efficiency. Policy change could be achieved with an individual's assessment of circumstance. However, elasticity also diminished accountability and prioritised pragmatism over principle (Strøm et al 2003). Rather than a clear mandate for action, governments increasingly sought forgiveness for their behaviour after the fact (Whitefield 2006). Clear promises, grounded in principle and ideology, have been rejected by successive generations of lawmakers in favour of a 'what matters is what works' scaffolding. It was policy without politics, in that indeterminate law has no undergirding thesis on how power may be used, or why its use is justifiable. As such, policy was made and the battles over its legitimacy came later. As Theodore Lowi (1972: 299) put it, 'policies determine politics'. It leads to the book's primary empirical contribution: that increasing reliance on indeterminate language in legislation – especially adjectives, adverbs, conditional conjunctions and the modal auxiliary verb 'may' – reduced policy effectiveness.

A further nuance to this argument is that legislative language had independent effects – independent, that is, from the forces that created the language. Of course, one could say that it is political uncertainty that created indeterminate legislation, which is the ultimate cause of policy ineffectiveness. However, it will be demonstrated that the language of politics had independent effects on policy delivery, exacerbating but also separable from the forces that created the indeterminacy in the first place. Legislation operates at a meso-level, between social and political inputs, and specific policy outputs that attempt to assign value authoritatively (Easton 1965). This book aims to lift the lid on the precise mechanism by which social demands are converted into language that then affects policy outcomes. A principal requirement of institutional and policy effectiveness is for language to coordinate and communicate between institutions, and from institutions to citizens. Yet, this component of institutional operation (and failure) has been somewhat overlooked in existing empirical research as being either ephemeral or entirely contingent on forces higher up the causal chain.

Policy effectiveness – the dependent variable – is difficult to measure. It can also be difficult to prove, that is, if the intended effects of policy are described so broadly that any and all outcomes count as effective. As such, it will specifically be demonstrated that indeterminate parts of speech affect the feasibility and desirability of policy (Pollitt and Bouckaert 2004; Christensen 2008). These broad headings are further refined into four observable facets. Indeterminate policy language, it is argued, undermines feasibility by affecting the delegation and accountability of power (Strøm et al 2003). In other words, indeterminate language in legislation enables significant 'bureaucratic drift', where policies are subject to many and varied interpretations (McCubbins et al 1987). Indeterminate language will also affect the desirability of policy by specifically undermining coherence and legitimacy (March and Olsen 1989), with coherence here denoting not only the internal coherence of a policy, but its connection to other public policies, and legitimacy here referring to voters' ability to comprehend and authorise policy.

Where feasibility looks to the coordination of policy among state actors, desirability looks to the public's response. It is the feasibility of policy for which the majority of analysis and evidence is offered, simply because this offers the more readily observable effects of changing language. The research strategy employed here has been to test hypotheses on how interpretations of policy 'work' in the presence and absence of indeterminate language. By focusing on policy interpretation, there is detailed analysis of the decisions reached by courts, local government administrators and private litigants. All of these actors attempt to establish a lasting interpretation of indeterminate legislation.

However, before judges and others can interpret language, the first-order effects of changing legislation are to the interpretative space available. This interpretative space can be stretched, narrowed and repositioned with indeterminate language. The following parts of speech are especially important. First, adjectives and adverbs used in legislation allow key concepts to be stretched or narrowed. This is important not only as regards the delegation and accountability of policy power, but also as regards its broader coherence and legitimacy. Concretely, it will be shown that adjectives and adverbs have allowed local authorities to narrow the interpretations of 'vulnerable' and have thereby limited the duty owed to homeless applicants. Second, conditional conjunctions affect the coordination of policy between state institutions. These, again, allow interpretative space to be stretched or narrowed, but have particular impact on how legal texts relate to context. By stringing together ifs, ors and ands, a law will expand the potential range of contexts in which the language can be applied. This will likely encourage dispute between institutions (such as between the government and the courts) in determining to what extent the law can or should be stretched or narrowed. Concretely, conjunctions will be shown to have instigated battles between the government and the courts over immigration policy. Indeed, the courts will more often rule against the government when immigration law contains indeterminate conjunctions. Third and fourth, modal auxiliary verbs and enabling verbs (as in 'the Secretary of State *may make*') create the possibility of repositioning interpretative space. The Secretary of State *may* decide to *make* new language that offers new challenges for interpretation. In addition, modal and enabling verbs create significant intertextual indeterminacies. This is where the interpretation of primary law is set against large quantities of secondary legislation and administrative rules. It is also likely that discretion for executives to interpret language will affect the timing and specific application of policy. Pulling together the threads, when interpretative space is not fixed by authority, it undermines inter-institutional coordination and empowers individuals with the power to determine meaning in line with their interests, or the perceived exigencies of context.

The aim here is not to present a moral case; this is an empirical work. What follows is the story of how UK policymaking and delivery have developed over more than a century. The work is founded on robust statistical analyses. Indeterminacy in law is not indicative of personal failings. Civil servants and politicians who draft legislation are not at fault for seeking to reconcile demands for policy change with the complex reality of what can be achieved.[7] This is not to say that indeterminacy is inevitable; choices can be made. However, more precise evidence is needed so that citizens and practitioners can see the consequences of indeterminate language in legislation. While efficient policy change may appear desirable in an uncertain world, there are significant consequences to policy effectiveness that undermine any gains from efficiency. This book provides evidence to buttress these claims. To do so, it opens up the policymaking black box so that we may peer at the medium used for communicating and authorising policy change. This book could be described as a history of democratic cybernetics, with political cybernetics describing any coding language used to coordinate state and society. Language is an under-studied variable affecting British policymaking. A focus on this essential ingredient of democratic politics is the principal contribution of this work.

State of the art

This is a history of the operation of language in British politics. So, what specifically does the book contribute to the existing literature? Theoretical, empirical and practical contributions are offered. This section begins by describing the book's theoretical framework. This broadens to a description of recent research on language in politics. After which is a discussion of the literature on policy effectiveness and its social impacts. This, in turn, segues to analysis of how democratic theory can be enhanced by studying language. The final paragraphs of this section describe the book's interdisciplinary utility and justify an empirical focus on the UK.

The centrality of language to democracy has been most notably emphasised by Vivien Schmidt's work on 'discursive institutionalism' (Schmidt 2008, 2010). Her theoretical framework anchors this book, and these pages offer detailed evidence of the phenomena she theorised.

[7] The 'Good Law' initiative of the Office of the Parliamentary Counsel makes plain that civil servants value well-crafted statutes (see, for instance: https://www.gov.uk/guidance/good-law). In addition to which, the Law Commission regularly advises on improving the quality of laws, and there are subject-specific experts empowered to review and report on legal quality, such as the Independent Reviewer of Terrorism Legislation.

Discursive institutionalism emerged from the 'new institutionalisms' of the 1980s and 1990s (Hall and Taylor 1996), as well as the 'turn to ideas' in political science and constructivism in International Relations (Hay 2008). Schmidt identified two keys discourses – coordinative and communicative – that mediate interactions between institutions, and between institutions and citizens, respectively. Schmidt's focuses on inter-institutional and extra-institutional discourses brought together strands of other institutional theories. As Schmidt (2008: 310) put it herself:

> Political scientists tend to focus on a particular part of the public sphere; some investigate the policy sphere, in which policy actors engage one another in a 'coordinative' discourse about policy construction, while others look at the political sphere, in which political actors engage the public in a 'communicative' discourse about the necessity and appropriateness of such policies.

Building on Schmidt's argument, indeterminacies in coordinative and communicative discourses undermine a 'logic of communication'. Such a logic is dependent on a funnelling process, where broad philosophies are translated into policies, which are, in turn, further specified into programmes of action (Schmidt 2008: 306–7). My findings demonstrate increasing rates of indeterminacy in coordinative and communicative discourses, to the extent that programmes of action come without obvious connection to policies or philosophies. The funnel has been upended, and a logic of communication is increasingly replaced by analogic reasoning. Practice dominates theory, in other words. The social impacts of this diminished logic of communication are significant, as will be demonstrated.

Alternative institutional theories propose different logics. Rational choice institutionalism, for one, describes a 'logic of consequences'. Under this logic, institutions and actors chase after their most-preferred policies in competition with other institutions and actors. Competing institutions (such as the executive and legislature) coordinate when there exists a policy that is more acceptable to them both than the *status quo* (Hall and Taylor 1996; Shepsle and Bonchek 1997). The issue with such theories is explaining behaviour when actor preferences are uncertain, or subject to ambivalence. It is these forces that encourage indeterminate communication. As such, studies of inter-institutional rationality can be significantly enhanced by analysis of their uses of language (Hönnige 2011).

A second powerful institutional theory to offer a logic is historical institutionalism. This school describes a 'logic of path dependence', where actors abide by well-established practices unless and until a major shock to the system undermines well-worn modes of thinking and acting (Pierson and Skocpol 2002). This theoretical frame can also benefit from analysing language. While continuities or sudden and significant moments of change are well-theorised, historical institutionalism is less helpful in explaining the slow and barely perceptible decay of institutional practices. By observing the language used by institutions, we can track these subtle alterations, which additively contribute to major changes in institutional operation and performance.

A further theoretical contribution of the 'logic of communication' is in assessing the connection between public demand and policy supply. The process of translating demands into authoritative language is not only an essential task for institutions, but also provides the first opportunity for institutions to fail in their broader task of distributing power and valuable services. If public will is indeterminately expressed, there are increased risks of moral hazard in policy implementation. There is also an increased emphasis on individual competence and discretion over the authority of shared ideas. This can further explain phenomena such as the 'presidentialisation of politics', where politicians' personalities dominate policies (Poguntke and Webb 2005). It can also help explain why policy decisions are often incomprehensible to voters, and can sometimes be pursued under a shield of secrecy (Mettler 2011). Put simply, the language used by institutions is a crucial variable, which, besides the rules and origins of institutions, will contribute much to our understanding of day-to-day democracy. Democracy is a process for connecting facts, values and actions.[8] This all depends on shared language. Peter Hall's quote from Charles Anderson captures the point: 'the deliberation of public policy takes place within the realm of discourse … policies are made within some system of ideas and standards which is comprehensible and plausible to the actors involved' (Hall 1993: 279).

As regards the consequences of different policy languages, it has been argued, persuasively, that indeterminate policy language has important advantages. Rather than holding fast to plainly stated,

[8] Robert Dahl argued that democracy requires control of the agenda. To achieve this, there has to be a peaceful exchange of ideas, culminating in a clear communiqué that is broadly acceptable. Language is of utmost importance to all steps in this mechanism of agenda control (Dahl 1989).

but rigid commitments, policymakers can adapt 'vague' language as needed (Endicott 2011). Indeterminate language can be tailored to specific problems with minimal outlays of scarce resources, such as political capital. However, besides potential gains to specificity, and efficiency, there are the following core consequences to policy effectiveness. First, the meaning of indeterminate policy will more often, and more successfully, be challenged by different institutions, such as courts. Second, interpretation will be dominated by those institutions and private individuals sufficiently powerful to fight over the meanings of words. Might, in other words, is right. Third, policy will lack a sustained core meaning that endures over the long term, that is, meaning will be lacking without the intervention of courts, bureaucrats or powerful citizens, whose interpretations can deviate from those intended by policymakers.

There are five further moral implications of indeterminate legislation. First, and most broadly, yielding the determination of policy meaning to context is dehumanising. Policymakers have increasingly orientated their decisions to what Michael Freeden (1996: 344–5) has described as 'extra-human factors'. Legislative language does not express intent or will, but signals submission to circumstances. This has weakened the relationship between citizens and the state, and thereby affected trust in public institutions.[9] Second, indeterminate instructions have meant that accountability for decision-making has become more difficult to establish. Third, as judges would say, 'hard cases make bad law', and so, conversely, 'bad laws make hard cases'. Without clear authorisation from Parliament, there has been a need for more frequent and substantive interventions from other authoritative interpreters of political language – most notably, courts and bureaucrats. When taken with the dehumanising effects of indeterminate law, it should be no surprise that human rights law has become an important tool for trying to determine the meaning of policies (on 'new constitutionalism', see Stone Sweet 2000; Hirschl 2004).[10] Fourth, unclear law begets more law. Just as an incomplete line of computer code creates bugs, indeterminate legislation will create unintended errors in policy

[9] For a further critical theory angle to this discussion, see the debate over 'systems theory' between Jürgen Habermas and Niklas Luhmann (1971).

[10] McCubbins, Noll and Weingast (1987) found, in this vein, that the US Administrative Procedure Act and Freedom of Information Act enabled more effective oversight of regulatory agencies. By placing procedural and substantive requirements on agencies, these Acts reduced opportunities for agents to shirk their duties.

administration that will need to be fixed with more legislation.[11] This is an inefficient use of time and political resources. Finally, indeterminate law has raised an awkward question: what are legislators even for in the 21st century? If Parliament, on the advice of the government, enacts law of indeterminate meaning, it raises the question of whether this signals a legislature that is ill-equipped to deliver 21st-century policy. While much has been written on executive dominance under the Westminster model, less reported is how the Mother of Parliaments' declining power of speech contributes to her own irrelevance (see, eg, Richards 2008).

My interest in the language of policy was particularly inspired by two books, one by David Epstein and Sharyn O'Halloran, the other by John Huber and Charles Shipan. Epstein and O'Halloran (1999) used transaction cost analysis to explain how and why legislators delegated power to the executive, through more or less discretionary language. Building on this, Huber and Shipan (2002) argued that politicians will either draft very detailed legislation so as to micromanage policy implementation, or else they will draft 'vague' legislation to enable bureaucratic discretion. They focused on four variables that explain the granting of discretion through policy language. These are: policy conflict; the capacity to write detailed statutes; the bargaining environment; and the effect of non-statutory factors. My argument is that while lawmakers have reasons and impulses to draft indeterminate legislation, there are significant costs to policy effectiveness that are incurred by failing to establish a logic of communication. While, in many cases, discretion will enable the effective handling of complex policy, evidence suggests that legal indeterminacy leads to high-profile failures of institutions to achieve their policy goals over the long term.

Besides this general contribution are two further theoretical additions to Huber and Shipan's work. First, longer laws do not necessarily achieve greater clarity, and therefore 'micromanagement'. More important than word length are the parts of speech used. 'Garrulity' can, indeed, change the mode of communication (Voigt 2009; Bjørnskov and Voigt 2014). However, more important than word count is sentence structure and lexicon. It is the clarity by which key concepts are presented, organised and developed that counts most. The

[11] The so-called regulatory state entails the delegation of law-making powers to agencies, commissions and regional political authorities. This much is well known, and documented. However, less well known is the effect of specific parts of speech on the delegation of power, or the relative importance of delegated powers and powers that are indeterminately framed, undifferentiated or multifunctional.

addition to texts of, in particular, adjectives, adverbs, conjunctions, modal auxiliary verbs and enabling verbs typically disrupts plain exposition. Second, 'vague' laws do not necessarily indicate a desire to delegate decision-making power. Vagueness can also be the product of uncertainty or ambivalence. Vagueness can, therefore, be indicative of a refusal to take a firm decision, with a desire to nonetheless be seen as active lawmakers. This is an example of non-decision-making, as described by Bachrach and Baratz, and Steven Lukes (1974). Lawmakers sometimes prefer to kick the can down the road.

Besides the theoretical contributions, this book also offers empirical contributions. Most notably, the data frame used comprises very nearly the entire legislative output from over a hundred years. There has been no need for sampling or inferential statistics because the data set is as close to the universe of data as it is possible to be. This analysis of 41.5 million words required modern machine-reading technologies. It has allowed a variety of analyses to be conducted that are presented in succeeding chapters. Not only have all primary Acts of Parliament undergone discourse analysis, but so too, separately, have all immigration laws, all legislation pertaining to homelessness, all secondary legislation pertaining to anti-discrimination from 1987 to 2010, and every word from each Organisation for Economic Co-operation and Development (OECD) constitution (a further 644,422 words). This is the most comprehensive analysis of language in politics to date.

Machine reading has the added benefit, besides scale, of accurately measuring specific parts of speech. Modern NLP software is able to demarcate the differences between homophones. For example, a word like 'free' can be used as a noun, an adjective or a verb. NLP software can accurately distinguish these forms through a process of sentence 'chunking'. It makes for a more accurate appraisal than would be possible with word counts alone. This facility allows me to draw out specific hypotheses as to the effects of individual parts of speech. Also, by testing links between legislative language and policy outcomes, the book contributes to interdisciplinary studies of political language. The book, for instance, adds to the field of 'politico-linguistics', which crosses disciplinary divides, while remaining resolutely political in focus (O'Barr and O'Barr 1976). This book also contributes to an exciting intersection of theory and technology, which could be described as 'political cybernetics', with cybernetics here referring to legislation as a command language, designed to evaluate diverse inputs down to specific outputs (Deutsch 1966). The book also offers theory and data of use to academics and practitioners in law and public administration.

This segues to a specific, personal aim, which is to impress on my students the importance of law to politics. Undergraduate students of political science have few accessible texts that explain how legal language encodes a hotly contested policy, and how the language used can affect the administration of that policy and the accountability of its interpreters. There is also limited explanation for students of why policies fail for procedural reasons, and why judges increasingly intervene. Law needs to be analysed as an important explanatory variable, and not just as a constant or an unimportant medium.

As for the empirical frame, most of the literature on legislative language has focused on the US. This research agenda should therefore cross the Atlantic, with improved machine-reading technology, tailored theory and new data. This book focuses predominantly on the UK, albeit with a chapter on OECD constitutions. Language is an especially significant variable in British politics precisely because there is no higher-law constitution available as an interpretative aide. Each new Act of Parliament contains the sovereign's voice, undiluted. Variations in the clarity of this voice can have major repercussions for the agents of Parliament. This speaks to key debates in contemporary British politics. Specifically, it allows assessment of how, exactly, the sovereignty of Parliament operates and has historically operated. There are implications for the changing relationship between Parliament and the government,[12] and the partial transfer of sovereignty experienced during Britain's membership of the European Union (EU) from 1973 to, as seems likely at the time of writing, 2019 (Nicol 2001). Besides the conceptual considerations of what sovereignty has meant and currently means, there are more tangible findings, most notably, that the poor definition of legislative intent disproportionately hits the weakest, those who are less able to fight for their preferred interpretations of political language. So, in addition to arguing for the merits of taking back sovereign power from the EU, policymakers ought to consider the clarity of the sovereign's voice within the UK. In British politics, words are cheap. The legislature can change legal language with relative ease. As a resource, legislation is perhaps not considered with as much care as in other countries where the legislative text can be subject to a greater degree of inertia. This is not to say that parliamentarians are blasé about legislative language, just that the incentives and resources for backbenchers to assert clarity on the rule of law are relatively limited.

[12] See, for instance, Rod Rhodes' (1996) work on governance and the 'hollowing out' of British politics.

Besides the Westminster model, the other major civic innovation from the British Isles – common law – is also implicated. The increased enactment of legislation has partially codified areas of law that were hitherto open to judge-made construction (Merryman 1981). Yet, the increasing indeterminacy in legislation, and the subsequent need for analogic reasoning (comparing like cases alike), has meant that policy delivery increasingly entails methods that would be familiar to common law judges. As Alec Stone Sweet (2000: 204) put it with regard to a different context, there has been a historic shift in policy towards 'governing like judges'. Yet, despite the focus on British politics, with its idiosyncrasies, the theory and findings are relevant to any students of institutional politics and policy effectiveness. Inferences can be drawn from the findings as to the effects of indeterminate language. If we accept that democracy depends on the accurate transfer of shared language between institutions, it is reasonable to expect that variations in that language will affect the operation of public policy. Further to which, one corrective to heightened indeterminacy in legislation in the UK has been the enactment of constitutional statutes, such as the *Human Rights Act 1998*. This move towards enshrining basic legal rights matches a pattern towards a 'new constitutionalism' seen across new and advanced democracies (Hirschl 2004). Thus, neither problem nor solution are uniquely British.

It is worth noting what has been deliberately omitted from the book. This is primarily an empirical work, with little to say on how language should work. Thus, deliberately omitted from the book will be extended analysis of normative political theory, including critical philology and post-structuralism (à la Connolly 1974; Foucault 1988). Nor will the book contribute much to sociolinguistic debate (à la Labov 1972). Analysis of 41.5 million words could add to these literatures. For instance, one could analyse changing patterns in conceptual markers, such as the now-defunct 'working class' concept used in pre-war legislation, or one could look for the collocation of socio-economic concepts with qualifying descriptors, such as in 'reasonable needs'.[13] Also deliberately omitted from the book will be extended analysis of jurisprudence, with notable contributors to the debate on legal language including Ronald Dworkin (1986), Brian Bix (1993) and Timothy Endicott (2011). While analysing the effects

[13] See, for example, section 24 of the *National Health Service (Scotland) Act 1978*: 'Regulations may make provision … (a) for requiring … reports as to – (i) the number of medical practitioners required to meet the *reasonable needs* of their areas and the different parts of those areas'.

of language on policy and society will draw out moral and social implications, this is not the primary aim.

A potential flaw in this positivist approach is, ironically, whether 'indeterminacy' means anything itself. Brian Flanagan has argued that there is no literal meaning to any legal text. Law is language that shapes, but does not reflect, reality. Law is a form of social technology, designed to help change society, but it is not reliant on accurate, or plainly worded, social theory. If no law is determinate, then all law must be to some extent indeterminate (Flanagan 2010). Such a conclusion would render the book's various hypotheses as unfalsifiable. My resolution is to accept that there is no such thing as objectively determinate law that faithfully and unambiguously encapsulates social reality. However, when considered intersubjectively, as in the degree to which discussants can comprehend each other, there is more or less determinable legislation. This argument relies on the theory of 'post-positivism' espoused most clearly by the late Neil MacCormick (2005). He submitted that language is the primary source of law's meaning, but the language is only persuasive, not demonstrative. Pure positivism, as in objective law, is impossible. However, more or less comprehensible language can be observed and measured. This is why legislation is best considered as a form of discourse. It is a means of sharing information in a mutually understandable medium. However, that information does not need to be factually correct, or morally unimpeachable. Capturing this point is section 3 of the *Representation of the People Act 1983*: 'A convicted person during the time that he is detained in a penal institution in pursuance of his sentence is legally incapable of voting at any parliamentary or local government election'. This language is straightforward to interpret. The policy can therefore be executed faithfully. It cannot, however, be said that the language is objective in the sense of describing an incontestable ethical proposition. Indeed, trying to unpack the meaning of these sentences for an earth-visiting Martian would be extremely difficult. However, the language is plain. It encapsulates a clear 'logic of communication'. In that, those implementing the policy will be able to use the language in a wide range of cases with minimal risk of misinterpreting what the sovereign Parliament intended to say. It is this connection of intention to action through language that is fundamental to the 'logic of communication'. However, this is increasingly missing from legislation.

Operationalisation, research design and chapter summary

There are three parts and nine chapters in this book. The first part describes and explains changes to the language of British legislation by analysing every word enacted between 1900 and 2015. The second part of the book assesses policy effectiveness at three levels of government: central government powers to administer immigration law; local authority duties to enforce homelessness law; and individual anti-discrimination and equality rights derived from EU law. The third part of the book analyses how indeterminacies in the law are, or can be, attenuated. The first chapter of this final part provides international comparisons of constitutional language, and the clarifying potential of higher constitutional law. This chapter also details some of the effects of indeterminacy in these constitutional texts on economic performance and corruption. Following from this is a chapter looking at one of the UK's prominent 'constitutional statutes' – the *Human Rights Act 1998* – to gauge its success in removing, or clarifying, indeterminacies in other laws. The final chapter concludes by evaluating the theoretical, empirical and normative implications of the work.

Two key concepts used in succeeding pages describe the dependant and explanatory variables. These are, respectively, policy effectiveness and legislative indeterminacy. Policy effectiveness, as mentioned earlier, is operationalised as inter-institutional coordination, consistency and coherence in policy delivery. First, for powers, Chapter Four on immigration law looks to how well different state institutions can jointly comprehend legislative language and coordinate in its delivery. In this chapter, coordination between the government and the courts is analysed. Second, as regards duties, Chapter Five on homelessness law looks to the consistent application of the duty to house across different local authorities. Finally, with regards to individual and communal rights, Chapter Six on anti-discrimination law looks to how language affects the coherence of rights, and at how private individuals can and have fought for their preferred interpretations. To link with Schmidt's theoretical framework, these chapters consider, in turn, coordinative discourses (for immigration and homelessness) and communicative discourses (for rights). In addition to considering different modes of policy in powers, duties and rights, these chapters also assess different nodes of government at central, local and supranational levels.

As for the explanatory variables, 'indeterminacy' denotes language where more than one interpretation is possible without misreading (Dyevre 2005; MacCormick 2005). This is similar to the 'ambiguity' of language (Empson 1953). However, where ambiguity typically concentrates on semantics, 'indeterminacy' broadens the area of study to include what semioticians describe as pragmatics (Morris 1946; Kurzon 1986). Pragmatics considers how meaning is established in context. Certain lexical and grammatical features of a text can enable widely varied interpretations in context. Where ambiguity denotes confusion resulting from how words can be defined, and what was intended by the individual using them, indeterminacy considers, in particular, the disconnection between text and context. It is the difference between intrinsic and extrinsic sources of meaningfulness (Hiltunen 2012; Poscher 2012). Words may have intrinsic definition, but they cannot be reconciled neatly with real-world signifiers. Thus, in legislation, a section of an Act may be unambiguous and yet the true meaning is dependent on context and interpretative norms. A famous example of this possibility was offered by H.L.A. Hart. His thought experiment outlined a law banning all vehicles from a park. This would, he argued, create a sticking point if a decommissioned military jeep was to be used as a statue (Hart 1958). The sentence 'no vehicles are allowed in the park' is not ambiguous, and yet it is still capable of indeterminacy. 'Indeterminacy' will therefore be used throughout to describe key parts of speech whose meaning is incomplete or elided. As such, this book pursues a different research agenda to previous works on legislative language that have focused more on the meaning of language in itself. These works have conceptualised unclear language variously as displaying 'ambiguity' (Edelman 1992), 'indefiniteness' (Freund 1920),[14] 'irrelevant considerations' (Taylor 1976)[15] and 'vagueness' (Post 1994).

Here is a deliberate attempt to measure potential causes of meaninglessness, rather than meaning. Meaning is not a fixed, exogenous, variable that can easily be measured across a century. However, those parts of speech that contribute to meaninglessness (such as adjectives, conjunctions and modal verbs) can be measured and will consistently rely on circumstance and discretion to be made meaningful. Of course, through repeated use, some of these parts of speech will be subject to interpretative norms – such as the adjective 'reasonable' or the conjunction 'or' in 'the protection of health or

[14] This concept has been used in the dicta of US judges. It was famously declared in *Winters v New York* 333 U.S. 507, 524 (1948) that 'indefiniteness is not a quantitative concept'.

[15] Relevant and irrelevant considerations are more common to the British judicial review tradition (see Woolf et al 2007).

morals' from Article 8 of the *European Convention on Human Rights*. However, because the sovereign Parliament has not determined the meaning of these words, they are still capable of reinterpretation as and when new circumstances, or new interpreters, emerge. It is difficult to imagine many situations where a good lawyer could not convince a judge that either 'health or morals' were under threat, and the conjunction of these nebulous concepts creates further confusion. Do 'health or morals' apply to individuals or groups? To what degree of conjunction, or disjunction, are these factors to be applied? Words like this only enjoy transitory meaningfulness.

While a law may be greater than the sum of its individual words, these individual parts of speech nonetheless yield a significant impact on meaning. Measurement of individual words and their likely effects is a form of discourse analysis. This is a method associated with Michel Foucault and post-structuralism (Crowley 1989). However, besides these theoretical works, discourse analysis can also be used for analysing massive data sets by coding and isolating those parts of speech that discourse will depend on. This method of analysis is similar to content analysis, where two or more coders, or a coding algorithm, determine what a text means (Krippendorff 1980). The primary difference is that my method of discourse analysis does not seek to determine what laws mean, but rather seeks to establish which laws are more likely to mean nothing, and therefore require post-enactment interpretation. In addition to which, my use of computer-assisted coding requires no inter-coder reliability tests, and can be replicated with ease.

The causal mechanism linking indeterminacy and policy effectiveness is focused on the impact of meaninglessness. The requirement for significant post-promulgation debate as to meaning has a significant impact on who gets what, when and how (Lasswell 1936). However, the causal mechanism is not straightforward. The book's title – *How Language Works in Politics* – leans on the preposition 'in'. Legislative language does not unilaterally create outcomes, as might be inferred from a title such as *How Language Works on Policy*. There is a messy interaction of legislative language with, *inter alia*, history, culture and ideology. Pragmatic linguistics – where text depends on context to be meaningful – is coincident with pragmatic governance. Those governments seeking to 'travel light'[16] when it comes to ideology will intuitively prefer legislation whose meaning can be subject to reinterpretation, should the need arise. As such, the language of law is

[16] Ian Gilmour, a minister in the Thatcher governments, is quoted as saying: 'the wise Conservative travels light'.

created by broader social and political impulses. There is also potential for reverse causation, where ineffective policy spurs the creation of indeterminate policy language.

Despite language being nested within broader social forces, and despite the possibility of reverse causation, it is still theoretically plausible, and empirically testable, that different parts of speech affect policy delivery. Careful research design has nonetheless been necessary. This is so as to enable rigorous hypothesis testing, and the acknowledgement of complex causal mechanics. Different methods are used to test specific causal claims (on the merits of mixed-methods research designs, see Laitin 2002). Methods used include very large-N descriptive statistics, logistic regression analysis of court cases (for immigration), a natural experiment with difference-in-differences analysis (for homelessness), qualitative process tracing of changes to the interpretation of legislation (for anti-discrimination law), comparative regression analysis (for analysis of constitutional texts) and further process tracing (for analysis of the *Human Rights Act 1998*). Each method is described further in its corresponding chapter. What brings all of these methods together is the desire to offer a contemporary history of legislative language and its effects.

Conclusion

Some of the most impactful legislation of the past century has been constructed from short, plainly worded sentences. The *Parliament (Qualification of Women) Act 1918*, for example, has just two sections and 43 words:

> 1 A woman shall not be disqualified by sex or marriage for being elected to or sitting or voting as a Member of the Commons House of Parliament.
>
> 2 This Act may be cited as the Parliament (Qualification of Women) Act, 1918.

It is certainly not the case that modern legislation never attains pithiness. Take the momentous *European Union (Notification of Withdrawal) Act 2017*. This is also just two sections long, whose operative part, section 1, is a mere 45 words:

> (1) The Prime Minister may notify, under Article 50(2) of the Treaty on European Union, the United Kingdom's intention to withdraw from the EU. (2) This section has effect despite any provision made by or under the European Communities Act 1972 or any other enactment.

The only indeterminacy in this tiny statute is the modal verb 'may'. It was legally possible for the Prime Minister to have decided not to notify the UK's intention to withdraw from the EU. While this was hardly likely given the political climate of March 2017, it is not unheard of for ministers to construe 'may' as 'may not',[17] and it is typical for 'may' to be interpreted as 'may decide when it suits the government'.

Nonetheless, this 2017 Act is anomalous. More typical are the following three excerpts of powers, duties and rights enacted in various 2015 statutes. This was a year where the average statute was 32 sections, 66 pages and 12,000 words long. For powers, let us consider the *Criminal Justice and Courts Act 2015*, section 62A:

> Release on licence etc: compulsory electronic monitoring conditions
> (1) The Secretary of State *may* by order provide that the power under section 62 to impose an electronic monitoring condition must be exercised. (2) An order under this section *may* – (a) require an electronic monitoring condition to be included for so long as the person's release is required to be, *or may* be, subject to conditions *or* for a *shorter* period; (b) make provision *generally or* in relation to a case described in the order.

Italics identify the indeterminate parts of speech. In executing this power, there has had to be significant post-promulgation debate as to the whats, whens and hows of policy implementation.

Similarly, with regard to duties, section 36 of the *Counter-Terrorism and Security Act 2015* offers a striking example: '(1) Each local authority must ensure that a panel of persons is in place for its area – (a) with the function of assessing the extent to which identified individuals are *vulnerable* to being drawn into terrorism'. Local authorities 'must' empanel persons, whose function is to implement policy not by logical

[17] *R v Secretary of State for the Home Department ex parte Fire Brigades Union* [1995] 2 AC 513.

deduction, but analogic induction. Specifically, they will have to, by law, assess the relative vulnerabilities of different identified individuals to be drawn into terrorism. Again, implementation of this policy will be affected by the indeterminacy in its authorising statute.

Finally, for rights, section 9 of the *Consumer Rights Act 2015* also requires reasoning by analogy, rather than logical application:

> (1) Every contract to supply goods is to be treated as including a term that the quality of the goods is *satisfactory*.
> (2) The quality of goods is *satisfactory if* they meet the standard that a *reasonable* person would consider *satisfactory*, taking account of – (a) any description of the goods, (b) the price *or* other consideration for the goods (*if relevant*), *and* (c) all the other *relevant* circumstances.

In any dispute between a consumer and a producer, several indeterminate adjectives will need defining. The words 'satisfactory', 'reasonable' and 'relevant' have no clear meanings, and must be determined in disputed cases by comparison to like cases. This is statute law that operates more like common law. Rather than providing a statement of sovereign will, the statute allows principles to develop and adapt through use.

This book will describe and explain over a century's worth of change in the logic of communication used between and beyond British institutions, and despite the near-universal data set of primary legislation, these data skim the surface. Also important are private and hybrid Acts of Parliament. Notably, the *High Speed Rail (London–West Midlands) Act 2017* is hybrid legislation allowing for the construction of the 'HS2' line. This law is, on its own, close to 150,000 words long. There is also subordinate or secondary legislation, often referred to collectively as statutory instruments. This is legislation created by the government under powers in primary legislation. A portion of these instruments will be analysed with regard to anti-discrimination policy in Chapter Six, but the vast volume of this law is beyond the scope of this preliminary survey of legislative language. As Lord Phillips of Sudbury put it in a House of Lords debate:

> I am grateful to my noble friend for that reply, but is he aware that we legislate at between 200 and 400 per cent the rate of any comparable country in Europe? Is he aware that the cumulative effect of making legislation at the rate of between 11,000 and 13,000 pages a year over the past

> 15 years has been a state of indigestion in this country that some might call citizen constipation, which has parlous consequences?[18]

In addition, the government publishes significant quantities of administrative rules. In sum, there is a surfeit of law, spread through different formats. This creates inter-textual confusion, which, in turn, manifests as inter-institutional confusion. As the former UK Supreme Court Justice Lord Toulson put it (Ormerod and Laird 2015: 19): 'To a worryingly large extent, statutory law is not practically accessible today, even to the courts whose constitutional duty it is to interpret and enforce it'.

It is clear that a greater portion of our daily lives are touched by the long arm of the law. However, as argued, the volume of law is less impactful on policy effectiveness than its linguistic indeterminacy. If there was a glut of precise instructions of the form 'if *A*, then *B*', there would be little room for discretion or reinterpretation in response to events. The consequences for policy effectiveness, and, more broadly, parliamentary sovereignty, can be seen from a significant ruling reached following a judicial review of executive action. The case was *R v Secretary of State for the Home Department ex parte Simms.*[19] The Law Lords decided that rules banning interviews between prisoners and journalists breached a basic right to investigate the soundness of a conviction. The Home Secretary had declared the rules in secondary legislation. He had done so, he believed, in accordance with the parent legislation – the *Prison Act 1952* – which did not mention access to journalists. However, judges had to assume that without explicit authorisation, Parliament could not have intended for prisoners to be denied contact with journalists. As per Lord Hoffmann:

> Parliamentary sovereignty means that Parliament can, if it chooses, legislate contrary to fundamental principles of human rights.... But the principle of legality means that Parliament must squarely confront what it is doing and accept the political cost. Fundamental rights cannot be overridden by general or ambiguous words.... In the absence of express language or necessary implication to the contrary, the courts therefore presume that even the

---

18 House of Lords Hansard for 17 January 2011, Column 3 (retrieved 18 May 2011).

19 [1999] UKHL 33, [2000] 2 AC 115, [1999] 3 All ER 400.

> most general words were intended to be subject to the basic rights of the individual.

Using 'most general words' to frame policy creates confusion that requires extra-parliamentary actors to determine what must have been said. There are therefore striking implications of indeterminacy for the contemporary sovereignty of Parliament. The doctrine that all political authority derives from Parliament is a pillar of British constitutionalism. Yet, the comprehensibility of sovereignty is a significant variable, not a constant. Without a codified constitution to elaborate general predispositions, the fallback refrain in British statecraft is to 'make do and mend'. However, this lackadaisical refrain advantages those with the patience to make do, and with the resources to mend. The principle of parliamentary sovereignty certainly does not give much illumination to the questions of why policies increasingly face unpredictable application and see rapid turnover, and why politicians sometimes shirk accountability. A common complaint is that politicians cannot be trusted to hold a commitment, but a significant factor in public disengagement is that firm commitments are not even being made in the first place. This book will consider how Parliament's language is central to our understanding of sovereignty, and hence the contemporary workings of the British constitution. The next chapter lays bare the extent of the changes across 115 years and 41.5 million words.

TWO

Past: how has Parliament's use of language changed?

> Clearness is the main object to be aimed at in drawing Acts of Parliament. Clearness depends, first, on the proper selection of words; secondly, on the arrangement and construction of the sentences.
>
> An enactment in its simplest form is a declaration of the legislature, directing or empowering the doing or abstention from doing of a particular act or thing.
>
> *Thring 1902: 61*

In this opening quote, Lord Thring states what he believed to be the essential purpose of an enactment: 'An enactment … is a declaration of the legislature'. This conceptualisation was, as Thring admitted, simplistic. It nonetheless captured an essential position of legislation in the British constitution. Legislation was an instrument to resolve a problem in the common law (Goldsworthy 2004). A commandment or 'statutum' (the origin of the word 'statute') is, under this conception, a declaration of intent from Parliament to the courts, as well as government. If this was still true today, we would expect 'clearness' in the 'selection of words' and the 'arrangement and construction of the sentences'. However, as this chapter will demonstrate, legislation has undergone a change in linguistic form.

Lord Thring was the first ever head of the Office of the Parliamentary Counsel. That is the civil service team principally responsible for drafting government Bills. In collaboration with the sponsoring department and ministers, these legal specialists craft legislative language before sending it across to Parliament for debate, scrutiny and amendment. In Thring's time, most parliamentary counsellors were former conveyancing lawyers. They therefore brought fastidiousness from their world of drafting property deeds. That style of drafting favoured long sentences, with minutely detailed exposition. Take, as an example, one of the last Acts of Parliament that Thring would have overseen in his long career – section 1 of the *Ecclesiastical Assessments (Scotland) Act 1900*:

> Where in any parish it shall be necessary to impose an ecclesiastical assessment which, according to previous use and wont in the parish, would fall to be imposed according to the valued rent, but which it would be competent to impose according to the real rent, it shall be lawful for any valued rent heritor to request the clerk to the heritors to summon a meeting of valued rent heritors in the manner prescribed by section twenty-two of the Ecclesiastical Buildings and Glebes (Scotland) Act; and …

This sentence goes on for another 54 words, making for a total sentence length of 140 words. Some judges complained in the late 19th century that Acts of Parliament were excessively detailed, making it difficult to apply law to borderline cases. Of course, not all law attained the sort of clearness that Thring advocated. Clearly, one should not measure modern legislation against an unrealistic, or ahistorical, benchmark. Rather, the aim of this chapter is to demonstrate the significant increase in the degree of indeterminacy in legislation. Clear legislation is still enacted today, just as indeterminate legislation was enacted in 1900. However, the increases in volume and per section proportions of indeterminate language are such that legislation can no longer be described as, in essence, declaratory. Legislation is increasingly speculative and enabling of discretion. This chapter provides a quantitative and descriptive history of changes to legislative language between 1900 and 2015. Findings point to a significant change in the degree of indeterminacy, and support the conclusion that legislation has changed in kind, not just degree. Specifically, over half the sections of legislation from 1960 onwards had either of the two most impactful sources of indeterminacy: adjectives and conditional conjunctions. Having a majority of sections rely on these parts of speech is a reasonable basis for concluding that legislation has changed by degree and in kind.

Changes by degree and in kind

Parliament's use of language has changed significantly. To establish this thesis, there must be incontrovertible evidence of both changes by degree and in kind. This is, in turn, essential for the overall claim that changes to legislation have had implications for policy effectiveness. The changes are a result of, in particular, increased reliance on adjectives and adverbs, conditional conjunctions, indeterminate modal verbs, and verbs that enable discretion. The penetration of these parts of speech into sentence structure constitutes a different 'logic of communication' to that familiar to Thring and his contemporaries. This is despite notable efforts to improve the comprehensibility of modern statutes, such efforts including the publication of explanatory notes with Bills, as well as more comprehensible page layouts and increased opportunities for the pre-legislative and post-legislative scrutiny of texts.

The changing logic of communication points to increased difficulty in connecting policy ideas to action through the medium of legislation. This depends on four components of legislative language that correspond to the primary parts of speech analysed:

1. The substance of policy can be elasticated by adjectives and adverbs. These parts of speech qualify the meaning of nouns and verbs, respectively. This thereby requires the subject of the sentence (be it the government or a private citizen) to first resolve the conceptual fuzziness before acting on the power, duty or right established by the legislation (Goertz 2006). This is fundamentally important to ascertaining what the aim of policy is. An example is section 4 of the *Road Traffic Act 1988*:

   > a person shall be taken to be *unfit* to drive if his ability to drive *properly* is for the time being impaired. (6) A constable may arrest a person without warrant if he has *reasonable* cause to suspect that that person is or has been committing an offence under this section.

2. The substance and the procedure by which law is implemented are affected by conditional conjunctions. How law is reconciled with the facts of a case is especially important. These parts of speech call for disparate conditions to be conjoined before action on the language can be taken. Each conjunction of conditions can implicate the potential scope of law, and necessitates analysis

as to the correct degree of conjunction between facts and law. This has especial importance for the object of sentences (be it a power, a duty or a right). This is thereby of the greatest importance for ascertaining how far a policy can be extended. This expansive potential can be seen in Article 8 of the *European Convention on Human Rights*, which was incorporated into UK law via the *Human Rights Act 1998*:

> Everyone has the right to respect for his private *and* family life, his home *and* his correspondence. There shall be no interference by a public authority with the exercise of this right except such as is in accordance with the law *and* is necessary in a democratic society in the interests of national security, public safety *or* the economic well-being of the country, for the prevention of disorder *or* crime, for the protection of health *or* morals, *or* for the protection of the rights *and* freedoms of others.

3. The extent and timing of policy implementation is implicated by which modal verbs are used. Where 'may' enables broad discretion as to the extent and timing, 'shall' or 'must' are obligatory modal verbs. This can be seen with the *Human Tissue Act 1961*, section 1:

> the person lawfully in possession of the body of a deceased person *may* authorise the removal of any part from the body for use for the said purposes if, having made such reasonable enquiry as *may* be practicable, he has no reason to believe – that the deceased had expressed an objection to his body being so dealt with after his death.

4. Other verbs used also establish discretion, but are more important for changing policy substance. Notable in this regard are enabling verbs such as 'make' and 'amend' when tied to a specified agent. The most noted use of these verbs in legislation come with so-called Henry VIIIth clauses. These allow the government to amend primary legislation without needing to go through the usual parliamentary procedure for enacting new laws, as in the *Ceylon Independence Act 1947*, section 4:

> His Majesty may by Order in Council *make* such further adaptations in any Act of the Parliament of the United Kingdom of an earlier session than this Act, or in any

> instrument having effect under any such Act, as appear to him necessary in consequence of section one of this Act.

These four parts of speech (adjectives and adverbs are taken together) concern the operation of the subjects, objects and verbs of policy language. They also implicate the aims, scope, extent, timing and discretionary range of policy. The four can be grouped into two broad linguistic factors: contextual and discretionary. Adjectives, adverbs and conjunctions describe what the law is and how it may be reified in varied contexts. Modal verbs and enabling verbs describe how the law could be changed by discretion. All four parts of speech have the capacity to interact, but their effects are additive not multiplicative. It is not the case that an absence of one linguistic form negates the effect of all others. Also, as will be demonstrated in succeeding chapters, the four parts of speech typically have effects independent of each other, and do not significantly interact to effect case outcomes. Even 'may' and 'make' do not significantly interact in immigration policy, where there are many more instances of the modal verb 'may' than there are of the enabling verb 'make'.

A key operational definition for this chapter is 'change in kind'. How much change in the indeterminacy of legislation is sufficient for us to conclude that legislation has changed in kind? Focusing on those parts of speech that create contextual indeterminacy (adjectives, adverbs and conjunctions), a change in kind will be defined as being where there are better than even odds of a section of legislation containing either adjectives and adverbs, or conjunctions. This would mean that a majority of legislative sections contain one or both of these sources of indeterminacy.

However, it must be noted that meaninglessness in law can be attenuated. Legislation often contains sections that define key words. For instance, section 21 of the *Anti-terrorism, Crime and Security Act 2001* states: '"terrorism" has the meaning given by section 1 of the *Terrorism Act 2000* (c. 11), and "suspected international terrorist" means a person certified under subsection (1)'. There is even a whole Act devoted to clarifying indeterminacies in other statutes. The *Interpretation Act 1978* provides in its First Schedule a glossary of terms that provides definitions in the following manner: '"Bank of England" means, as the context requires, the Governor and Company of the Bank of England or the bank of the Governor and Company of the Bank of England'.

Despite these definitional sections, Parliament's voice typically remains indeterminate when couched in the parts of speech outlined earlier. Indeed, the literature on statutory construction attests to ongoing difficulties in confirming the sovereign's will (Cross et al 1995). Consider again the definition of 'terrorism' given by the 2001 Act. It refers us to section 1 of the *Terrorism Act 2000*, which provides the following definition. Indeterminate parts of speech have been highlighted:

> (1) In this Act 'terrorism' means the use *or* threat of action where – (a) the action falls within subsection (2), (b) the use *or* threat is designed to influence the government *or* to intimidate the public *or* a section of the public, *and* (c) the use *or* threat is made for the purpose of advancing a *political, religious or ideological* cause. (2) Action falls within this subsection *if* it – (a) involves *serious* violence against a person, (b) involves *serious* damage to property, (c) endangers a person's life, other than that of the person committing the action, (d) creates a *serious* risk to the health *or* safety of the public *or* a section of the public, *or* (e) is designed *seriously* to interfere with *or seriously* to disrupt an *electronic* system.

Again, it is worth stressing that no moral case is being advanced in this book. I am not arguing that the language used to define terrorism is inappropriate or immoral. The definition of terrorism is, in fact, reasonable, and the definition's adaptability is no doubt useful. The 2000 Act was written primarily with Irish terrorism in mind, and the 2001 Act, which draws on the same definition of terrorism, had religious extremism as its target. The aim is not to judge parliamentarians and parliamentary counsel for their drafting habits, but to describe how complex policies are framed and to consider what effects these framings can have.

Of the four parts of speech identified as impactful, the most important are hypothesised to be adjectives, adverbs and conjunctions. These implicate the aims and scope of policy. They are the principal causes of indeterminacy, where modal and enabling verbs create legal discretion, but create less linguistic confusion. In other words, modal and enabling verbs are legally indeterminate, but linguistically clear. Adjectives, adverbs and conjunctions are both linguistically and legally indeterminate. My argument is that linguistic indeterminacy is more impactful on policy than is the deliberate delegation of power by modal verbs or enabling verbs (Huber and Shipan 2002). It is reasonable to manage policy uncertainty with discretion delegated in law. What is less effective is discretion achieved through linguistic indeterminacy as this requires the construction of meaning, and thereby adds a level of policymaking that will be opaque and unaccountable.

What are the specific expectations? First, it is expected that there has been a significant increase in the volume of legislation enacted. This trend will not be linear as it is expected that a slight decline in output will be observable after the devolution of legislative competencies during the first New Labour government from 1997 to 2001. Second, as regards the degree of indeterminacy in law, again, increases on all four measures are expected. The theory expects that those parts of speech that affect the substance of policy (adjectives, adverbs and enabling verbs) will have undergone a linear increase in per section application, whereas those parts of speech that also affect the process of policy implementation (conditional conjunctions) will have undergone a quadratic path, with an overall rise, but a slight fall in more recent years. The split in results between substance and process matches the claim made in the Chapter Three that indeterminacy is a result of a mismatch between policy ambition and capacity. The ambition to attain significant policy change in response to uncertain circumstances has risen without abatement. Hence, there has been a linear increase in parts of speech that enable policy substance to be changed. It could alternatively be argued that a logarithmic growth is more likely, where policy ambition trails off with more and more policy instruments to hand (Cohen et al 1972). However, my expectation is that ambition to develop policy substance, despite constraints, has not trailed off. Indeed, besides ambition, indeterminacy itself creates a need for more indeterminate law, such that an important driver of increased indeterminacy in law is to manage past indeterminacies in law. This feedback loop could be expected to have caused an exponential increase in substantive indeterminacy. However, any exponent is likely to be very small as the primary driver of indeterminacy is ambition to develop adaptable policy, not to correct past mistakes. Therefore, the parts of speech expected to have a linear growth are adjectives, adverbs and enabling verbs. These parts of speech most affect what the policy is, rather than how it will work.

As regards the implementation of policy, conjunctions and modal verbs are more impactful on the hows and whens, rather than the whys and whats. The reason that these are expected to have risen in use before falling slightly is primarily because of decentralisation. Policy implementation has, in some domains, been decentralised to local authorities, devolved assemblies, executive agencies and non-governmental organisations. Parliament lacks the capacity to determine all policy outcomes in the peripheries to which it sends instructions. Tightening the range of possible implementation options is one approach at attempting to ensure its faithful execution. Indeed, changing public management attitudes of the past 30 years have, in theory, emphasised cost efficiency and managerial decentralisation. However, in practice, the UK model of 'new public management' has emphasised cost efficiency, and Whitehall has retained much of its power to manage policy outcomes (Hood 1991). As such, it is expected that the language used to implement policy will have loosened, then tightened again between 1900 and 2015.

Besides the expected per section changes to primary legislation, it is expected that a similar trend in adjectives, adverbs and conjunctions is observable in the preambles to all 6,694 statutes. This suggests that even describing laws in introductory terms is becoming more challenging for Parliament. One would not expect discretionary language, such as 'may' or 'make', to appear in a preamble, or, if these did appear, they would not be accepted as formal delegations of power. Finally, legislation concerning the public finances – the annual Finance Act(s), Appropriation Act(s), Consolidated Fund Act(s) and Supply and Appropriation Act(s) – will have fewer indeterminacies per section in general, and declining discretionary language ('may' and 'make') in particular.

Data and methodology

One of the most challenging aspects of this research was the collection and processing of an enormous corpus of legislative language. In order for the language to be analysed by the Natural Language Toolkit (NLTK) software, all 6,694 Acts had to be collected in plain text form, that is, text without any of the usual embellishments found on websites. To make text easy on the eye and accessibly presented, websites use 'mark-up' languages, such as hyper-text mark-up language (HTML) or extensible mark-up language (XML). A long process of web scraping was therefore required to extract all of these rich mark-up languages and convert files into plain text. The websites used for finding digital copies of legislation were legislation.gov.uk and justis.com. Together, these websites offer a comprehensive database of legislation. All laws can now also be found in plain text form on the website associated with this book.[20] Conditions on use and reuse of these data are provided under an Open Government Licence.[21]

Having transferred laws into useable formats, it was then necessary to analyse them. As mentioned earlier, the methodology is best described as discourse analysis. This method relies on a codebook of hypothetically important parts of speech. My approach has built on existing analyses of legal language. This includes seminal work by Brenda Danet (1985). She demonstrated that legal language is 'frozen' by relying on archaisms. She also demonstrated the use of common terms with uncommon meanings, the use of tautological doublets ('null and void'), the use of unusual prepositional phrases and a frequent use of 'any'. Some of her earlier work looked more to syntax than the parts of speech used (Danet 1980). She described a pattern of 'whiz' deletion, where the wh-words in sentences of law are often omitted, for example, 'an agreement [*which is*] herein obtained or applied'. Another inspiration was Marita Gustafsson (1975), who demonstrated that legal documents employ many more clauses per sentence than other structured languages. Also important, as regards legal syntax, are the prevalence of prepositional phrases (Charrow and Charrow 1979). From a policy perspective, Butt and Castle (2007) launched a campaign for plain language drafting. A particular problem that they highlighted was the use of 'may' as a modal verb in place of 'shall'. This is a facet of legal texts that is further explored here. Also of inspiration for this book was the analysis of complex conditional phrases formed by the use of conjunctions such as 'if', 'when', 'or' and 'and' (Crystal and Davy 1969).

For this book, there were two methods used for taking measurements from language. The first was the manual coding of samples of law. This method was used to inform the second method: the comprehensive computer analysis of all enactments. For the manual coding, 5,878 sections of legislation from 1920 to 2015 were analysed by hand, with 5% reanalysed to ensure the consistent application of the coding method. Two parts of speech – adjectives and conjunctions – were identified as either present or absent (coded as a binary 0/1) in a section of law (Williams 2016, 2017a, 2017b). The results do not give a sense of relative degrees of indeterminacy within sections, but they do describe the proportion of sections in a year that relied on indeterminate parts of speech. Every single section enacted in 1920,

[20] Available at: http://www.matthewlippoldwilliams.com

[21] See: http://www.nationalarchives.gov.uk/doc/open-government-licence/version/3/ (accessed 20 March 2017).

2010 and 2015 was so coded. Between 1920 and 2010, 5% of sections were sampled from five-year intervals, starting at 1925 and ending with 2005.

The computer-assisted coding relies on natural language-processing capabilities in NLTK software. Much of this is achieved through counting 'tokens'. To analyse a corpus of language, it is typically necessary to 'tokenise' the text into separate parts of speech. Notable words, such as the verb 'may', can then be counted. This works much like an ordinary word count, except that the program is able to distinguish when 'may' is used as a verb, and therefore avoids counting the month of May. The program also returns results in milliseconds from an enormous set of documents. Even more sophisticated is the analysis of parts of speech, rather than individual words. Most notable in this regard are adjectives, adverbs and conjunctions. NLTK is able to assess, with reasonable accuracy, what grammatical function an individual token is performing in each sentence. This is done by assessing the words around the target word, as well as its position in a sentence (so-called 'sentence chunking'). Due to its sophistication, NLTK extracts all words it believes to be adjectives, adverbs and conjunctions. This will include adjectives such as 'British' and the determinate adverb 'not'. As such, the program used to analyse the texts had to be adapted so as to subtract the number of words that did not contribute to indeterminacy. These words I identified from samples of law taken from 1899 and 2016. These years, being outside the data set, could be used to develop a more bespoke coding frame without affecting the results of laws analysed from 1900 to 2015. These adjustments to the NLTK code were limited, and the code used was kept deliberately simple to allow for easy replication and to minimise the likelihood of systematic observation errors. An excerpt of the code used for this chapter is displayed in Figure 2.1.

Figure 2.1 displays an excerpt of the code used to extract all adjectives and adverbs from the texts. These variables are labelled as allAdj and allAdv, respectively. These parts of speech have the special NLTK codes 'JJ' and 'RB'. Conjunctions are extracted in the same manner, under the variable label 'CC'. In the excerpt in Figure 2.1 are two more variables: allAdj2 and allAdj3. The former are specially selected adjectives that I argue create significant indeterminacies in law. However, the frequencies of these words are not displayed in the graphs that follow. The data extracted from allAdj2 are nonetheless available in the online appendices. More important to this study is allAdj3, which counts all adjectives that I argue do not create indeterminacies, such as 'administrative' and 'architectural'. In short, the program used to

Figure 2.1: Excerpt from the discourse analysis program

```
while True:
    print('Enter the number of sections, if known. If not, simply enter "1" to find
        the totals rather than the averages.')
    sec = int(input())
    class SampleApp(tk.Tk):
        def __init__(self):
            tk.Tk.__init__(self)
            self.title("Discourse Analysis")
            self.entry = tk.Entry(self)
            self.button = tk.Button(self, text="Analyse", command=self.on_button)
            self.button.pack()
            self.entry.pack()
        def on_button(self):
            raw = self.entry.get()
            tokenizer = RegexpTokenizer(r'\w+')
            tokens = tokenizer.tokenize(raw)
            sents = sent_tokenize(raw)
            print('Length: ' + str(len(tokens)) + ' words.')
            print('Length: ' + str(len(sents)) + ' sentences.')
            print('The average section is ' + str(len(tokens)/sec) + ' words long.
                ')
            tagged = nltk.pos_tag(tokens)
            allAdj = [word for word,pos in tagged if pos in ['JJ']]
            allAdv = [word for word,pos in tagged if pos in ['RB']]
            allAdj2 = (tokens.count('additional') + tokens.count('average') +
                tokens.count('bad') + tokens.count('beneficial') + tokens.count
                ('capable') + tokens.count('competent') + tokens.count('competent')
                + tokens.count('consistent') + tokens.count('convenient') + tokens.
                count('dangerous') + tokens.count('defective') + tokens.count
                ('effectual') + tokens.count('efficient') + tokens.count('equitable
                ') + tokens.count('excessive') + tokens.count('expedient') + tokens
                .count('extraordinary') + tokens.count('fair') + tokens.count
                ('favourable') + tokens.count('fit') + tokens.count('further') +
                tokens.count('good') + tokens.count('gratuitous') + tokens.count
                ('great') + tokens.count('harsh') + tokens.count('imminent') +
                tokens.count('impossible') + tokens.count('improper') + tokens.
                count('incidental') + tokens.count('insufficient') + tokens.count
                ('necessary') + tokens.count('poor') + tokens.count('possible') +
                tokens.count('practicable') + tokens.count('principal') + tokens.
                count('proper') + tokens.count('proportionate') + tokens.count
                ('reasonable') + tokens.count('residuary') + tokens.count
                ('satisfied') + tokens.count('special') + tokens.count('sufficient
                ') + tokens.count('superior') + tokens.count('supplemental') +
                tokens.count('supplementary') + tokens.count('ultimate') + tokens.
                count('unconscionable') + tokens.count('unconscionable') + tokens.
                count('unjust') + tokens.count('unnecessary') + tokens.count
                ('unreasonable') + tokens.count('vulnerable') + tokens.count
                ('conducive'))
            allAdj3 = (tokens.count('absolute') + tokens.count('administrative') +
                tokens.count('annual') + tokens.count('architectural') +  tokens.
                count('central') + tokens.count('chargeable') + tokens.count('chief
                ') + tokens.count('chronological') + tokens.count('circular') +
```

analyse the texts is simple and rests largely on counting key words and relying on the capacity of NLTK to extract specific parts of speech, such as adjectives, from vast quantities of text.

Various more sophisticated techniques, such as lemmatisation, sentiment analysis and n-gram collocation, were deliberately not used. Lemmatisation is required when the roots of words need to be identified so as to attain the essence of meaning across a variety of texts. This will be necessary where processes such as declension or conjugation do not abide by systematic rules. Such will be the case when analysing medieval texts from different regions (see, eg, Widner 2016). Sentiment analysis is a built-in tool that allows NLTK users to assess subjectivity in a text. This is achieved by weighting words as more or less subjective, such as the word 'good' (see, eg, Pang and Lee 2008). Sentiment analysis is not used here because, as highlighted by Danet, commonly used words such as 'good' have uncommon meanings in law. For instance, the word 'good' is typically used as a noun in law, rather than an adjective, as in 'the public good'. Due to these uncommon meanings, it is not appropriate for the purposes of this study to use sentiment analysis on legal texts. Finally, n-gram collocation allows a researcher to assess the frequency by which certain words appear together, where 'n' describes the number of words that commonly appear together; as an example, 'public good' is a bigram, and 'null and void' is a trigram. Again, this method is geared to analysing content rather than discourse.

The aim in this book is to assess how effectively messages are transmitted between sender and receiver, rather than what it is that is communicated. Hence, the aim is to measure the causes of meaninglessness, rather than meaning. This is because meaning is neither fixed nor exogenous to the language used (Loughran and McDonald 2011). Text-mining the entire legislative output between 1900 and 2015 could not establish meaning from the words alone. However, identifying those parts of speech that qualify meaning, and always have, is achievable. Certain parts of speech, such as adjectives, qualify the interpretation of nouns by omitting information regarding context and the will of the interpreter. It is for this reason that nouns are not coded, such as 'justice' or 'good'. These words can be of indeterminate meaning but their communication is often clear. Thinking back to the radio reception metaphor, my interest is the degree of clarity, not the content. Other methods of content analysis, such as Wordfish and Wordscores, were therefore not used (Laver et al 2003; Evans et al 2007). This meant that there was no need to code a reference text, against which 'virgin' texts would be assessed (Martin and Vanberg 2008).

As discussed in the previous chapter, two works provided specific models for the text coding techniques used in this book. First, David Epstein and Sharyn O'Halloran (1999) coded laws as 'vague' and 'specific'. They coded from a sample of 257 laws identified in David Mayhew's (1991) seminal book *Divided We Govern*. For each legislative provision, they isolated 'delegation measures' and 'constraint measures'. This was all achieved with manual coding and inter-coder reliability checks. John Huber and Charles Shipan (2002) similarly took samples of law and coded 12 types of policy instruction, including 'general policy language' and 'client issues'. Their samples were from Medicaid managed care (MMC) legislation from US states between 1989 and

1998. They also analysed 30 statutes pertaining to labour from 12 countries, drawing on the International Labour Organisation (ILO) Natlex database. My coding design is more straightforward but it thereby allows for a significantly larger data set, greater scalability and easier replicability. By using manual coding as well as text-mining software, I have ensured accuracy with scale. Similar text-mining approaches that were instructive for this research include the Object-oriented Parsing and Analysis of Legislation (OPAL) project (Van Gog and Van Engers 2001). Also instructive were text-mining analyses in literary studies and critical legal studies (see, eg, Moretti 2013).

All of the methodological choices made for this book were designed to maximise replicability by minimising human error. That is not to say that the computer coding is infallible; the program does misclassify words on occasion. However, there is no reason to believe that this error is concentrated in any particular time frame. In other words, the errors are likely to be homogeneous across the period. An example of the program's output, and the intermittent errors that can emerge, is displayed in Figure 2.2. The output describes indeterminacies in section 11(3) of the *Extradition Act 1989*:

> (3) Without prejudice to any jurisdiction of the High Court apart from this section, the court shall order the applicant's discharge if it appears to the court in relation to the offence, or each of the offences, in respect of which the applicant's return is sought, that – (a) by reason of the trivial nature of the offence; or (b) by reason of the passage of time since he is alleged to have committed it or to have become unlawfully at large, as the case may be; or (c) because the accusation against him is not made in good faith in the interests of justice, it would, having regard to all the circumstances, be unjust or oppressive to return him.

The program concludes that there are nine adjectives and adverbs, and five conjunctions. These are all listed, in order, in the three final lines of the output. Eleven words are listed as adjectives and adverbs, but because I manually instructed the program to disregard 'not', it is not included in the tally. The error one can see is that a lone 's' is identified as an adjective. It would not be appropriate to instruct the program to count and subtract all uses of 's' because, in most cases, NLTK will not misclassify it. The reason that an individual 's' has been tokenised is because it was considered a separate word from 'applicant' in one of the instances where it is used with an apostrophe.

Figure 2.2: Example of the discourse analysis output

```
Length: 121 words.
Length: 1 sentences.
The average section is 121.0 words long.
On average there are 9 adjectives and adverbs per section.
On average there are 5 conjunctions per section.
On average there are 1 indeterminate modal verbs [may, might] per section.
On average there are 1 determinate modal verbs [shall, will] per section.
On average there are 0 enabling verbs [make, amend] per section.
['applicant', 's', 'trivial', 'large', 'good', 'unjust', 'oppressive']
['apart', 'unlawfully', 'not']
['or', 'or', 'or', 'or', 'or']
```

The output shows that per section averages are calculated by the program. With only one section used for this example, the results are obtained by dividing everything by 1. However, why is the total number of sections an appropriate denominator? First, dividing the incidence of significant parts of speech by the number of words would be inappropriate because changes to the numerator would directly affect changes to the denominator. Each conjunction would, for instance, be counted both above and below the dividing line. Second, sections are akin to sentences. They are the essential building block of all laws. As section 1 of the *Interpretation Act 1978* puts it: 'Every section of an Act takes effect as a substantive enactment without introductory words'. Third, assessing the frequencies of different parts of speech from the total quantity of words enacted would be testing different claims, such as with regards to the increased garrulity of the legislature (Voigt 2009). The aim of this book is to test whether the circuitry of legislation has gaps in it. Each section should provide a complete statement of law. Gaps therein are more impactful than the proportion of indeterminacies across the entire word count of all law. Finally, using sections of law as the denominator has precedent, being the approach used in Huber and Shipan's (2002: 49) seminal work.

Results

There are three sets of results to be discussed. These are changes in the volume of enacted legislation, the manual coding results and the machine-reading results. Figure 2.3 describes changes in the quantity of law enacted.

Figure 2.3 displays an increase in the number of words enacted by Parliament (as measured on the secondary y-axis), but in a gradually decreasing number of statutes (as measured on the primary y-axis). The curvilinear trend line describing the changing number of statutes takes the formula $y = -0.0092x^2 + 0.9562x + 43.531$, with $R^2 = 0.30284$. There are sharp changes in the number of statutes enacted from one year to the next, but the general pattern is of a post-war decline in the number of enactments, although there were only 20 laws enacted in 1912. This trough is unsurprising given the raging extra- and intra-parliamentary battles over women's enfranchisement, Irish Home Rule and public finances in that year. It was 1939 when the greatest number of laws was enacted, with 120. Since 2000, there have been around 30 Acts passed per year. The pattern is therefore of fewer statutes enacted, with much greater word lengths. The formula describing the increased number of words is $y = -29.055x^2 + 8446.5x - 3663.8$, with $R^2 = 0.58553$. Variability in this formula (as measured by the

Figure 2.3: Changes in the quantities of enacted legislation, 1900–2015

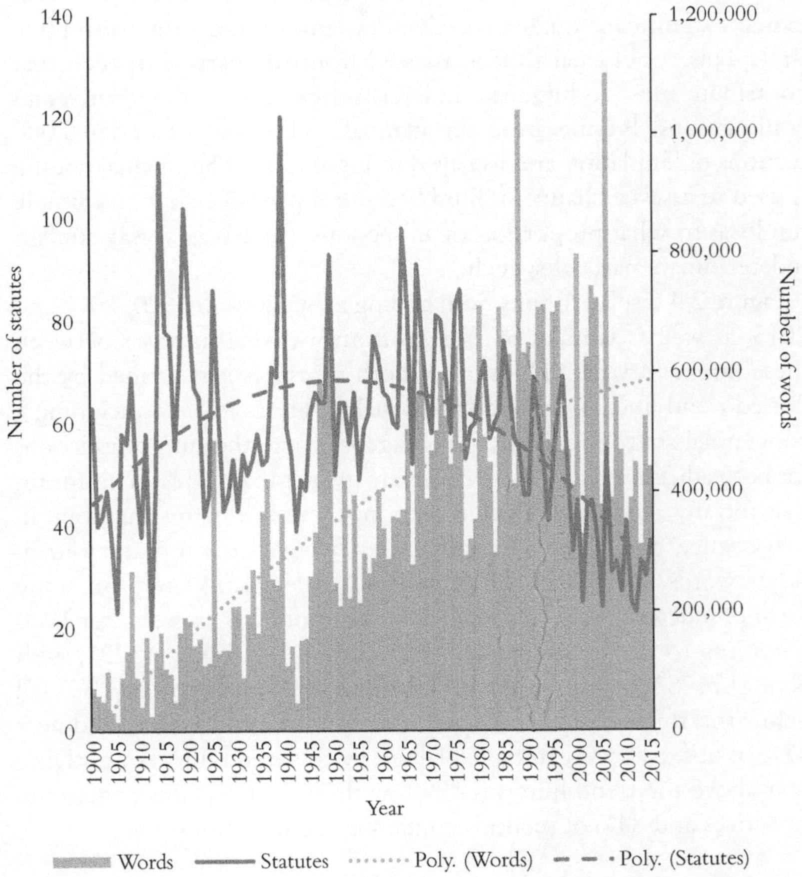

R^2) is lower than with regard to statutes. Nearly 60% of observations are described accurately by the trend line. The changes are striking: only 15,771 words of legislation were enacted in 1905 in 23 statutes. That makes for a little under 686 words per statute. In stark contrast was the output of 2006. In that year, 1,101,706 words were enacted in 55 statutes. Each statute was, on average, just over 20,000 words in length, although 2006 was an outlying year, with all succeeding years seeing a total average output of over 400,000 words. Similarly outlying, but of note, is the longest statute enacted in the 20th century. This is the *Income and Corporation Taxes Act 1988*. At 1,317 pages and 390,797 words long, it is, on its own, 25 times greater than the entire legislative output of 1905. As mentioned, these data only describe public Acts of Parliament. Not included are other important sources of law, including private Acts, hybrid Acts, legislation of the European Union, secondary legislation and Measures of the Church of England's general synod.

Besides the quantitative changes to legislation, this book's thesis expects significant qualitative changes, amounting to a conceptual shift. This conceptual shift is assessed from the parts of speech that contribute most to linguistic indeterminacy: adjectives, adverbs and conjunctions. Results from the manual coding of just under 6,000 sections of legislation are displayed in Figure 2.4. The manual coding is used to assess a change in kind because it provides clear and simple results as to what proportion of all sections enacted in a year contain indeterminate parts of speech.

Figure 2.4 displays results from coding all sections in 1920, 2010 and 2015, as well as samples of sections from five-year intervals between these bookend years. The sum of both measures is described by the dotted trend line. As argued, a reasonable threshold for concluding a conceptual shift in legislative language is where the sum proportions for both adjectives and conjunctions are greater than 100%. This means that for any randomly selected section, there is a better than one in two chance of it relying on either an adjective or a conjunction. In other words, a majority of all sections of legislation rely on some form of indeterminate language. This threshold was crossed after 1960 according to the trend line ($y = 0.0038x^2 - 14.155x + 13227$, with $R^2 = 0.76783$), although the observations for both 1965 and 1975 fall below this threshold. Nonetheless, the upward trend is clear, and near 77% of observations can be explained by this trend line. An outlying year above the trend line was 1990, with 74% of sections containing adjectives and 84% of sections containing conjunctions.

Figure 2.4: Changes in the proportion of sections containing indeterminacies, 1920–2015

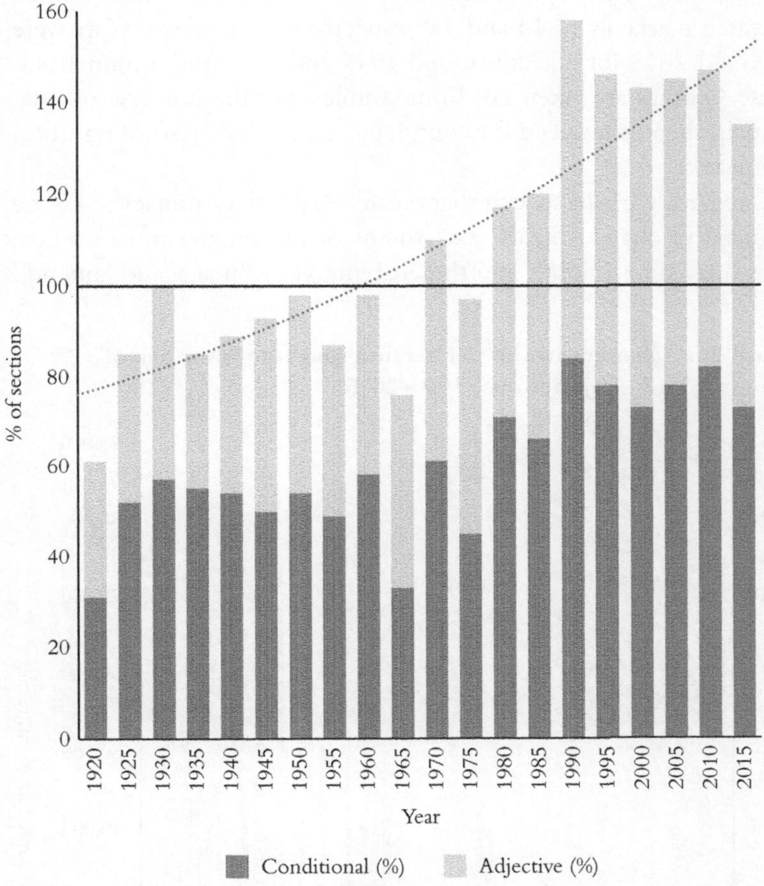

For assessing the impact of indeterminate legislation on policy, it is more useful to know how indeterminate sections are relative to each other. This requires analysis not of whether or not a section relies on indeterminate parts of speech, but of how many such parts of speech are used. These data are taken from the machine-reading analysis.

Figure 2.5 provides the first set of results from the machine-reading analysis. Displayed are the per section and total incidences of adjectives, adverbs and conjunctions enacted in every single year between 1900 and 2015. The results match the patterns uncovered in the manual coding, but provide significantly more detail. As described earlier, the pattern of per section incidences of conjunctions is curvilinear, with a decline after the early 1990s ($y = -0.0012x^2 + 4.7224x - 4626.4$, with $R^2 = 0.45232$). For adjectives, the trend is unrelentingly upward and linear ($y = 0.0649x - 119.73$, with $R^2 = 0.73308$). These are strong findings. On average, sections of legislation in 1900 had two adjectives and seven conjunctions; by 2015, these averages had increased markedly to 13 and 14, respectively. Superlative years were 2014 and 2015 for adjectives, and 1947 and 1990 for conjunctions. These findings are taken not from samples, but the universe of data. As such, there is no need for confidence intervals or tests of statistical significance.

As regards parts of speech that create legal indeterminacies, Figure 2.6 displays changes in the enactment of the indeterminate modal verbs 'may' and 'might', and the enabling verbs 'make' and 'amend'.

Figure 2.5: Changes in the per section and total number of adjectives and conjunctions, 1900–2015

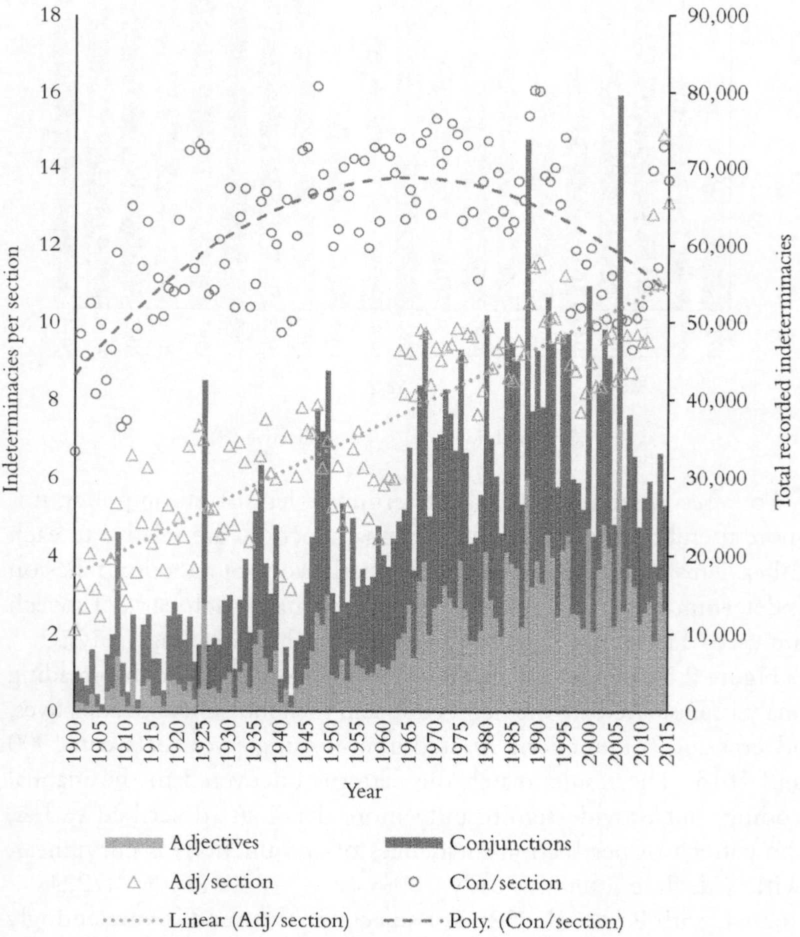

Both have increased with upward and moderately curvilinear trend lines ($y = -0.0001x^2 + 0.4919x - 485.83$, with $R^2 = 0.47003$ for indeterminate modal verbs, and $y = 3E\text{-}05x^2 - 0.1231x + 116.1$, with $R^2 = 0.76855$ for enabling verbs). Both of these parts of speech are recorded with significantly lower frequencies than adjectives, adverbs and conjunctions. Nonetheless, the increases in per section and total use are striking. The superlative years were 2012 for indeterminate modal verbs (2.98/section), and 2014 for enabling verbs (1.12/section). The story for determinate modal verbs is very different, as Figure 2.7 shows.

Interestingly, the use of the determinate modal verbs 'must' and 'shall' declined sharply after the war ($y = -0.0009x^2 + 3.5374x - 3442.6$, with $R^2 = 0.78678$). Turn of the millennium decline was especially rapid; there were only 143 uses of 'must' or 'shall' in 2015. That is an astonishingly small count from a total legislative output of 359,110 words: just four hundredths of 1%.

The overall patterns in legislative language, therefore, have been sharp increases in indeterminacy after the Second World War, coincident with the decreased use of determinate modal verbs. Of the indeterminate parts of speech, only conjunctions and indeterminate modal verbs have declined in use, after peaking post-war. As argued, these patterns constitute, in sum, not only change by degree, but also change in kind. In addition, the indeterminacies are not confined to legally operative language; Figure 2.8 tracks changes in preambles.

Preambles have increased in length and indeterminacy. Of the indeterminacies, only adjectives, adverbs and conjunctions are relevant as no delegations of power can be achieved by use of 'may' or 'make' in a preamble. Both trend lines describe continuous growth, albeit at a decreasing rate from the mid-1970s onwards ($y = -0.0002x^2 + 0.9175x - 915.4$, with $R^2 = 0.73395$ for conjunctions, and $y = -9E\text{-}05x^2 + 0.3613x - 366.25$, with $R^2 = 0.68795$ for adjectives and adverbs). In 1900, the average preamble was just 17 words long. Preambles used to be short and unadorned. As an example, the preamble to the *Mines (Prohibition of Child Labour Underground) Act 1900* describes no more than the statute's title: 'An Act to prohibit Child Labour Underground in Mines'. In 2014, by contrast, the average preamble was 61 words long and contained, on average, two adjectives and four conjunctions. Illustrative is the preamble to the *Immigration Act 2014*:

> An Act to make provision about immigration law; to limit, or otherwise make provision about, access to services, facilities and employment by reference to immigration

Figure 2.6: Changes in the per section and total number of indeterminate modal verbs, 1900–2015

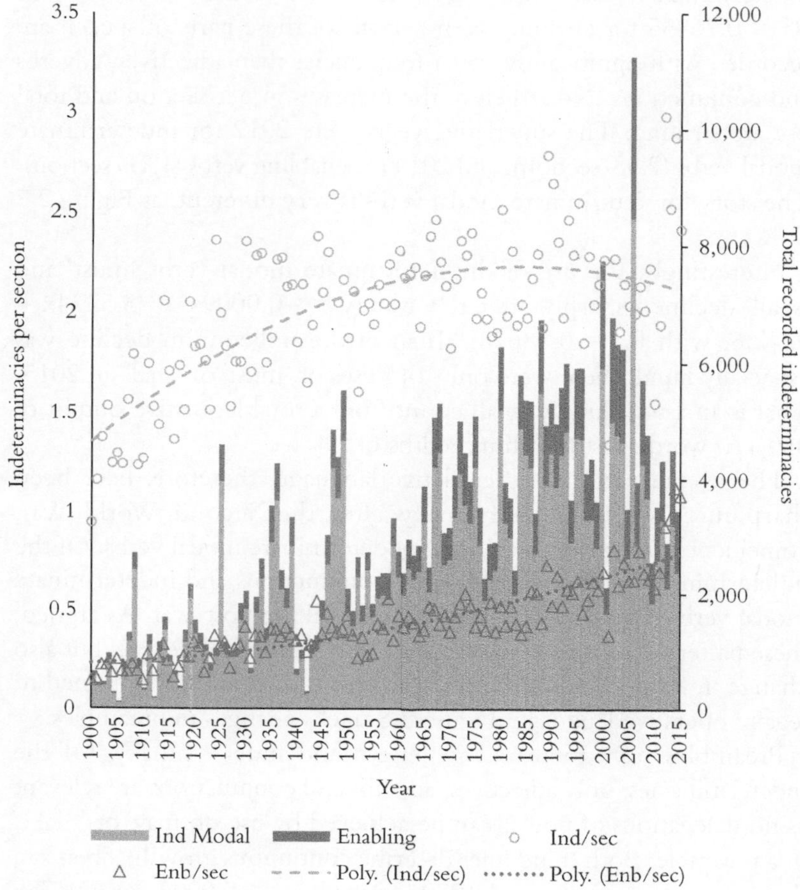

status; to make provision about marriage and civil partnership involving certain foreign nationals; to make provision about the acquisition of citizenship by persons unable to acquire it because their fathers and mothers were not married to each other and provision about the removal of citizenship from persons whose conduct is seriously prejudicial to the United Kingdom's vital interests; and for connected purposes.

This preamble has no legal force, but its length, complexity and use of indeterminacies such as 'seriously prejudicial … to vital interests' demonstrates the difficulties in succinctly describing policy ambitions.

Figure 2.7: Changes in the per section and total number of determinate modal verbs, 1900–2015

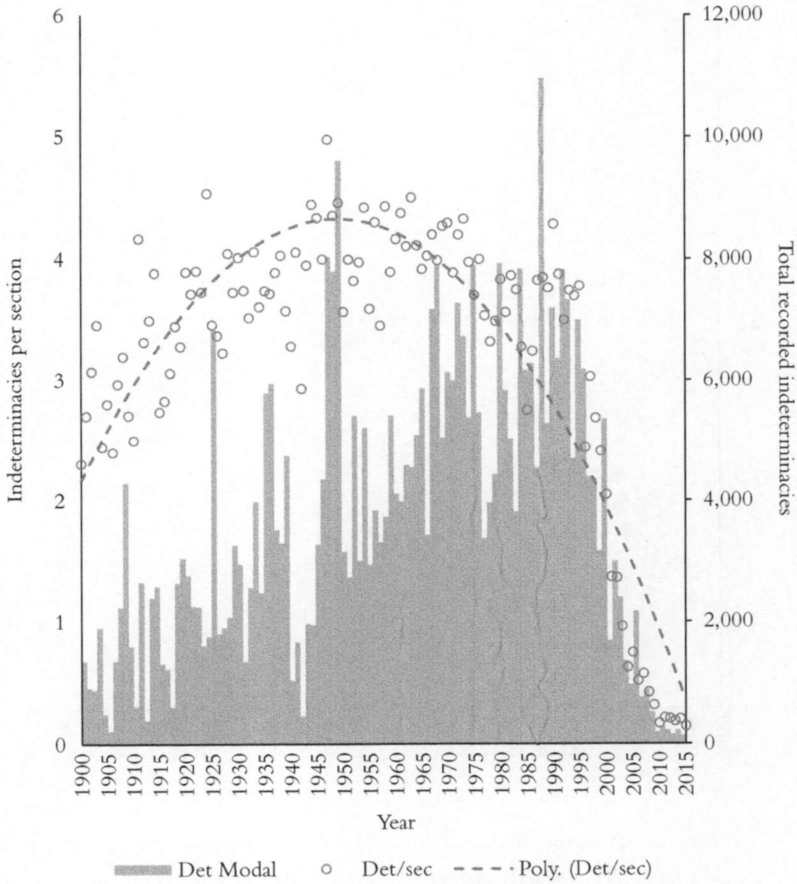

However, it must be stressed that not all legislation has become indeterminate with time. Legislation that authorises and manages public finances relies far less on indeterminate parts of speech, as Figure 2.9 demonstrates.

Figure 2.9 displays similar trends in the use of adjectives, adverbs and conjunctions in financial legislation as were seen for all other legislation in Figure 2.5. Where adjectives and adverbs start from a low base, they have increased in use with almost linear consistency across the period ($y = 9E\text{-}05x^2 - 0.2275x + 122.65$, with $R^2 = 0.67486$). The per section incidence of conjunctions started from a higher base but declined after the late 1960s ($y = -0.0024x^2 + 9.3637x - 9192$, with $R^2 = 0.40797$). The use of these indeterminate parts of speech is nonetheless markedly lower than for all other legislation. The election

Figure 2.8: Changes in the per preamble number of adjectives and conjunctions, 1900–2015

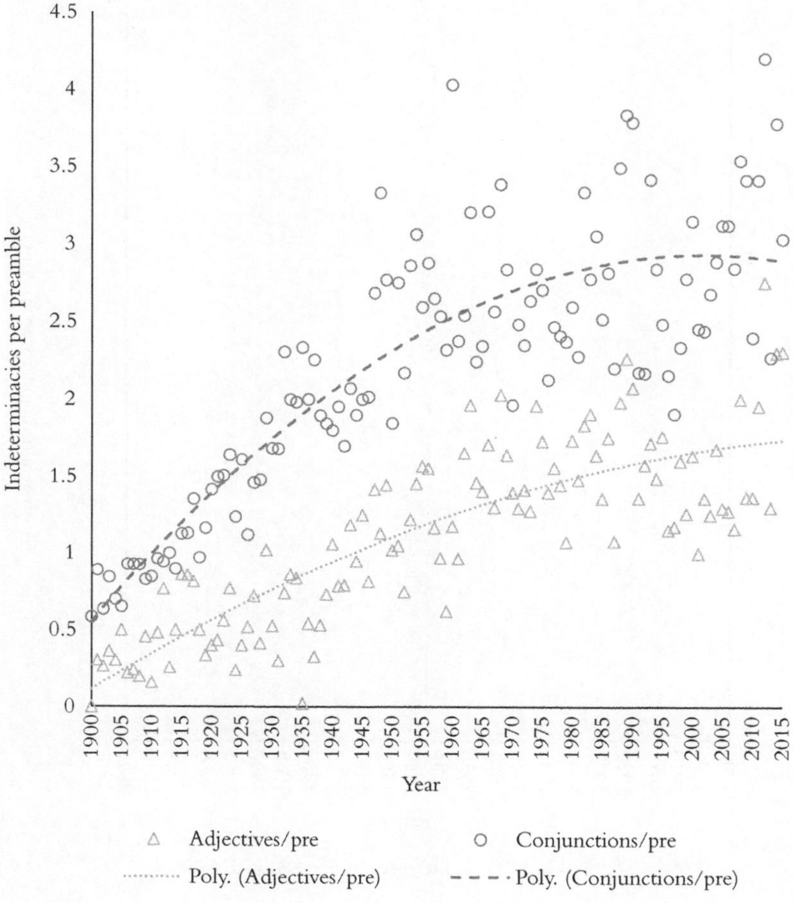

year of 2015 was anomalous for the levels of indeterminacy in financial legislation, so 2014 is a safer point of comparison. In that year, there were, on average, nine adjectives and adverbs, and 10 conjunctions, per section of financial legislation. However, there were 15 adjectives and adverbs, and 15 conjunctions, for all other legislation. The divergence is even more striking when we consider parts of speech that delegate or deny discretion.

Figure 2.10 demonstrates that indeterminate modal verbs ('may' and 'might') have decreased in their use ($y = -7E\text{-}05x^2 + 0.2793x - 269.55$, with $R^2 = 0.11791$). The use of enabling verbs ('make' and 'amend') has increased, but from a near-zero starting point and by a tiny amount ($y = 3E\text{-}05x^2 - 0.1023x + 97.604$, with $R^2 = 0.53157$).

Figure 2.9: Changes in the per section number of adjectives and conjunctions in financial legislation, 1900–2015

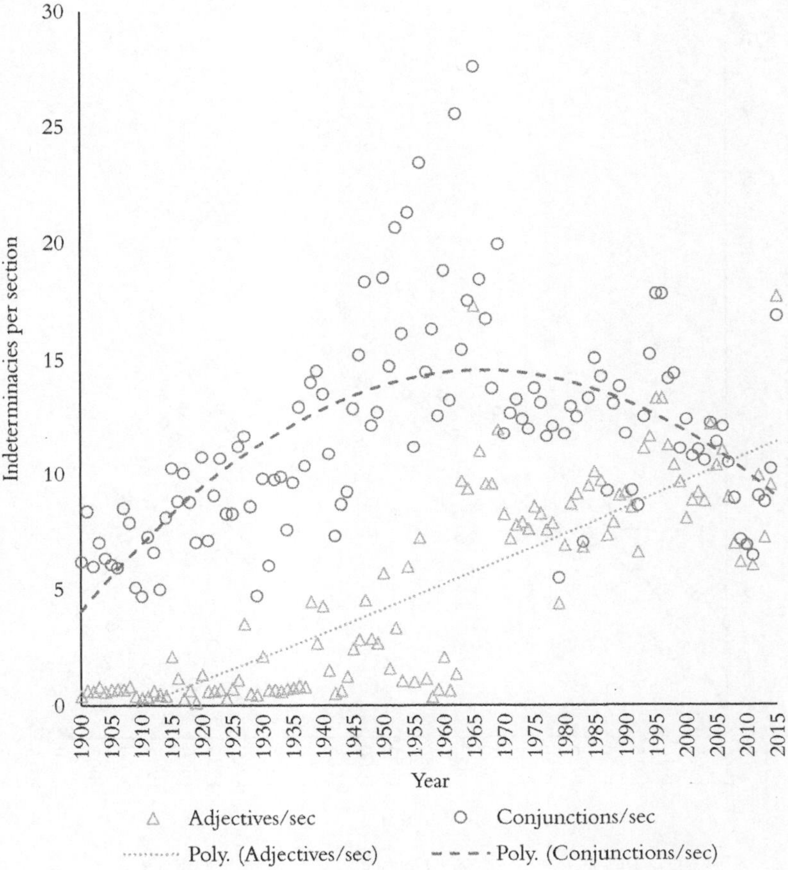

By contrast, the use of determinate modal verbs ('must' and 'shall') has seen a significant increase, albeit with a sharp decrease after the millennium ($y = -0.0014x^2 + 5.4123x - 5295.2$, with $R^2 = 0.58168$).

These findings are important. They suggest that while the substance of public policy is increasingly indeterminate, the means of financing it are increasingly clear. This, in turn, suggests that indeterminacy is not a failure of drafting, or an unconscious shift in linguistic norms. Indeterminacy and determinacy are used deliberately to achieve flexibility, on the one hand, and fixity, on the other.

Exemplifying the relative clarity of financial legislation is the *Finance Act 2009*, which attempted, after the global recession, to ensure improved transparency and higher standards of behaviour from those employed in financial administration:

Figure 2.10: Changes in the per section incidences of indeterminate modal verbs, determinate modal verbs and enabling verbs, 1900–2015

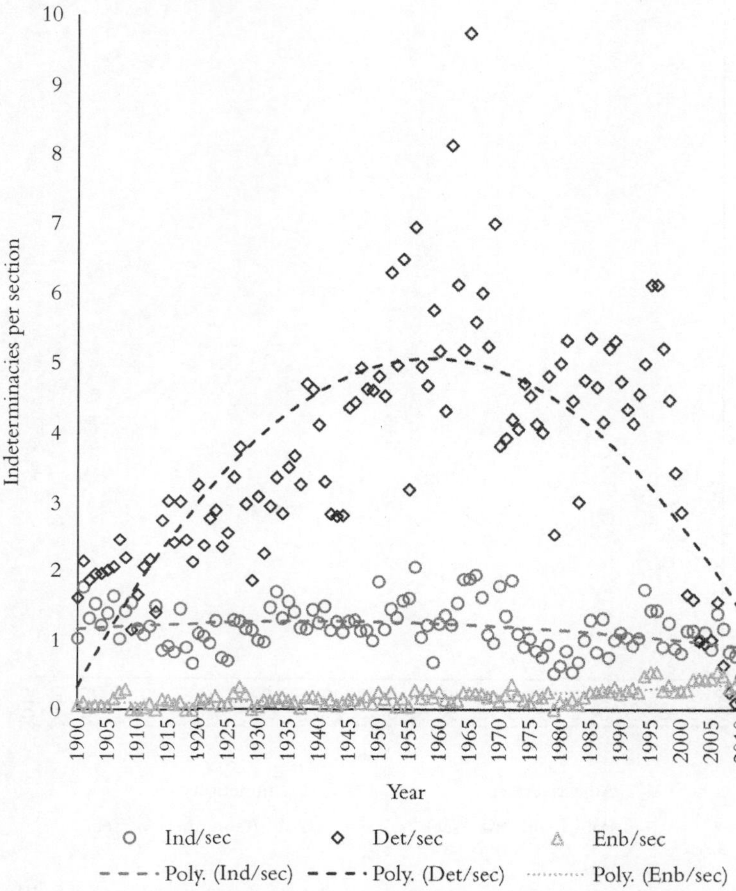

92 (1) The Commissioners [of HMRC] must prepare a Charter. (2) The Charter must include standards of behaviour and values to which Her Majesty's Revenue and Customs will aspire when dealing with people in the exercise of their functions. (3) The Commissioners must – (a) regularly review the Charter, and (b) publish revisions, or revised versions, of it when they consider it appropriate to do so.

While the adjective 'appropriate' gives some superficial latitude to the Commissioners in deciding when to publish revisions to their Charter, the immediately succeeding subsection (4) makes plain that an annual report 'must' be made, reviewing the standards of behaviour.

So, financial legislation is closer to the model of plainness advocated by Henry Thring. Over one of Parliament's core competencies, therefore, there remains a tight grip. This is unsurprising given that it is in the interests of the government to retain clear, programmatic instructions for managing public finances. A similar theory underpins the Dutch Program for an Ontology based Working Environment for Regulations and legislation (POWER) (Van Gog and Van Engers 2001). The Dutch Tax and Customs Administration implemented a method for ensuring that new financial legislation conforms precisely to formal economic models. The language of Dutch financial legislation is therefore intended to be as close as possible to a formal algorithm. While UK financial legislation retains many indeterminate parts of speech, the significant divergence between financial and non-financial legislation suggests that the former accords to a different model of inter-institutional communication. Financial law is, as Huber and Shipan (2002) would note, largely attempting a 'deliberate delegation' of power.

Conclusion

Quantifying patterns in parliamentary language is far from simple. Conclusions must therefore be drawn tentatively. Not every adjective, adverb, conjunction, modal verb or enabling verb in a statute will undermine clarity. Indeed, plainness of exposition can itself create confusion in determining the sovereign's will. Take the proposed opening section to the *Wild Mammals (Hunting with Dogs) Bill 1997*, a Bill intended to stop the practice of fox-hunting with hounds: 'Any person who uses, causes or permits any dog to hunt any wild mammal shall be guilty of an offence'. This superficially plain language never made it to the statute book. Had it done so, some rather perverse consequences would have been possible. For instance, 'any person' who 'permitted' their dog to chase squirrels in the park would have been committing an offence. It is therefore true that, in some cases, enumerating conditions and qualifications can make language easier to interpret. Ultimately, the *Hunting Act 2004* opted for the following construction: 'A person commits an offence if he hunts a wild mammal with a dog, unless his hunting is exempt'. The exemptions were then enumerated in the Act's first schedule. These exemptions are replete with conditional conjunctions and adjectives. Some of these conjunctive and descriptive elements helped clarify the intended operation of the law. However, the key point of this chapter is not that these parts of speech never improve interpretability, but rather that they have a significantly greater potential in undermining interpretability than would simple, unadorned, subject–object–verb constructions. For instance, the fifth condition on exempt hunting with dogs is framed in the following indeterminate language:

> The fifth condition is that – (a) reasonable steps are taken for the purpose of ensuring that as soon as possible after being found or flushed out the wild mammal is shot dead by a competent person, and (b) in particular, each dog used in the stalking or flushing out is kept under sufficiently close control to ensure that it does not prevent or obstruct achievement of the objective in paragraph (a).

Any hunter wishing to avoid prosecution would simply need to establish that 'reasonable steps' were taken, such that 'as soon as possible', a flushed-out mammal was shot by a 'competent person' accompanied by a dog 'kept under sufficiently close control'. A hunter could also skirt the dividing lines between various conjoined conditions: 'found or flushed', 'stalking or flushing' and 'prevent or obstruct'. It is little wonder that so few prosecutions have succeeded under this legislation. Henry Thring was aware of the problems caused by these parts of speech over a century ago. He emphasised the interpretative difficulties caused by parts of speech that intervene in the connections between legal subjects and predicates in language. Indeed, he presents one of his clearest theses, somewhat subtly, in a footnote:

> The most frequent cause of ambiguity in Acts of Parliament is the want of an adjectival inflexion. For example, the expression 'Every factory and every workshop subject to this Act', raises the question whether 'subject to this Act' applies to both or to the last only of the nouns. If it is intended to apply to the last only, the ambiguity is avoided by placing the qualified noun before the unqualified, that is to say, by reading the sentence 'Every workshop subject to this Act and every factory'. To make the qualification certainly apply to both the form of sentence must be altered somewhat in this way, 'Where a factory and a workshop are subject to this Act they shall'.
>
> *Thring 1902: 77, fn 1*

The aim in this chapter has not been to assert, without justification, that the language of legislation is indeterminate to explicitly stated degrees. The aim was to establish relative and probabilistic theses. Legislative language increasingly relies on parts of speech that have the potential to communicate partial meanings. Patterns in language suggest changes both in degree and, crucially, in kind.

There exists no more comprehensive analysis of legislative language. With a corpus of 41.5 million words, the findings are by necessity broad. However, analysis across a *longue durée* has great utility in revealing changes to how subjects, objects and verbs are connected in legal language. The wide angle offered in this chapter will be reinforced by close-up analyses of specific effects of indeterminate language in succeeding chapters. However, first, we must consider in further detail why the language of legislation has changed.

THREE

Present: why has Parliament's use of language changed?

> Consider what effects, which might conceivably have practical bearings, we conceive the object of our conception to have. Then, our conception of those effects is the whole of our conception of the object.
>
> *Charles Sanders Peirce's maxim (Peirce 1992:132)*

> 47 (1) Where a local authority – (b) have reasonable cause to suspect that a child who lives, or is found, in their area is suffering, or is likely to suffer, significant harm, the authority shall make, or cause to be made, such enquiries as they consider necessary to enable them to decide whether they should take any action to safeguard or promote the child's welfare.
>
> *Section 47 of the* Children Act 1989

Introduction

A local authority cannot know what 'significant harm' means from the words of the *Children Act* alone. It is only through repeated use that meanings for 'reasonable cause', 'likely to suffer' and 'significant harm' have emerged. The concept of causing harm to children is, therefore, understood from its effects. It has no clear *prima facie* meaning, and it succeeds in attaining the pragmatists' maxim of Charles Sanders Peirce that the 'conception of … effects is the whole of our conception of the object'. So, why might this approach to framing policy be useful to policymakers? When legislation is indeterminate in meaning, its words can be used flexibly to address a variety of problems, both predicted and unforeseen. In other words, context determines text. In a similar vein, post-structuralists argue that words often precede their meanings (see, eg, Lyotard et al 2006). Policymaking is cheapened by this use of language in that the same supply of language can perform multiple tasks and can allow legislation to be promulgated despite incomplete information on what policy tools are desirable.

This, in essence, is why Parliament's use of language has changed. The increased indeterminacy in legislative language, as observed in Chapter Two, can be explained by a theory of increasing pragmatism in policymaking. Steady increases in the use of adjectives and adverbs have allowed policy concepts, such as the meaning of 'harm', to be altered. Conjunctions, by conjoining multiple conditions on policy, allow policy implementation to be shaped by variable contexts. As an example, action under the 1989 Act can be taken when a child 'is suffering, or is likely to suffer', harm. Indeterminate modal verbs – 'may' and 'might' – allow for the timing of policy and other procedural matters to be altered in accordance with discretion. Ultimately, flexible language comes with enabling verbs – 'make' and 'amend' – which allow powerful individuals to replace language with relative ease. This will be necessary where the text simply cannot be reconciled with context, despite its indeterminacies. As noted in Chapter Two, there have always been indeterminacies in legal language, but there has been a change in degree, as well as in kind. Statutes were shorter and more focused in 1900, but legislation increasingly enables, indeed requires, ongoing redefinition.

Referring back to the theoretical frame of this book, legislation accords more to a 'logic of consequences' than to a 'logic of communication'. According to the latter logic, communication is derived from principle. After principles are established, concrete decisions on how to act are framed in language. Like a funnel, broad principles are narrowed to specific decisions. Connections between intention and action will then be obvious. Conversely, the logic disintegrates if there is disconnection of intention and action. This will happen if, instead of beginning with principle, decisions are taken on the basis of expediency and are justified retrospectively. This logic of consequences is described by rational choice theory (Hall and Taylor 1996). It can be stated more plainly as a 'what matters is what works' approach to policy. However, pragmatic language in legislation is symptomatic of powerlessness, both real and perceived. The issuance of indeterminate commands simply masks this powerlessness, rather than resolving its underlying causes.

How has this powerlessness shown itself through British political language? As Chapter Two demonstrated, major changes to legislative language were observed post-war. Given this timing, the changes to language mirror changes in the demands for, and the available supply of, public power. Indeterminate legislation allowed successive governments to address heightened demands for public policies while adapting to circumstances that increasingly lay beyond their control. Being indeterminate, the language of law could evolve with the times, or be changed by discretion. These facilities of language were especially useful to those politicians wishing to provide or withhold public services in specific cases. Indeterminate legislation increased, therefore, by necessity at first, in response to Britain's relative economic decline post-war. However, indeterminacy was later motivated by choices taken to 'roll back' the state and allow policy to adapt to changeable market conditions.

This chapter begins by elaborating the theory. This is followed by tracing the historic patterns in language use since 1900. These patterns of use are then explained through three case studies. These look to court records and declassified Cabinet papers, from which we can see how and why choices were made to change the language of the law.

Government by circumstance and discretion

Politicians must address voters' demands while also managing market forces, press scrutiny and diplomatic considerations. This juggling act is performed within the time constraints of an electoral cycle, and with politicians relying on imperfect information. These demand- and supply-side constraints are fundamental to understanding political language, as well as its change. Most notable have been changes to supply. The public have increasingly looked to the state to solve their problems, despite severe constraints on what can be delivered. Capturing policy goals in tight, determinate language is increasingly difficult as a result.

The very 'concept of law' – that is, law's role in society – has changed. Legislative language is akin to an argument. It is, more specifically, a thesis on power. It describes what power exists, who should wield it and how it will be used. Indeterminacy in legislation is tantamount to an incomplete argument. Elision and omission of information on the face of the law makes for an incomprehensible theory of power (Robertson 2010). As argued previously, indeterminate language cannot easily frame logical propositions. Instead, the language must typically be interpreted analogically. Stated literally, analogic means 'up to a standard'; it is regression to the mean. Observation and experience help to flesh out the meanings of words like 'significant harm', but the words have no clear meaning of themselves. This mode of communication is especially interesting when coming from an indefeasible sovereign, such as Parliament. The sovereign has created scaffoldings for power but has not fully decided what powers do, or should, exist. Without delving too deeply into analytic jurisprudence, it may be argued, tentatively, that the findings of Chapter Two suggest that both John Austin's and Herbert Hart's works could be described as empirically correct, despite their divergent conclusions (see, eg, Freeman, M.D.A. 2008): in the past, statute law offered mostly clear commandments, backed by Parliament's authority (à la Austin); since the war, however, legislation has increasingly offered instruments that facilitate wide-ranging social action, backed by communal norms (à la Hart). Hence, the concept of law is time-dependent, and has varied significantly as democracy has matured.

Yet, of course, distilling the data from Chapter Two into a singular concept of law would be reductive. Law is, and achieves, many things. What can be claimed is that legal language is increasingly capable of adaptation, such that Parliament's will is difficult to ascertain. This is, in truth, more a statistical rather than a conceptual proposition in that we cannot say that 'legislation is always indeterminate'. Yet, because we can say that a majority of legal sections are now indeterminate, the statistical shift amounts to a conceptual shift. In modern legislation, there remain great quantities of plain and easily determinable legislation. Indeed, these remaining determinate laws provide useful points of comparison. What they tend to communicate are very specific, or unambitious, goals. As an example, the *Term and Quarter Days (Scotland) Act 1990* states its ambition in the following terms: 'An Act to regulate, in relation to Scotland, the dates of Whitsunday, Martinmas, Candlemas and Lammas; and for connected purposes'. Also, plain legislative language can be found when addressing a specific pathology in the common law, as in the *Law of Property (Miscellaneous Provisions) Act 1989*:

> An Act to make new provision with respect to deeds and their execution and contracts for the sale or other disposition of interests in land; and to abolish the rule of law known as the rule in *Bain v. Fothergill.*

Where policy ambition is greater, it is still possible to find determinacy in language when there is broad cross-party consensus and little need or desire for events to determine policy content. This can explain why financial legislation is significantly more determinate than all other laws. Not only have the parties broadly agreed on fiscal policies since the war, but there are few incentives for Parliament or the government to enable flexible rules on tax collection or public spending. Apart from anything else, finance Acts are enacted annually, and it is not unusual for there to be more than one such Act passed in a year, so even if there is a clear financial commitment enacted that quickly falls out of favour, it does not take long to expunge it.

A reiteration of what indeterminacy means is needed. Four parts of speech have been identified as significant to the determinacy of a text: noun/verb qualifiers, conjunctions, modal auxiliary verbs and enabling verbs. However, do these elements work collectively, or severally, with regard to comprehensibility? They have the potential for collective effect but will also operate independently. Put arithmetically, their effects are additive, not multiplicative. The absence of one indeterminacy will not negate the impact of others. Put grammatically, this can be explained as the four elements operating on different parts of sentence structure. First, adjectives and adverbs have the greatest effect on the connection of subject and object. 'Significant harm' in the *Children Act* describes the conceptual coupling of the subject (a child) and the object (harm). Second, conjunctions focus more exclusively on the object of a sentence. By conjoining conditions on interpretation, the object of a sentence (be it a power, a duty or a right) can be extended or restricted in scope. Third, modal verbs, being auxiliary to the principal verb of a sentence, will influence the interpretation of the principal verb. Fourth, enabling verbs are not auxiliary and will independently affect interpretation. In policy terms, the four elements have the following principal effects. Adjectives and adverbs create conceptual indeterminacy. That means that variables (such as harm) are capable of adaptation. This has especial importance for the substance of policy. Conjunctions are most impactful on the process of implementing policy, rather than its substance. By conjoining multiple conditions or information, policymakers are able to adapt the text to multiple contexts. Modal verbs affect agency. If agents of Parliament 'may' act, rather than 'must' act, there is a significant impact on the timing and extent of policy implementation. Finally, enabling verbs are examples of the deliberate delegation of policymaking authority from a principal (Parliament) to an agent (such as the government).

The policy benefits of these four elements can be described by analogy to a learning algorithm. A simple computer program will achieve a basic outcome with only a few lines of code, reliant on a sparse number of variables (which describe inputs and outputs) and basic flow control (which describes how variables interact). For instance, a pacemaker relies on fewer than 100,000 lines of code as the function performed by a pacemaker must remain carefully regulated and predictable for the sake of the patient. By contrast, social media platforms rely on millions of lines of code. Facebook, for one, is assembled on 62 million lines of instructions (Desjardins 2017). The variables and flow control needed to operate Facebook are complex and, importantly, have a learning capacity. The code uses outputs to develop new inputs. There is no fixed code, but an adaptive algorithm that traces statistical patterns and optimises for future use. By this analogy, we can see both why legislation has increased in volume and, yet, is less comprehensible. The language of legislation also includes a learning facility. As with social media, this learning is driven by statistical regressions to the mean, as well as individual discretion. As Andrew Schotter (1981) has put it, political institutions are 'machines for thinking'. Also pertinent are Deutsch's (1966) descriptions of 'cybernetic' government, and Polanyi's 'spontaneous order' (Heclo 1974; Freeman, R. 2008: 383). Yet, until now, these political cybernetics have not been traced through the historical record.

Who benefits from this? Epstein and O'Halloran (1999) and Huber and Shipan (2002) stress that individual policymakers shape legislative language in line with their policy preferences, as well as their desire to win votes. Epstein and O'Halloran, as mentioned, identified 'delegation measures' and 'constraint measures', whose application depended on a transaction cost analysis by the legislator (in their case, the US Congress). Huber and Shipan described various forms of policy language, such as 'general policy language' and 'client issues'. Their theory also focused on individual legislators' will as they describe a process of deliberate delegation from principals (legislators) to agents (bureaucrats). My theory synthesises, in part, structural and agency explanations. Indeterminate commands are, fundamentally, evidence of power lost. This is the structural change. However, loss of power can also be deliberate. Sometimes, ceding responsibilities can be desired on ideological grounds (so as to shrink the state), or as a means to shed off unimportant ephemera and focus on big issues (Dunleavy 1991). By considering the historical record, I submit, in broad terms, that power to determine language was lost at first, but then later given away by choice, although it is important to take care when asserting that power was lost. I am describing Parliament's power to determine the meaning of laws as being lost or given away. The government, on the other hand, have benefited considerably from Parliament's relaxed grip on language. Also, Parliament has ceded power to determine meaning, but the range of its responsibilities has grown dramatically. The complexity of modern governance is far beyond that which would have been familiar to politicians a century ago. Powers have not straightforwardly disappeared, but increased expectations from voters have been less easily met by state capacity.

The following is an admittedly wry example, but nothing even close to the *Sunbeds (Regulation) Act 2010* could be imagined passing a Victorian, Edwardian or Georgian Parliament. Section 1 of that Act demonstrates a portion of the conceptual and regulatory complexity of modern governance:

> (2) 'Sunbed' means an electrically-powered device designed to produce tanning of the human skin by the emission of ultra-violet radiation. (3) A 'sunbed business' is a business that involves making one or more sunbeds available for use on premises that are occupied by, or are to any extent under the management or control of, the person who carries on the business; and those sunbeds are the sunbeds to which the business relates.

As this Act suggests, describing a secular loss of state power would be plain wrong. However, the point is not that the aggregate level of power has declined, but that the relative capacity to meet demands for policy has declined. Important is the interaction between rising demand for action and the ability to meet said demands amid global and domestic constraints.

One absent constraint in the UK is divided government. Where US congressmen may send rigid instructions to an executive controlled by an opposing party (Mayhew 1991), British parliamentarians face fewer incentives from separated executive and legislative powers. By extension, it is reasonable to claim that the British government have predominant control over the language of public Acts of Parliament. The civil service Bill teams will draft what their political bosses desire (Hood and Dixon 2015), and Parliament will amend Bills but almost always with the government's approval (Dixon and Jones 2017). As such, indeterminacy in legislation should almost exclusively be considered as of a benefit to Her Majesty's Government, which means that this book offers only a partial synthesis of structural and agency factors. Predominantly, the move to indeterminacy has been driven by individual choices. However, the difficulties faced by successive governments in managing policy constraints shaped these choices. The principal theme of post-war British politics has been managed decline (see, eg, Gamble 1981). A slow ebbing of faculties was extraordinarily difficult for policymakers to deal with. Expectations of voters, who were often unaware of the extent of decline, did not walk in step with reality. A series of crises faced by governments from the 1950s through to the 1980s must, in part, be described as unavoidable structural constraints (see, eg, Wickham-Jones 1998). This complex interplay of forces, with indeterminacy in law as both a necessity and as a choice, can be seen from the discourse analyses.

Historic patterns

'Critical junctures' – significant and sudden shocks – triggered rapid change in legislative language (Collier and Collier 2002). These juncture points can be identified as moments of crisis, as well as the choices taken to resolve the crises. In British politics, a conjunction of crisis and ideology has been described, not without controversy, as a period of policy consensus. Consensus implies that in response to events, governments made choices that ultimately became acceptable to opposition parties, and thereby endured up to the next critical juncture. The idea of consensus is somewhat ill-fitting with the presence of indeterminate legislation. If the underlying philosophy of new policies is, indeed, adopted consensually, there should be little need for language that can be adapted by the discretion of agents to unforeseen circumstances. To ensure the faithful application of policy consensus, one would expect governments to favour clear legislation that successor governments will have limited discretion to alter, and that will not yield to changes in circumstance. So, as Ben Pimlott and others have argued, the 'post-war consensus' was, to an extent, asserted rather than real (Pimlott et al 1989). The period from 1945 to 1979 saw rapid increases in the enactment of indeterminate legislation, although, as can be seen from the following graphs, the subsequent 'Thatcherite' era (roughly 1979–2007) was even more dependent on indeterminate and adaptable legislation. This reinforces the argument that 'Thatcherism' is more an approach to governing than a coherent set of policy ideas (Bulpitt 1986). Figures 3.1 and 3.2 highlight moments of rapid change in legislative language.

Figure 3.1: Rates of change (ROC) in per section incidence of indeterminacies

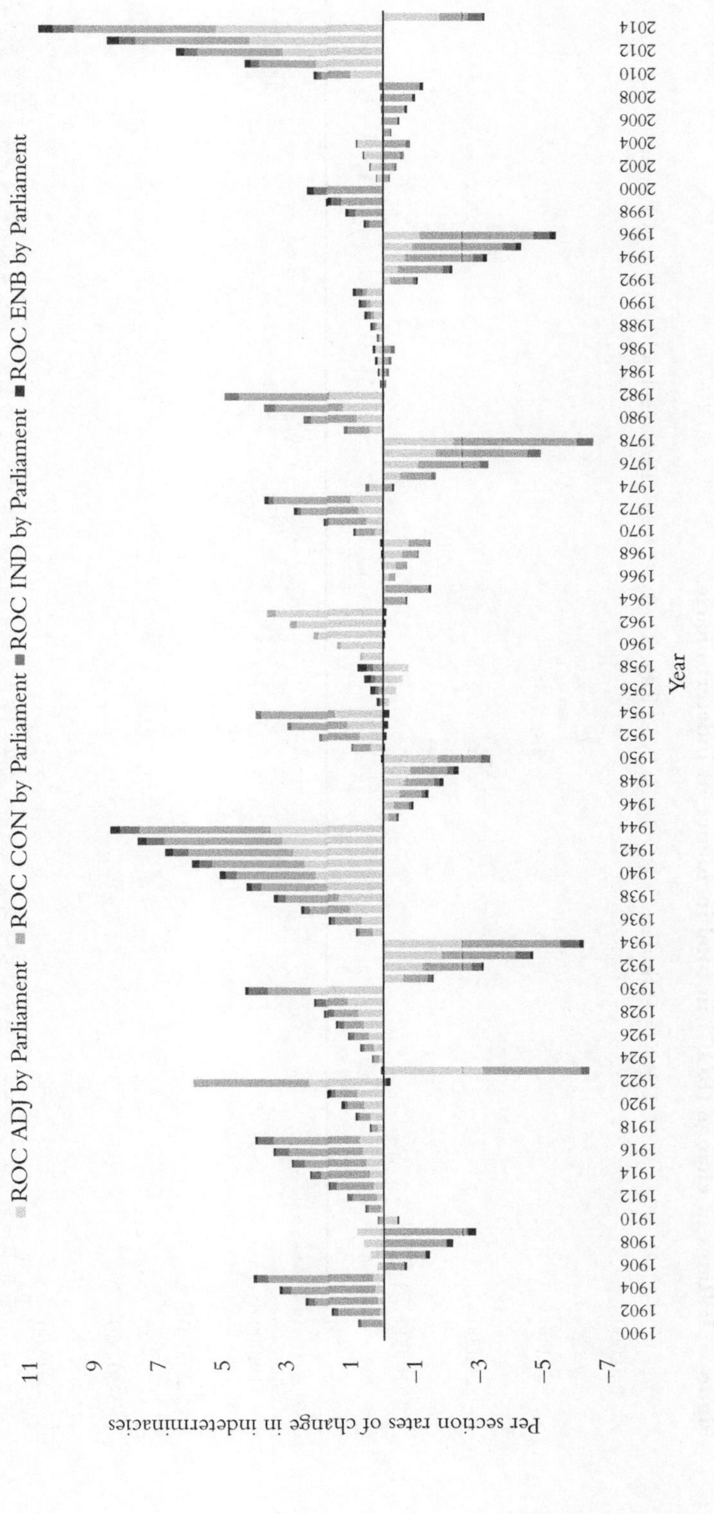

Figure 3.2: Rates of change (ROC) in total incidence of indeterminacies

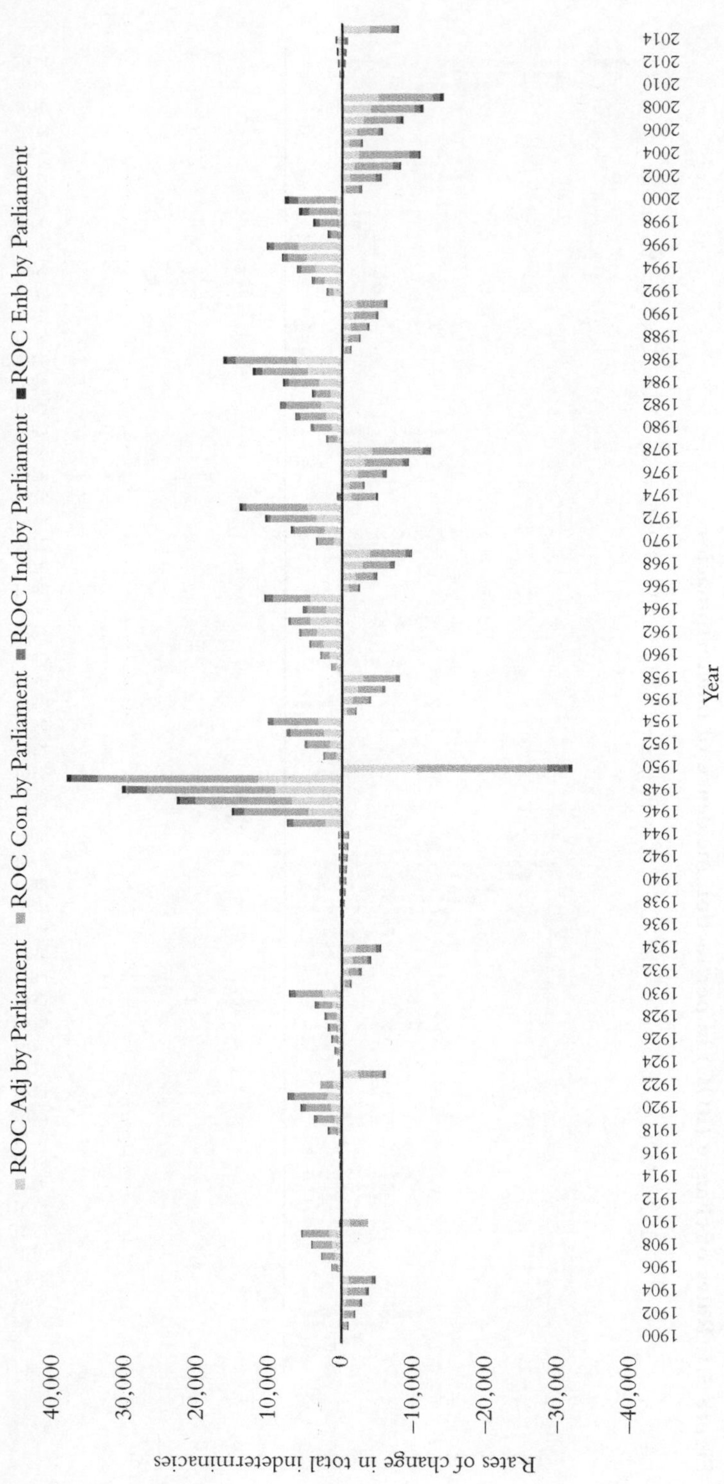

Figures 3.1 and 3.2 display the rates of change from one Parliament to the next. For each Parliament, the average rate of change per year has been calculated. This annual average is shown building additively to the total change for each Parliament. This is, of course, not what actually happened, as the graph simplifies the story and makes clear which Parliaments saw net increases or decreases in indeterminacy, as well as the degree of change from the preceding Parliament. So, for example, Figure 3.1 shows that the 1979–83 Parliament saw an average rate of change of +0.7 conjunctions per section per year. That made for a total increase of 2.8 conjunctions per section when compared with the preceding Parliament. It should be noted that there is no need for tests of significance in comparing years because the data represent the entire available data set. As such, confidence intervals are not required. Also, the reason for focusing on Parliaments, as opposed to individual years, is so that the patterns in language change come into sharper focus. Changes in Parliament often coincide with times of economic and international discombobulation. They also capture changing ideological currents and shifts in party leadership. As such, a single Parliament is a useful unit of historical change.

Figure 3.1 shows volatility in the rates of change before the war. However, as Figure 3.2 shows, the real-term changes at this time were modest. It is after the war when indeterminacy in legislation really took off. Bankruptcy, US geopolitical dominance and imperial retreat were the primary causes of Britain's post-war decline in power. The intersection of these factors caused particular difficulty for policymakers. Crucial constraints included the need to manage the trade deficit and the value of sterling simultaneously. The US demanded that sterling be pegged in value to the dollar. This artificially inflated the pound's value, thereby applying pressure on exporters and other commonwealth countries reliant on sterling. It was a toxic mix of an uncertain political economy and status readjustment, all set in the context of a country that had practically bankrupted itself on the path to victory. Britons, meanwhile, had suffered extraordinary privations and had inflated expectations for lavish public services. These were driven, in particular, by the publication in 1942 of William Beveridge's report on post-war reconstruction. The welfare state, national insurance and the National Health Service (NHS) were enhanced or created anew by the post-war Attlee governments (1945–50, 1950–51), despite the less-than-favourable political and economic contexts.

All post-war governments instructed Parliament to frame policy competencies in loose language. Yet, interestingly, Conservative governments were more reliant on indeterminate language than were

Labour governments in the period 1945–79. A plausible theory for this is that Conservatives are more instinctively pragmatic, whereas the Labour Party is rather more wedded to principles. Labour also had stronger institutions and internal democracy, which could ensure that commitments to principle were upheld. Put in the language of this book's theoretical framework, Labour historically relied more on a logic of communication than the Conservatives. However, as the 1970s progressed, attention to what the public wanted switched to increased consideration of what governments could practically provide. The constraints of industrial relations and inflation crises were felt by Labour and the Conservatives. From 1979, interest in the government's waning capacity to supply was driven, in part, by ideology, not just acceptance of limitations. The Thatcher governments' ideological commitments are difficult (and intellectually dangerous) to pinpoint, but can be loosely described as adhering to neoliberal positions. The state was seen more as a facilitator of private enterprise than a guarantor of demand and employment. Public services were therefore 'rolled back' to make way for free enterprise. Although, as suggested, describing these governments as coherently neoliberal is unwise, it was a neoliberal approach to economic management, with some British idiosyncrasies. First, there was no stomach to abandon the welfare state. The NHS, public housing, pensions and benefits were modestly subjected to market forces, but none were entirely removed from the public sector. The second idiosyncrasy was patriotism. Policy was meant to boost national pride, so there was no rolling back of the state in matters of defence and internal security. Indeed, illiberal means were, on occasion, used to fight both foreign and domestic enemies. The third uniquely British characteristic of neoliberalism undergirded the other two: the core executive was enhanced (Rhodes and Dunleavy 1995). Markets would be freed by a strong central government smashing barriers to competitiveness (Gamble 1988). These three idiosyncrasies of British neoliberalism called for legislation that could be adapted to circumstance with discretion. Less palatable would have been tight parliamentary oversight of law and policy.

It is therefore interesting to note from Figures 3.1 and 3.2 that the New Labour governments from 1997 to 2010 oversaw modest increases in indeterminate legislation at first, followed by decreasing reliance on indeterminacy in the last two Parliaments (2001–05, 2005–10). These decreases came before further sharp increases in the per section rates of change under the Coalition government (2010–15). Also of note from Figure 3.1 are findings anticipated in Chapter Two, namely, the post-millennium decrease in the use of conjunctions as compared with, in particular, adjectives and adverbs. How can these changes be explained? The New Labour governments sustained some of the policy ideas and governing practices of their Conservative predecessors, but there were significant changes in the language of policy, especially after the 2001 election. The explanation is, of course, multifaceted. The primary motive was to modernise public services. This began before the New Labour governments by the Major governments of 1990–1997, but the agenda was accelerated after 2001. The key changes under New Labour were procedural reforms. The goals were, among others, to provide more cost effectiveness and accountability for public services. This was achieved by delegating policy implementation to arm's-length agencies and thereby 'hollowing out' much of the policy work of central government (Rhodes 1994). However, interestingly, while the Major and Blair governments were keen to delegate the delivery of public services, they were less keen to cede control over its content. This has been described as 'bureau shaping', where policy delivery is separated from policymaking (Dunleavy 1991). Christopher Hood (1991) has described public sector reform in the UK as focused on cost effectiveness and accountability, while shying away from managerial reform that would see the centre relax its grip on policy content. By this theory, we can explain why indeterminacy in law fell somewhat in the 1992–97 and 2001–10 Parliaments, and yet the use of conjunctions fell faster than other parts of speech. If the aim was to delegate limited discretion to deliver policy, using fewer conjunctions would make the law marginally more determinate in its execution. This would help ensure increased accountability. If, simultaneously, the aim was to retain or enhance central control of policy content, using more adjectives would allow for this expanded capacity. This theory would also predict somewhat fewer indeterminate modal verbs, and somewhat more enabling verbs. This is what Figure 3.1 displays for the 2001–05 Parliament. This Parliament had much the same pattern as the 1983–87 Parliament. Indeterminate modal verbs could allow broad discretion for non-governmental agents to act, whereas enabling verbs almost exclusively empower the central executive to change the law.

It should also be noted that the function of legislation is a variable, as will be explained further in Part Two. If law enumerates a new power, then conjunctions will allow expansive application of that power to multiple, indeterminately conjoined contexts. Hence, in establishing powers for agents of government, it is in the centre's interests not to use too many conjunctions. Adjectives and adverbs have less effect on the application of power, where they are more susceptible to definition by judges. Adjectives and adverbs are more important for enumerating duties and rights because they allow for concept stretching, which will be less susceptible to judicial constraint. In other words, judges will less easily prove a negative (that a duty was shirked) than notice a positive (that an indeterminate power was used).

Notable peaks in indeterminate legislative language came at times of uncertainty. At these times, a gap grew between what voters wanted and what governments could, or wanted to, provide. The mid-1920s saw a spike in the enactment of indeterminate language, and the greatest rates of change were recorded between 1960 and 2000, as Figures 3.1 and 3.2 demonstrate. Also of note are the sharp changes in direction from indeterminate to more determinate language recorded when Conservative and Labour governments exchanged power (see, for instance, the decreased proportionate use of indeterminate language recorded in 1965, 1975 and, to a lesser extent, 2000). Conversely, moves from Labour to Conservative governments, as well as changes of Conservative prime minister, were coincident with the increased use of indeterminate language (see 1970, 1980 and 1990). So, the greatest use of indeterminate language coincides with Conservative rule in the late 20th century, albeit that the four forms of indeterminacy did not change uniformly, and Labour governments in 1965, 1975 and 2000 were coincident with an increased use of adjectives and adverbs.

The upshot is that changes to legislative genre were greatest under Conservative-led Parliaments, as measured by rates of change per section. This, in part, reflects that party's ideological pragmatism and moves to centralise policymaking power. Although Labour-led Parliaments enacted increased numbers of adjectives and adverbs, this likely reflects the Labour Party's interest in concept formation in law, which is especially important to establishing public sector duties and rights. Furthermore, besides changes in per section levels of indeterminacy, significant changes in legislative output (measured by total changes in the number of indeterminacies) are most common at the dawning of new consensuses. So, significant changes in degrees of indeterminacy were led by structural forces, while significant changes in kind were more the result of ideological choices.

Case studies

Three case studies describe how, exactly, context and individual choice combined to encourage the adoption of different forms of legislative language. The three cases look to instances of Parliament creating new powers, new duties and new rights.

On powers: the Anisminic *case*

An excellent source for discovering what meanings were intended by legislative language are court cases. The government, as defendant or appellant, will explain what they think is the correct interpretation of legislative language. As such, let us consider arguably the most important case in the post-war renaissance of judicial review: the 1969 case of *Anisminic Ltd v Foreign Compensation Commission*[22] (Blom-Cooper et al 2009). In this case, the Appellate Committee of the House of Lords supposedly ignored Parliament's explicit instruction and ruled that the actions of the Foreign Compensation Commission were illegal (*ultra vires*). It was argued at the time that the court had breached the British constitution by defining limits to Parliament's sovereignty (Elliott 2000: 344). However, if we look in detail at the language of the legislation that was under dispute, we can see indeterminacies that needed to be constructed into meaningful law. These indeterminacies were deliberately inserted to maximise the powers available to the government.

The details of the case are that Anisminic Ltd, a British-owned mining company, had lost property in Egypt worth £4,000,000 during the Suez Crisis. In 1957, Anisminic agreed to a sale of their assets to an Egyptian company named TEDO for £500,000, but reserved a right to future compensation. In 1959, the British and Egyptian governments ratified a bilateral treaty that included the payment of a lump sum by the Egyptians to compensate those who had lost property. Control of this money was granted to Her Majesty's Government by Parliament via the *Foreign Compensation Act 1950.* Appeals against compensation decisions were entrusted to a government-appointed tribunal, the Foreign Compensation Commission. The decisions of this Commission had been intentionally protected from judicial review by any court through an 'ouster' clause in section 4(4) of the 1950 Act: 'The determination by the Commission of any application made to them under this Act shall not be called in question in any court of law'.

This section contains none of the indeterminate parts of speech measured for this book. It is plainly worded. The reason for ousting the courts' jurisdiction was to ensure that the Commission's work in dividing a limited pot was not frustrated or delayed by appeals. The 1950 Act also made provision for the government to pass secondary legislation so as to refine the compensation rules as and when it was felt necessary to do so. The government did so with the *Foreign*

[22] [1969] 2 AC 147, [1969] 2 WLR 163.

Compensation (Egypt) (Determination and Registration of Claims) Order 1962. The Order established a right to compensation for those persons or companies listed in Annex E of the 1959 Anglo-Egyptian treaty. Listed were those who had lost property or were successors in title to property lost. The Foreign Compensation Commission relied on the 1962 Order when dismissing Anisminic's claim to compensation. It was ruled that because Anisminic had sold their holdings, they had thereby forfeited any right to compensation. The House of Lords ruled that this determination by the Commission was null and reversed it. They reasoned that the words 'successor in title' had no meaning if the original claimant still survived. The Commission had made a legal error that was in excess of their jurisdiction (therefore, *ultra vires*). So, the Lords ruled that no legal determination had been made at all and the ouster clause at section 4(4) could not stop the court ruling over the case.

For John Griffith (1977: 123–4), a noted critic of judicial overreach, the Lords were acting unconstitutionally by explicitly ignoring Parliament's instructions in the 1950 Act. However, the 1950 Act was extraordinarily indeterminate. Section 4(4) was clearly constructed, but it was nested in a scheme of law riddled with omissions and ellipses. The major problem was with section 2(2), which established the power for a government minister to create Orders in Council. These Orders needed to establish what a valid 'determination' of the Commission was, and what the legal jurisdiction of the Commission was. The 1962 Order, challenged by Anisminic, failed on counts because the 1950 Act was indeterminate:

> Without prejudice to the generality of the preceding subsection an Order in Council under this section may provide – (a) for defining the persons who are to be qualified, in respect of nationality or status, to make applications to the Commission for the purpose of establishing such claims as aforesaid, and for imposing any other conditions to be fulfilled before such claims can be entertained.

In drafting an Order under this section, the government had wide discretion, without tethers to determinate language. This discretion was established by the modal verb 'may', the enabling power to establish Orders in Council and a liberal application of conditional conjunctions. For example, qualifying persons can be defined 'in respect of nationality *or* status', with status undefined. In addition to which, the Commission could define who could bring applications '*and* for imposing any other conditions'. This language was intended to maximise the government's flexibility in managing compensation claims. Furthermore, the 1962 Order, rather than clearing up confusion as to the Commission's powers, further muddied the waters. Lord Reid complained at paragraph 214 of his judgment in *Anisminic* that language was, indeed, the primary cause of confusion:

> The meaning of the important parts of this Order is extremely difficult to discover, and, in my view, a main cause of this is the deplorable modern drafting practice of compressing to the point of obscurity provisions which would not be difficult to understand if written out at rather greater length.

The meaning of important parts of the Order, and, by extension, the parent Act, had to be constructed by judges. As a result, the ruling in *Anisminic* adapted administrative law by abolishing a technical distinction between administrative errors made within jurisdiction and those made beyond jurisdiction (Taylor 1976). The 1950 Act was legally indeterminate because it established near-unfettered power for the government, but Parliament cannot remain as sovereign when a rival has unfettered power. It is a logical impossibility. The government could, by Order, lay down any conditions it saw fit for the Commission to use, and nothing of this could be reviewed by the courts. For Sir William Wade (1969), a lifelong champion of Parliament's sovereignty, this sort of statutory language was the foundation of tyranny, and totally at odds with Parliament's sovereignty under the rule of law. Nevertheless, successive governments have instructed Parliament to enact more and more ouster clauses in order to protect their policies from review by the courts (Loveland 2006: 84–7). However, ouster clauses can only work if the power they support is plainly established.

On duties: the Franklin *case*

With regard to duties, it is in governments' interests to ensure that statutory duties are flexible. Clearly established duties are important for ensuring the faithful and accountable execution of policy. However, if set in rigid language, duties can frustrate policy action in response to changing circumstances or individual discretion. A court case from 1947 describes the interplay of these motives. The case of *Franklin and Others v The Minister of Town and Country Planning*[23] was heard by the Appellate Committee of the House of Lords. At issue was whether Stevenage should be designated as a new town. This 'new town' designation gave planning control to a development corporation, answerable to Whitehall rather than to local authorities or affected communities. Statutory duties to consult were imposed in broad terms by section 1 of the *New Towns Act 1946*:

> (1) If the Minister is satisfied, after consultation with any local authorities who appear to him to be concerned, that it is expedient in the national interest that any area of land should be developed as a new town by a corporation established under this Act, he may make an order designating that area as the site of the proposed new town.

Note that 'after consultation with any local authorities' is a subordinate clause. The main sentence clause empowers the Secretary of State with the opaque adjective phrase 'expedient in the national interest'. Further detail on the duty to consult was set out in Schedule 1(3) of the Act:

> If any objection is duly made to the proposed order and is not withdrawn, the Minister shall, before making the order, cause a public local inquiry to be held with respect thereto, and shall consider the report of the person by whom the inquiry was held.

So, while the power to designate new towns was indeterminate, the duty to consult on said designation was clear: 'the Minister shall … cause a public local inquiry to be held'. In the case of *Franklin*, the appellants submitted that the Minister had pre-judged the outcome of the local inquiry. Lord Thankerton transcribed the exchange between the Minister and the local residents in his ruling. These are the Minister's words:

> [4] … in due course Stevenage will gain. Local authorities will be consulted all the way through. But we have a duty to perform, and I am not going to be deterred from that duty. While I will consult as far as possible all the local authorities,

[23] [1947] UKHL 3, [1948] AC 87.

> at the end, if people become fractious and unreasonable I shall have to carry out my duty – (Voice: Gestapo!).

The Gestapo comparison was far-fetched, but the Minister was clearly determined not to change his mind. In response, the court curled into a ball:

> [7] In my opinion, no judicial, or quasi-judicial, duty was imposed on the Respondent [the Minister], and any reference to judicial duty, or bias, is irrelevant in the present case … the Respondent was required to satisfy himself that it was a sound scheme before he took the serious step of issuing a draft order … I am of opinion that no judicial duty is laid on the Respondent in discharge of these statutory duties, and that the only question is whether he has complied with the statutory directions to appoint a person to hold the public inquiry, and to consider that person's report.

It was not, according to the Law Lords, improper for a policymaker to reach a snap decision on the basis of their personal political beliefs. The duty to consult in the 1946 Act clearly stated the need for an inquiry. However, the extent to which the government had to follow the findings of such an inquiry remained indeterminate. Technically, the Minister held an inquiry, was called a Nazi and designated Stevenage as a new town all the same.

On rights: the Immigration Act 1971

Court cases make clear what the government think legislation means. Another, more candid, source are Cabinet papers pertaining to draft legislation. This case study looks to when automatic rights to citizenship changed from connection to the land, to connection by blood: 1 January 1973. It was the *Immigration Act 1971* that came into force on that day, and changed UK citizenship law from *ius soli* to *ius sanguinnis*. The 'law of soil' grants citizenship to anybody born in the nation's territory. It is a policy principle that still applies in the US, and explains how even illegal immigrants can give birth to new citizens. The 'law of blood' is the more common model among rich nations. It dictates that only a relationship by blood to a current or deceased citizen can grant automatic citizenship. The policy shift came, in part, as a response to Enoch Powell's 'Rivers of Blood' speech, and the public reaction to increased migration from East Africa, in particular. Individuals coming from East Africa could previously take advantage of the *ius soli* principle, set out in the *British Nationality Act 1948.* This granted British citizenship to citizens of Kenya and Uganda on account of their being born in Commonwealth territory.

There is no question that race relations were a consideration in changing this formula for granting citizenship. The 1971 Act deliberately distinguished between the so-called 'Old Commonwealth' of mostly white nations (such as Australia, Canada and New Zealand) and the 'New Commonwealth' in Africa, Asia and the West Indies. To make this distinction the following statutory language was used in section 3:

> (1) … where a person is not patrial – (a) he shall not enter the United Kingdom unless given leave to do so in accordance with this Act; (b) he may be given leave … either for a limited or for an indefinite period; (c) leave … may be given subject to conditions restricting his employment or occupation … or requiring him to register with the police, or both.

The conditional language ('or' is used four times) and modal verb used ('may' is used twice) allow wide discretion in deciding when to grant leave and when to issue ancillary benefits. However, it is the automatic right to citizenship that is of interest here. This applies to anyone who is 'patrial' – an esoteric adjective that had never previously been used in legislation. Declassified Cabinet papers from the Legislation Subcommittee reveal that much confusion was created by these seven letters. The following was recorded on 9 February 1971:

The Lord President [Willie Whitelaw] said he thought the word 'patrial' would get a bad press. The Lord Chancellor [Quintin Hogg, Lord Hailsham] said that he hated it … Sir John Fiennes [Chief Parliamentary Counsel] … had judged it better to use an unfamiliar word for a novel concept.… The Solicitor General [Geoffrey Howe] said that he and the Attorney [Peter Rawlinson] did not like the word much but had not been able to improve on it.[24]

Most telling here is Sir John Fiennes' position as Chief Parliamentary Counsel. It was his task to oversee the drafting of the Bill. He claimed

---

[24] W J Bohan B2 Div minutes of Cabinet Legislation Commt 9/2/71, National Archives HO 376/170.

in this account that it was best to use an unfamiliar term for a novel concept. This encapsulates how, in breaking policy ground, new language was considered necessary. Another motivation was doubtless to obscure the racial connotations, a point on which Lord Hailsham was less squeamish than his colleagues:

> the Lord Chancellor said that the government ought not to be so 'mealy-mouthed' as its predecessor in making administrative arrangements favourable to citizens of Australia, Canada and New Zealand. He commented that he could himself see no objection in principle to giving favourable treatment to people who had the same sort of ethnic connection with this country as ... President Kennedy had had with Ireland.[25]

Furthermore, an earlier memo captures the desire for near-absolute flexibility in policy implementation: 'The Prime Minister's argument [faded text] since the Home Secretary will have absolute discretion he will be able to admit any category you like'.[26] This flexibility was intended to secure exclusions for different persons: 'the Prime Minister will want to be able to say to the Prime Ministers of Australia and New Zealand ... that the Bill will not make any difference to Australians or New Zealanders'.[27] Exasperation, from some, at the policy's flexibility is captured here:

> I have been losing patience with the Foreign Office, who have a desire to secure exceptional treatment for all sorts of people. I think that we are showing great helpfulness over the Old Commonwealth. But they are still thinking about some points on Malta and the dependent territories.[28]

Above all, the motivation for introducing such an adaptive adjective as 'patrial' was electoral pressure. Minutes of a meeting between the Home Secretary and Mark Bonham-Carter (head of the Community Relations Commission) show the pressures brought to bear by media populism:

---

[25] See note 24.

[26] Brief to SSHD prior to full Cabinet by J H Waddell of No 10 4/1/71.

[27] See note 26.

[28] J H Waddell HO memo to Sir Philip Allen 22/12/70.

> The Home Secretary said that the Bill made the minimum changes consistent with the election manifesto. One of its objects was to remove the widespread feeling in the country that immigration was out of control: such views gravely prejudiced community relations.[29]

This perception 'that immigration was out of control' has not much changed in the intervening years. However, trying to craft a determinable rule of law amid such extraordinary demands for action clearly proved difficult. In the end, automatic rights to citizenship hinged on language that was difficult for claimants to determine, and this thereby helped with government efforts to constrain those rights.

Conclusion

Zygmunt Bauman (1991, 7–8) described sovereignty as the 'power to define and to make definitions stick'. What has been explored in this chapter is why a sovereign (in this case, Parliament) might cede this power to define. We have seen an increasing use of legislative language whose meaning must be established through analogy, rather than deduced from the logical progression of arguments in a text. In other words, the rule of law must increasingly be inferred from an individual's experiences, or by regression to a central tendency of meaning. The primary reason given for this ceding of sovereign authority is to attempt to address heightened demands for public services against diminished capacity to guarantee delivery. The findings suggest that structural constraints have, for the most part, forced Parliament to recognise its diminished power to define. No legislature in a small economy can plausibly attempt to define its nation's reality against the forces of globalisation. However, as well as being forced to accept a diminished power to define, some Parliaments, especially those led by Conservative governments, have pushed further. They have embraced the theory that no state can, or even should, define their citizens' realities. All arguments on power are, in this conception, transitory, and must be subject to adjustment when context demands it. By Steven Lukes' (1974) classic account, Parliament is using not its power to decide, but its power deliberately not to decide. It has deferred judgement to those who are, or will become, better placed to

[29] From minutes of a meeting held in Reginald Maudling's House of Commons office, 16 February 1971.

make definitions. Going further, this non-decision-making is tied, as Lukes would predict, to ideological power: the desire to be pragmatic and decide on the basis of what will likely work best. It is, as argued, an approach to language that is led by a logic of consequences, rather than a logic of communication.

It could be argued, plausibly, that travelling light on principle and taking the pragmatic course is found in the national DNA. Empiricism and pragmatism are prominent in British (especially English, but also some Scottish) political thought. The 'what matters is what works' style of government is unsurprising from a political culture wedded to ancient institutions, rather than committed to any timeless principles. A comparative example is the USA's second amendment, taken alongside the lesser-known, and vastly more indeterminate, article seven of the *Bill of Rights 1688*: 'the right of the people to keep and bear Arms, shall not be infringed'; and 'That the Subjects which are Protestants may have Arms for their Defence suitable to their Conditions and as allowed by Law'.

Notwithstanding that 'A well regulated Militia' is open to interpretation, the USA's gun laws are plain. Britain's (more properly, England's) version allowed the government, at any time, to take away its citizens' guns. The phrase 'as allowed by law' is almost entirely redundant as a phrase in law. It is a law whose meaning depends on future law. It is rather like Parliament defining power in the following terms: 'you may legally do *A*, unless *A* becomes illegal someday'. Indeterminacy is also created in article seven by conditional language (which, and, as) and adjectives (suitable).

However, despite this historic example, there is evidence that the enactment of indeterminate legislation has increased markedly since 1900. It cannot be claimed that the pragmatic maxim of Peirce has always led the drafting of British statute law. Plainness was, after all, the aim of Lord Thring in drafting statutes. Plainness would mean a loss of flexibility where the text could not easily yield to context. However, post-war governments, especially those seeking to 'roll back the state', have relied on language whose meaning turns on context and authority. This is not truly discourse at all, in that indeterminate legislation does not encourage shared and meaningful communication. Instead, indeterminacy allows authority and context to determine text.

Part Two: The social impact of Parliament's use of language

FOUR

Immigration: how Parliament's language affects central government powers

> Politicians don't actually say things, they indicate them.
> *George Carlin, National Press Club, 1999*

> This [decision] is reinforced by the constitutional principle requiring the rule of law to be observed. That principle too requires that a constitutional state must accord to individuals the right to know of a decision before their rights can be adversely affected. The antithesis of such a state was described by Kafka: a state where the rights of individuals are overridden by hole in the corner decisions or knocks on doors in the early hours. That is not our system.
> *Lord Steyn in* R (Anufrijeva) v Secretary of State for the Home Department and Another *[2004] 1 AC 604, at 621*

Introduction

George Carlin and Lord Steyn describe, in their own ways, how difficult it can be to understand politicians and their policies. An implication of this indeterminate communication is that judges often have to make sense of the law. This chapter looks specifically at judicial interpretation of immigration law. No other public policy domain has been subject to more litigation than immigration and asylum. It also dominates public debate. Battles over Brexit, economic growth, social care and national security have all circled round questions of who has a right to reside in the UK. This chapter grasps the nettle. Here, I analyse what impact indeterminacy in immigration law has had on the effectiveness of policy.

For this opening chapter of Part Two, the focus is on how legislative language affects central government powers. Immigration and asylum laws delegate power from Parliament to the government, and the aim is to track this inter-institutional coordination. An attempt by the government to act under delegated powers will be deemed to have been ineffective if it is declared illegal. So, the specific question for this chapter is as follows: why are government steps to manage immigration increasingly declared illegal in court? By focusing on judges' rulings, we can better understand what happens when politicians 'don't actually say [any]thing', as Carlin put it. The failed inter-institutional discourse between Parliament and the government stimulates a judicial response. Judges' rulings can therefore provide a logic of communication that was absent from the law.

How has judicial behaviour changed in this area? From 1970 – when immigration appeals were first allowed – up to 1994, there were 78 immigration cases brought to a superior appeal court, with appeal courts being the Court of Appeal, House of Lords (up to 2009) and the UK Supreme Court (after 2009). Of these 78 cases, the government lost 25 times. That is a rate of one loss per year, and a defeat rate of one in three. In just 17 years after 1994 up to 2012, 174 appeal cases were heard, of which the government took 90 defeats. Government decisions were declared illegal in over half the cases appealed, with ministers losing over five of these major cases per year. Part of this change can be explained by increased rates of immigration since the turn of the millennium. In addition, this demographic shift was coincident with judges wielding new powers to challenge government decisions under the *Human Rights Act 1998* (HRA). However, there remains a mystery: there being more immigrants does not plausibly lead to more government defeats in appeal cases. Yes, there have been many more cases brought to courts – including lower courts as well as appeal courts. However, why should simply increasing the supply of litigants change the behaviour of judges? It should not, and arguably has not. In addition to which, the HRA does not gift judges power to make new law. They have new powers to interpret legislation, but where that legislation is plain, they have nothing to gain from the HRA. So, it could be that government ministers are simply breaking the law with greater frequency. However, this is also implausible: ministers would not pursue a costly appeal if a decision of theirs was blatantly illegal. A more plausible theory for why governments increasingly lose appeal cases is because of problems with the law, not judges' wilfulness or government incompetence.

Increasingly indeterminate language framing immigration policy therefore helps explain changes in judicial behaviour. In this chapter, focus lies on how power is delegated. Legislation increasingly leaves indeterminate the exact content, scope and appropriate timing of power. Immigration policy is thereby adaptable, and less restricted by narrow 'policy windows' (Kingdon 1995). Yet, indeterminate legislation offers only an 'incomplete contract', and judges will need to interpret away any uncertainty. Of course, all law taken before an appeal court will be indeterminate to some degree (Dyevre 2010: 311–14). However, it is notable that this supply of ever-more indeterminate law has increased, with implications for policy effectiveness.

Recent attempts at modelling judges' behaviour have derived from theories of 'judicialisation'. These theories describe 'expansion of the province of courts or the judges at the expense of the politicians and of the administrators' (Tate and Vallinder 1995: 13). In this chapter, I dust off an older theory that has somewhat dropped out of favour: the legal model (Levi, 1948; Dahl 1957; Merryman 1981; Edwards 1984). Legal models of judicialisation predict that any 'expansion of the province of the courts' will be led by changes in law. Rival theories alternatively stress the changing preferences of judges as drivers of judicialisation. Judges are the principal components in both attitudinal (Schubert 1965; Gibson 1978; Sisk et al 1998; Segal and Spaeth 2002) and strategic models (North and Weingast 1989; Eskridge and Ferejohn 1992; Epstein and Knight 1998; Garrett et al 1998; Carrubba et al 2008). These attitudinal and strategic models assume that judges have policy preferences that inform their rulings. I accept these reasonable assumptions, but would add the caveat that judges are severely constrained, meaning that judges cannot advance their policy interests unless given an opportunity to rule on a case where the law is essentially incomplete. Acting on such opportunities is not inappropriate, *per se*, as it is squarely within judges' institutional competence to determine what law means when there is doubt. However, judges determining the details of immigration policy, against the government's interests, is an indication of policy ineffectiveness. Indeed, it is policy ineffectiveness with extraordinary political consequences.

Conditional conjunctions (if/and/or) in legislation are especially impactful when it comes to wielding power. These allow multiple conditions to be conjoined in various ways, and allow powerful actors to determine how language and reality can be reconciled. Conjunctions therefore elasticate the scope of policy. Judges will seek to narrow the potential scope with their rulings. Adjectives and indeterminate modal verbs have less of an effect on judges' behaviour. This is because these parts of speech affect content and timing, respectively, and can more easily be subject to binding precedent. For instance, an interpretation of an adjective at time *t* will affect interpretations at $t + 1$. Conjunctions are less delimited by a central tendency of meaning, and depend more heavily on contextual information. This will change from case to case, meaning that each individual use of a law requires a new interpretation of the rules. With regard to powers, conjunctions significantly undermine a 'logic of communication' (Schmidt 2008). In addition to which, legal fights over indeterminate law will often favour the weaker party – the immigrant – because where there is doubt, benefit is accorded to the party subject to power, not the party attempting to extend their power. This is a basic requirement of natural justice.

Attitudinal models, which predict judges' decisions on their preferences alone, have weak predictive power in the UK. This was comprehensively demonstrated by Chris Hanretty (2013). Variables other than the judges' personalities must explain their changing behaviour. Strategic opportunities to strike down government decisions have not notably changed either. Without entrenched constitutional law, British judges remain subservient to Parliament. So, legal language is a plausible variable. Changes to this inter-institutional discourse have theoretically profound effects on policy implementation (Hönnige 2011). Focusing on immigration policy can further be justified on two counts. The first is the enduring salience of immigration policy. Voters, media commentators and policymakers consider effective immigration control as both desirable and important. In addition, there is misplaced suspicion that judges are 'soft' on questions of immigration by changing policy without accountability. Second, immigration and asylum cases are the most common public law suit in British courts. As such, there are plenty of cases available to analyse.

Two methods of analysis are used in this chapter. First, to demonstrate that immigration law is increasingly indeterminate, all of the 1,233 sections of immigration legislation enacted between 1905 and 2016 have been put through the discourse analysis program used in Chapter Two. Second, results from multivariate logit regressions are presented. These regress data on legislative language and case outcomes. Other variables describe changes to the age of legislation, the use of human rights law, case facts and historical events. To capture historical events, period dummies are used to demarcate periods of reform to lower courts. These immigration tribunals manage thousands of immigration cases, of which only the most impactful make it to a court of appeal. Both fixed effects and random effects logit models were put together. Random effects models tested for the clustering of errors around individual judges, as well as clustering for each of the two courts in which appeals were heard. Data were taken from all 252 appeal cases heard from 1970 to 2012 at the Court of Appeal and House of Lords/Supreme Court. A fixed effects model relying on two language variables, and period dummies, has the greatest statistical significance. This model predicts 73% of judges' rulings. Models including random intercepts for judges or courts offer no improvements in model fit. So, legislative language and lower court administration best explain why judges increasingly frustrate the implementation of immigration policy.

Context

Immigration is a complex issue for modern democracies. Indeed, a primary component of sovereignty is the determination of who does and does not qualify for residency; much of the Brexit debate centred on 'taking back control' of borders and citizenship. Typically, immigration policies are set by governments on calculations of material self-interest (Bevan 1986). As such, there is considerable friction between the popularity of tough immigration policy, set against the benefits of mobile labour and wider concerns for human rights.

Randall Hansen (2009) identified three notable waves of immigration since 1800: first, Jewish immigration during the 19th century; second, Commonwealth immigration before the *Immigration Act 1971*; and, third, immigration from the European Union (EU) 'A8' countries since 2004 (Eastern Europe) and 'A2' countries since 2007 (Romania and Bulgaria). Making policy in response to these waves was complicated by intersecting questions of national security, social security, economics, culture and race relations. Consequently, policy to manage immigration and asylum lacked coherence (Freeman 1995). There have, however, been roughly identifiable phases in policy. An open-door approach was first established by the *British Nationality Act 1948*: any individual born in a Commonwealth country attained automatic British citizenship. This policy lasted until the enactment of the *Commonwealth Immigrants Act 1962*. This instigated a more restrictive phase in policy, which responded to public fears about community relations. Further restrictions were introduced with the *Commonwealth Immigrants Act 1968*. This Act was rushed through

Parliament in 48 hours to allow the issuance of immigration vouchers to East-African Asians. James Callaghan, Home Secretary at the time, confided to Cabinet that such an obvious attack on civil liberties would not be tolerated in any nation with a written constitution (Bevan 1986). Alongside these restrictive laws were measures to alleviate the effects of restrictive immigration policies, notably, the *Race Relations Acts 1965* and *1968*, and the first immigration appeals system inaugurated by the *Immigration Appeals Act 1969*.

As discussed in Chapter Three, a critical change came with the *Immigration Acts 1971* and *1981*. These removed common law immigration rules. The common law and royal prerogative had, up to that point, dominated citizenship law. However, mass immigration had made the medieval system not fit for purpose. The common law approach to citizenship was founded on feudalism, with fealty to one's lord by dint of birth in his domains (*ius soli*). However, since the *Immigration Acts 1971* and *1981*, modern immigration law rejected this formula, and citizenship was only guaranteed through blood relationship to another citizen (*ius sanguinis*) (Bevan 1986; Stolcke 1995). After 1997, immigration policy changed once more to reflect the economic benefits of skilled and unskilled migration. As such, entry conditions were relaxed. This liberal phase was short-lived in the aftermath of the terrorist attacks in New York on 11 September 2001. On top which, the decision to allow free migration from new EU member states after 2004 led to a significant backlash (Hansen 2009).

Theory and hypotheses

Before describing the theory in abstract, a concrete example will be helpful. In 2012, the UK Supreme Court put a hold on the deportations of seven men.[30] These Algerian citizens were deemed by the Home Secretary to be threatening British national security. However, the court was told of a significant risk of their being tortured if returned to Algeria. Evidence in support of this claim could only be admitted if a key witness could testify anonymously. This would mean that all court records relating to this testimony could never be published. Applying an indefinite injunction against publishing testimony was without precedent in such cases. Yet, the Supreme Court justices rejected the government's submissions, then ordered

[30] *W(Algeria) and another v Secretary of State for the Home Department; PP(Algeria) v Same; Z(Algeria) and others v Same* [2012] UKSC 8.

the testimony be admitted, imposed a permanent injunction against its publication and demanded that all seven cases be reheard in light of the new evidence. Theresa May, Home Secretary at the time, submitted that secret witness testimony could not properly be cross-examined. She relied in this submission on a ruling in her favour at the Court of Appeal. So, it was a case that saw appeal judges rejecting government descriptions of their own powers in the high-stakes context of national security. How can such a ruling be explained? Were the presiding justices just 'soft' and unwilling to deport individuals who may come to harm? Were they taking advantage of government weakness to push a policy agenda? Or, were they acting on reasonable doubts as to what the law allowed? It is this last rationale that I submit provoked the decision.

In these cases, barristers debated the meaning of highly indeterminate legislative language. Section 5 of the *Special Immigration Appeals Commission Act 1997* was the focus of dispute. It was legislation that established special courts for trying, in particular, foreign-born terror suspects. Legislation was needed to allow the government to use secret intelligence in court. Rather than the usual public scrutiny of evidence, special advocates would see material on behalf of the defendant, who would not be allowed access to it. This is known as a closed material procedure, and was regulated in part by the following legislation:

> (1) The Lord Chancellor may make rules – (a) for regulating the exercise of the rights of appeal … (b) for prescribing the practice and procedure to be followed on or in connection with appeals … including the mode and burden of proof and admissibility of evidence on such appeals, and (c) for other matters preliminary or incidental to or arising out of such appeals….
>
> (3) Rules under this section may, in particular – (a) make provision enabling proceedings before the Commission to take place without the appellant being given full particulars of the reasons for the decision which is the subject of the appeal, (b) make provision enabling the Commission to hold proceedings in the absence of any person, including the appellant and any legal representative appointed by him….
>
> (6) In making rules under this section, the Lord Chancellor shall have regard, in particular, to – (a) the need to secure

that decisions which are the subject of appeals are properly reviewed.

Justices had to determine whether rules describing the admissibility of evidence could include the admission of anonymous '*ex parte*' testimony. The will of Parliament on this point was indeterminate. We can isolate the parts of speech that created this indeterminacy. There is the modal verb 'may' and enabling verb 'make', which, together, granted the Lord Chancellor wide discretion to determine rules of court. Law-makers had also relied on several conditional conjunctions, such as with 'on or in connection with' and 'for other matters preliminary or incidental to or arising out of such appeals'. There are also indeterminate adjectives and adverbs in 'matters preliminary or incidental' and 'the need to secure that decisions which are the subject of appeals are properly reviewed'. With this law, the government could broadly determine the procedural rules for sensitive cases. However, crucially, it was not made clear by Parliament whether this power had to be consistent with commitments to other rules of law, such as the *European Convention on Human Rights* (ECHR). The Convention did not create the dispute in this case, but it was needed to resolve the indeterminacy in domestic law.

Before describing the theory, key concepts need to be defined. For this chapter, a binary dependent variable is used: loss for the immigrant (0) and win for the immigrant (1). A win for the immigrant is, as far as the government is concerned, a failure of policy. So, tracking the increased likelihood of immigrant victories is a latent measure of rising policy ineffectiveness. While this pro-/anti-government conceptualisation is simple, it is defensible for a large-N analysis, where alternative conceptualisations would be far more difficult to measure (Staton and Vanberg 2008: 505). It could, for instance, have been possible to broaden the conceptualisation to describing judges' decisions as ideologically slanted towards either liberalism or conservativism. However, a liberal-to-conservative spectrum cannot readily be observed. Reliable data on what motivates British judges do not exist. This is partly because judicial appointments in Britain focus on experience and merit, rather than an individual's politics. It is also, relatedly, because barristers and judges so rarely proclaim their political positions in public. Another conceptualisation of the dependent variable could have described decisions as 'activist' or 'restrained'. However, as with 'liberal' and 'conservative' adjudication, there is little agreement as to what judicial activism actually is, nor any reliable data from which to measure it (Roosevelt 2006). The safest concept is the 'judicialisation of politics', which can, in part, be captured by my simple binary. An anti-government/pro-immigrant ruling at a senior appellate court signals 'reliance on courts and judicial means for addressing core moral predicaments, public policy questions, and political controversies' (Hirschl 2008: 94). A common blind spot in analyses of judicialisation is, as argued by Christoph Hönnige (2011: 351), consideration of inter-institutional relationships. Focusing on inter-institutional discourse goes some way to addressing this. Interactions between judges and law-makers are important for understanding court rulings (Clayton and Gillman 1999: 5). Much existing research on judicial behaviour, drawing from theories and findings in the US, has tended to focus on judges and courts in isolation (Dyevre 2010: 301). Even strategic theories that look to how courts interact with other institutions have been founded on assumptions as to judges' isolated preferences. However, in Britain, judges are relatively weak and can only really affect policy when the sovereign Parliament makes way for them with indeterminate legislation.

As described in Chapter One, my causal argument concentrates on the meso-level. As such, I will summarise the notable factors operating at macro-, meso- and micro-levels in order to demonstrate the importance of the midsection. At the macro-level are broad forces of history, especially post-war increases in international migration and invigorated concern for human rights. For Britain, net immigration rose for the first time from the mid-1990s onwards. Even prior to this watershed, rising rates of immigration long led demands for policies to prevent incoming and facilitate outgoing. Despite these sustained pressures, policies have lacked coherence. Where public opinion generally wished to see rates of immigration fall, an increasingly expensive and under-productive workforce encouraged businesses to favour a more open-door approach. All of which is set in the context of heightened concern for individual and communal rights. So, the increasing rate of anti-government court rulings observed since 1995 coincide with rising net immigration and new human rights legislation. Most notably, the HRA offered protections against deportation to any state that practises the death penalty, torture or unlawful deprivations of liberty. Those threatened with deportation may also be able to prevent their removal on the basis that their family life in Britain will be unduly disrupted. However, as mentioned, increased immigration and new human rights laws cannot explain changes to judicial behaviour by themselves because, first of all, the recognition of human rights for non-citizens is far from new to British politics: the United Nations' (UN's) *Refugees Convention* and the ECHR have offered protections to immigrants since the 1950s. Second, judges simply could not quash a lawful use of power simply because human rights were threatened. Third, there is a complex causal mechanism linking an individual's attempt to enter the country and a court's anti-government ruling. Crafting models from these macro-level variables would not help us understand (a) why judges' behaviour has broadly changed and yet (b) anti-immigrant rulings remain far from unusual. If immigration and human rights were sufficient to encourage pro-immigrant court rulings, then the rate of such rulings would be far higher.

Missing from macro-level analysis is an identifiable cause of action; in other words, a specific opportunity for immigrants to bring successful litigation against the government. These opportunities come from indeterminate legislation. Legislative language is nestled between the macro-level historical forces that created it and micro-level interpretations of its meaning (Stone Sweet 2000; Dyevre 2010). Immigration law is, like most other laws, increasingly indeterminate because of policy ambition not keeping step with government capacities. Governments cannot straightforwardly meet public demands for immigration control without undermining the economy, or alienating other countries. These are consequences of globalisation. Legislative language cannot fully capture policy because there often is no determinate policy. Instead, Parliament has created spaces in the law to be filled according to short-term need, and with reliance on government discretion. Policymakers 'muddle through', using loose policy language that can be adapted as required (Lindblom 1959). Immigration policy must, in particular, be adaptable to unforeseen humanitarian crises, threats to international security and economic shocks.

The parts of speech in legislation that will encourage anti-government rulings will be those that create uncertainty as to what the legitimate power of the government is. Most important when it comes to power delegation will be conjunctions, whose meaning depends almost entirely on the context of each case. In linguistics, this would be described as pragmatic indeterminacy (Morris 1946). Put simply, the legitimate power of the government is not known until it is used. Semantic indeterminacy, on the other hand, at least offers a central tendency of meaning. Adjectives and adverbs, in particular, will need to be interpreted relative to context, but they have dictionary (and legal) definitions that provide some guidance. The meaning of conjunctions like 'if', 'or' and 'and' depend on what is being conjoined and how the conjunction of ideas relates to the reality of a case. Semantics can cause confusion, as did the word 'properly' in the Algerian case cited earlier. However, as Ronald Dworkin (1986) argued, the 'semantic sting' will be avoided if judges used better dictionaries. Every time an adjective or adverb from a particular law is litigated, its meaning will become more determinate. This process of clarification is far less likely with conjunctions. In addition to which, indeterminate modal verbs and enabling verbs also militate against determinate interpretations of law. Ministers can change the law using 'mays' and 'makes'. It is conjunctions, indeterminate modal verbs and enabling verbs in legislation that, when used to frame government powers, will create greater indeterminacy. Besides the length and subject matter of legislation, the determinacy of its language is crucial to explaining judges' behaviour (Huber and Shipan 2002; Staton and Vanberg 2008).

Besides legislative language, tribunal reform is another meso-level variable. Courts of first instance must pare down thousands of immigration cases, and, by doing so, they affect the caseload of their senior colleagues. Tribunals also mediate between macro-level changes in migration and micro-level case determinations on appeal. Three notable reforms reorganised tribunals in the period under study. Reforms were motivated by a growing backlog of unresolved cases, rising costs and a desire to curtail fruitless litigation. The first was the creation of an Immigration Appellate Authority (IAA), established under the *Immigration Act 1971*. This replaced immigration adjudicators, who had presided over appeals for just two years under the *Immigration Appeals Act 1969*. The two-tier IAA was itself unsuitable for managing vast numbers of cases, and was therefore replaced in 2005 by the Asylum and Immigration Tribunal (AIT). This single-tier set-up was then replaced in 2010 by the Asylum and Immigration Chamber of the First-tier Tribunal. IAA reform after 2005 improved case management efficiency and empowered these lower courts to dispose of more cases without need of further appeal. Data bear this out. Governments appealed against tribunal decisions 16 times between 1970 and 2012; 14 of these appeals came during the IAA set-up (1971–2004) and only two came after the lower courts were overhauled. This suggests that the government was increasingly pleased with decisions reached at lower courts after 2005, and felt less of a need to appeal. Pursuing an appeal at the Court of Appeal or Supreme Court needs the permission of those courts. Permission will only be given where an error of law is identified by the tribunal or the appellate court. By managing more cases, tribunal reform has affected the raw number of cases that can make it to appeal. These appeals have almost exclusively been brought by immigrants. However, besides the number of cases, the tribunals' increasingly pro-government deference can be expected to have affected the rate of government defeat at the higher courts. The deference of lower courts is not a sign of timidity or political bias. Lower courts simply have fewer powers to dispose of certain cases, and what powers they do have are entirely derived from statute. Higher courts have powers to change rules of law. By use of common law powers, these senior judges are capable of being less deferential to the government. So, tribunal reform will have increased the throughput of cases to appeal, and will have increased the rate at which those cases go against the government.

Following the macro- and meso-levels are the judges' appeal rulings at the micro-level. Indeterminate legislation makes anti-government rulings more likely according to three factors: the government's action, the immigrants' reactions and the court's interpretation. First of all, governments will typically act to limit immigrants' autonomy. This will include placing fetters on entry, residence rights and access to public services. Secondary legislation and rules can clarify primary law, but these subordinate laws cannot fully determine the extent of a power. Where there is indeterminacy in primary law, secondary laws do not have sufficient authority to resolve all disputes. Second of all, for immigrants, indeterminate legislation allows their barristers to claim that power used was not delegated by Parliament. Third, in their rulings, judges must provide a clear resolution to the dispute at hand. Where the law is indeterminate, ruling against the government will often be the more appropriate legal argument (March and Olsen 1989). This is because indeterminate powers are more likely to offend the rule of law. A power-constraining judgment will more likely fit with existing rules of law, and will uphold natural justice by giving the benefit of the doubt to the weaker party.

As described earlier, this is a legal theory of judicialisation: senior judges' rulings are predicted from the clarity of law and the administration of lower courts. Yet, other factors could be decisive at the micro-level. Attitudinal and strategic models should be tested relative to this legal model. The importance of judges' attitudes is often claimed as determinative by lawyers. They complain that who hears the case often matters more than what the law says (Robertson 1998). Strategic models also offer plausible explanations, reliant on game theory: judges act on their preferences, it is claimed, but only if the likelihood of being overruled is low (Ferejohn and Weingast 1991). Certain legal cases present greater opportunities for judges to rule against the government as the likelihood of a decision being overturned, or publicly disdained, is low. For instance, when an innocent immigrant's life is threatened by deportation to a tyranny, judges may feel more confident in ruling against the government without being overruled. Conversely, cases involving dangerous and unpleasant characters will embolden the government to challenge an unfavourable court ruling, perhaps relying on the court of public opinion. Therefore, to test a theory that indeterminacy in law best predicts anti-government court rulings, it will also be necessary to test whether the presiding judges and the nature of the dispute affect outcomes.

It is also worth acknowledging a possibility of reverse causation, in that anti-government court rulings may encourage Parliament to enact more indeterminate legislation. Losing major appeal cases could spur the government to seek more discretionary power from Parliament. Indeed, we have seen ministers declare publicly that they need more power and greater ability to curtail immigration appeals (Mitchell 2009). However, these declarations concerned the thousands of mostly minor appeals brought before tribunals, rather than the smaller number of weighty appeals brought before senior courts. The government could limit these higher appeals by 'ousting' these courts' jurisdiction. This would require Parliament's approval, which has never been granted for immigration cases, although an 'ouster clause' was very nearly enacted in clause 14(6) of the *Asylum and Immigration Bill 2004*. However, following severe backlash from judges, the government withdrew it: 'No appeal shall lie to the House of Lords from any decision of an appellate court in relation to the giving of an opinion under this section'. There is no mistaking this language. It would have removed secondary appeals from immigration cases, granting absolute supervision to the Court of Appeal. The point is that enacting more indeterminate legislation to respond to hostile court rulings would be utterly self-defeating. Clear statutory language is the only way to use legislation to control judges. As such, reverse causation – where senior court rulings lead to more indeterminacy in law – remains plausible, but would be irrational, as enacting indeterminate law to curtail court rulings would achieve the opposite.

Hypotheses

Hypotheses look to the observable implications of macro-, meso- and micro-level theories. For my theory – the legal model – it is expected that indeterminacy in legislation, especially conjunctions, will offer the best predictive power for immigrant wins and losses. This legal model also predicts that changes to the administration of tribunals will have accelerated the throughput to higher courts of cases that will more likely be resolved in favour of the immigrant. For all other variables, it is not expected that there will be evidence to reject the null hypotheses. Hypotheses and expectations are summarised in Table 4.1.

There are many other macro-level variables that could be considered relevant, such as the rate of immigration. This particular variable is omitted because it correlates with time, and would cause an endogeneity problem. Also, even if a time-independent measure of immigration was included, there is no reason why the raw number of immigrants ought to be relevant to the ratio of pro- to anti-immigrant rulings. A variable that is included is the age of the legislation disputed (H1). In response to increases in immigration, Parliament enacted a greater volume of legislation, at a quickened pace. The resulting volatility in immigration law could enable litigants, and their counsel, to defeat the government on the basis that there is no coherent rule

Table 4.1: Hypotheses

Level	Description	Hypotheses	Expectation
Macro	Socio-legal	H1 – Disputes over old legislation have a lower rate of government loss.	Null
		H2 – Disputes over human rights law have a higher rate of government loss.	Null
Meso	Legislative language	H3 – Disputes over legislation containing adjectives or adverbs have a higher rate of government loss.	Null
		H4 – Disputes over legislation containing conditions, signified by the conjunctions 'if'/'or'/'and', have a higher rate of government loss.	Evidence to reject the null
		H5 – Disputes over legislation containing the modal verb 'may' have a higher rate of government loss.	Evidence to reject the null
		H6 – Disputes over legislation containing the enabling verbs 'make' or 'amend' have a higher rate of government loss.	Evidence to reject the null
	Institutional reform	H7 – Tribunal reform increases the throughput of meritorious cases to appeal, which leads to increased government loss.	Evidence to reject the null
Micro	Case facts	H8 – Disputes over national security have a lower rate of government loss.	Null
		H9 – Disputes over a threat to the life of the immigrant have a higher rate of government loss.	Null
	Judicial	H10 – Senior judges lead courts to rule against the government.	Null

of law. Conversely, older laws might be expected to have more stable meanings, achieved through repeated interpretations. However, most indeterminate parts of speech always rely on context to be meaningful. So, an interpretation at time t cannot determine meaning at $t + 1$. As such, the age of legislation is not expected to be significant when compared to its language. Another macro-level variable included is the submission, by counsel, of a human rights violation (H2). Critics of human rights laws, including the government, contend that barristers use these instruments as trump cards to defeat otherwise legal government actions. My counter-submission is that the use of human rights law will not significantly correlate with government losses.

At the meso-level, indeterminate parts of speech that omit information on the law's scope (conditional conjunctions) (H4), timing (indeterminate modal verbs) (H5) and policy content (enabling verbs) (H6) are expected to have the greatest impact on case outcomes. Adjectives and adverbs (H3), having a central tendency of meaning, are not expected to have a significant effect on the delegation of powers. Of the linguistic variables, it is conditional conjunctions and indeterminate modal verbs that are expected to have the greatest predictive power across the whole period (H4, H5). This is because enabling language (H6), while creating policy indeterminacy, is more time-dependent than conditions and modal verbs. Specifically, more cases successfully contesting enabling powers will have come after tribunal reforms in 2005. These reforms led to a more deferential stance to government discretion from lower courts, and pushed more cases through to appeal. Conditional conjunctions and indeterminate modal verbs confuse the intersection of law and case facts, where enabling verbs also implicate government discretion. The reform of tribunals is therefore expected to have greater explanatory power than the presence of enabling language. Put grammatically, indeterminacy in the object (conditional conjunctions) and the verb of legislative language is less controversially challenged in a tribunal than language that enables the subject (the government). Hence, as well as measuring language at the meso-level, I have included dummy variables to capture reforms to the administration of lower courts. These reforms have affected the behaviour of judges on higher courts by increasing the number of meritorious cases they hear (H7).

At the micro-level, hypotheses test alternative strategic and attitudinal models. For the strategic model, hypotheses consider case facts so as to test whether pro-immigrant rulings are more or less likely given the chances of the ruling being reversed by Parliament or disdained by public opinion. To analyse this, disputes of an existential nature are considered. Threats to national security (H8) and threats to the life of the immigrant if deported (H9) are cases of the utmost importance. If judges were moved by case facts alone, we would expect them to defer to the government in national security cases and constrain the government when an immigrant's life was hanging in the balance. However, the expectation of my legal theory is that the gravity of a case is of lesser predictive power than the clarity of law. It would have been possible to include other case facts, such as where an immigrant was a convicted criminal or claimed to have an established family life in the UK. However, I have chosen to focus on the most diverting case facts, being those posing existential threats to national security or the immigrant. If even these momentous matters do not correlate with case results, then it is unlikely that matters of lesser implication will.

Finally, the attitudes of individual judges are analysed (H10) so as to consider the importance of who hears the cases. As discussed, there are difficulties in measuring judges' attitudes, but it is possible to observe whether the presence of individual judges consistently leads to outcomes favouring the government or the immigrant. In the Court of Appeal, there are typically three Lord Justices, including a senior judge, while the Supreme Court typically hears cases with five Justices, including a senior judge. These senior presiding judges have no power to compel their colleagues to rule a certain way. However, there are nonetheless possibilities for leadership, borne out of experience and intellectual authority. Some senior judges have unquestionably led their courts in new legal directions. Notable in this regard have been developments to administrative and civil law under Lords Reid, Wilberforce, Denning and Bingham in the post-war era (Blom-Cooper et al 2009). By assessing whether the presence of senior presiding judges is associated with patterns in wins or losses for the immigrant, we can go some way to test if the judges themselves matter for determining the result. What is being observed, specifically, are patterns in judicial leadership, rather than judges' attitudes. In a notable contribution, Chris Hanretty analysed individual judge's rulings using a hierarchical item-response model. The aim was to model judicial preferences within a unidimensional policy space. Evidence could not be found in that study to reject the null, reinforcing the argument that attitudinal theories have limited purchase in the UK (Hanretty 2013).

Thus, it is a legal model that is expected to have the greatest explanatory power. The specific model is presented formally by the following fixed effects logit formula, the results of which are presented under 'Model 3' in Table 4.4:

$$\text{Logit}\left(Pr_{PI}\right) = \alpha + \beta_1 CON + \beta_2 MOD + \beta_3 PD2 + \beta_4 PD4 + \varepsilon$$

Pr_{PI} describes the probability of a pro-immigrant/anti-government ruling. The four beta coefficients describe two language variables – conditional conjunctions (CON) and indeterminate modal verbs (MOD) – as well as two period dummy coefficients to capture reforms to the administration of immigration tribunals (PD2 = 2005–09; PD3 = 2010–).

Data and methodology

This chapter rests on discourse analysis and logit regression analyses. The same discourse analysis program used for Chapter Two tests the descriptive claim that immigration legislation has become more indeterminate. Logit regression analyses test the implications of this change for judicial behaviour. Included in the discourse analysis is every section of immigration legislation enacted, from the first-ever complete statute on the matter up to the most recent statute. That makes for a total of 1,233 sections analysed, from section 1 of the *Aliens Act 1905* to section 96 of the *Immigration Act 2016*. Total numbers of indeterminate parts of speech are reported. This gives information on both the increased quantity and declining clarity of legislation. The four separate measures of indeterminacy (adjectives/adverbs, conjunctions, indeterminate modal verbs and enabling verbs) are reported. The reason for not aggregating these four variables into a single indeterminacy factor is because they operate independently. Cronbach's α (0.56) and McDonald's ω (0.41) coefficients for internal consistency are too low to justify establishing an aggregate factor.

For the logit analyses, two techniques were used: fixed and random effects modelling. The data were taken from appeal case reports. Specifically, every appeal pertaining to immigration and asylum reported by the Incorporated Council of Law Reporting (ICLR) and the All England Law Reports was analysed. That makes for a total of 252 case reports across 42 years. To analyse the legislation disputed in each case, the specific sections that were central to the dispute were identified from the law reports, and these were coded using the natural language processing program. In each case report, a summary identifies the precise sections and words of legislation that were litigated. Typically, a case hinges on just one or two sections of domestic legislation, or a clause from an international treaty. Although counsel for the immigrant will typically try to establish breaches of several different laws, the case reports make clear the specific points of law that were most pertinent to the cause of action. The per section densities of each of the four parts of speech were recorded, and then normalised to between 0 and 1 so as to make for comparable regression coefficients. A section, like a sentence, encapsulates dominant and subordinate subjects, objects and verbs. The density of indeterminacy within this basic unit, whether in domestic or international law, is a legitimate basis for assessing the relative meaningfulness of language.

Data on all other variables for the regression analyses were also taken from case reports. The age of legislation was measured by subtracting the year of enactment of the disputed legislation from the year of the dispute. As a non-binary variable, this was also scaled to between 0 and 1 to ensure comparable coefficients. The submission by counsel of a human rights breach was coded as a binary where a human rights instrument was identified by case reporters as central to the dispute. Three period dummies were used to capture reforms to tribunals. Finally, to establish whether the case implicated national security or an immigrant's life, a binary coding was again used if either of these claims was made in submissions by counsel and confirmed in the factual summary provided by the case reporters.

All variables were first tested in bivariate logit regressions and then three multivariate models were run. Two are of primarily statistical interest, while the third model offers the principal evidence for this chapter. Model 1 is a fixed effects model including just the indeterminacy variables, excluding adjectives. Model 2 is a random effects model including the same linguistic fixed effects as Model 1 and also random intercepts for each senior presiding judge. This is to assess whether individual judges have had any notable effect on case outcomes. Model 3 is a fixed effects model that includes the conditional and modal variables, with period dummies to capture changes in the administration of tribunals. This is the model described by the equation set out earlier. It is expected to have the greatest statistical significance and it captures the argument of this chapter. Other random effects versions of Model 3 were run to assess for the clustering of errors by judge or court. These results are described in the results section but are not presented in the regression table (Table 4.4). Descriptive statistics are presented in Table 4.2.

With regard to data diagnostics, of principal importance is that the dependent variable be stationary rather than subject to time-series autoregression. A Priestly-Subba Rao test for stationarity offers a p-value of 0.83 for the null. This is insufficient evidence of autoregression, and suggests that the logit regression assumptions are

Table 4.2: Descriptive statistics for fixed effects

Variables	Min	Mean	Median	Max	SD
Dependent variable					
Anti-government ruling	0	0.46	0	1	0.5
Independent variables					
Age of legislation	1	20.84	13.5	61	18.03
Human rights claim	0	0.41	0	1	0.49
Adjectives or adverbs	0	1.19	1	4.5	1.14
'If'/'or'/'and' conditionals	0	1.58	1	5	1.63
Indeterminate modal verb 'may'	0	0.35	0	2	0.48
Enabling verbs 'make'/'amend'	0	0.15	0	1.5	0.29
National security implications	0	0.3	0	1	0.3
Threats to the immigrant's life	0	0.46	0	1	0.46

Notes: $N = 252$. Notes on clusters and period dummies: for clusters, there were 70 different senior presiding judges, 134 cases were heard at the Court of Appeal and 118 cases were heard at the House of Lords/Supreme Court. For period dummies, just under 52% of cases were heard in the first period (PD1 = 1971–2004), 24% were heard in the second period (PD2 = 2005–09) and another 24% were heard in the final period (PD3 = 2010–).

valid. With regard to the independent variables, Table 4.3 displays variance inflation factors (VIFs) for all variables. None present a factor greater than 2, so there is insufficient evidence to reject the null in favour of multicollinearity. If present, multicollinearity would have voided the independence assumptions of the logit method.

Table 4.3: Variance inflation factors for independent variables

Variable	VIF
Age	1.35
Human rights	1.33
Adjectives	1.52
Conditional	1.54
Modal	1.30
Enabling	1.38
National security	1.15
Threat to life	1.31
Period dummy 2 (2005–09)	1.09
Period dummy 3 (2010–)	1.30

Note: Only two of the three period dummies can be included in any single model. The two dummies included represent periods of significant reform for the immigration tribunals (after 2005). These time periods might be expected to present correlations with other predictors. However, as the table suggests, there are no grounds to reject the null hypothesis, and there is no significant interaction between variables.

Results

First, what evidence is there of changes to the language of immigration legislation? Changes in law are essential to the argument presented in this chapter. Figure 4.1 demonstrates changes on four measures of indeterminacy. The numbers of indeterminate parts of speech are summed into totals for every five years from 1905–09 up to 2015–.

Figure 4.1 presents the universe of data, without any sampling or confidence intervals needed. Indeterminate parts of speech have always been present in immigration legislation, but there has been a substantial increase in their application. Notably, there were 162 conditional conjunctions used in immigration law between 1905 and 1909. This figure increased by 24 times, to 3,883 conjunctions, in legislation a century later (2005–09). The other three parts of speech have also markedly increased in use.

Figure 4.1: Changes to the language of immigration legislation, 1905–2016

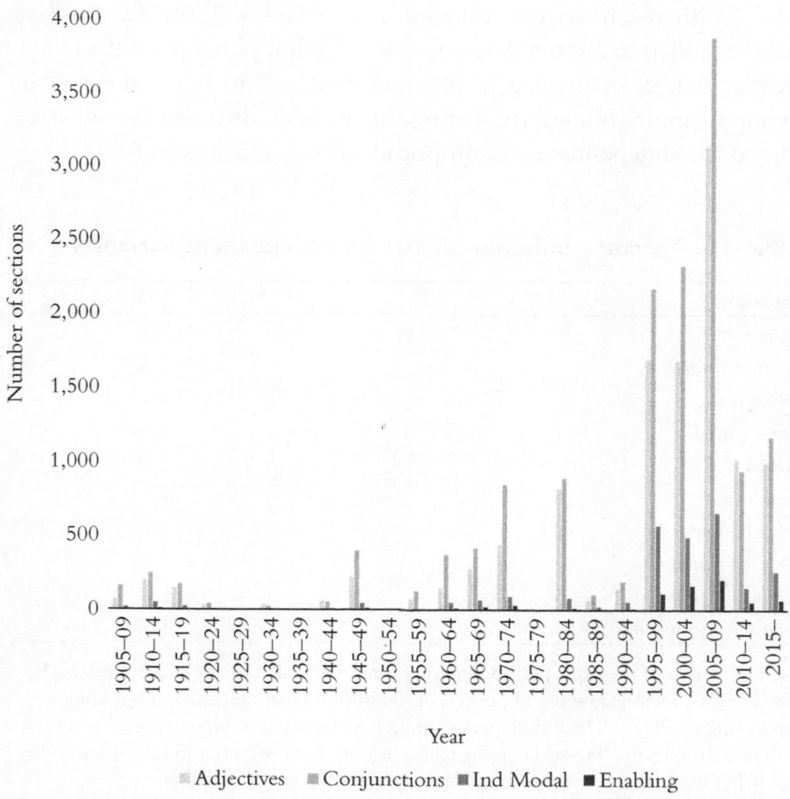

Table 4.4 displays results from bivariate regressions and three multivariate models, and also presents log odds of pro-immigrant/anti-government rulings for each variable. In the bivariate analyses, it is not possible to improve on the null with regard to the age of

Table 4.4: Log odds of anti-government rulings in fixed effects and random effects models

Variable	Bivariate	Model 1 (FE)	Model 2 (RE)	Model 3 (FE)
Age	0.43			
	(0.43)			
Human rights	0.43*			
	(0.26)			
Adjectives/adverbs	0.62			
	(0.50)			
Conjunctions	2.42***	2.71***	2.70***	2.63***
	(0.46)	(0.48)	(0.48)	(0.48)
Modal	1.56***	1.35*	1.42*	2.31***
	(0.56)	(0.77)	(0.85)	(0.69)
Enabling	2.19***	1.84**	1.75*	
	(0.73)	(0.92)	(1.01)	
Period dummy 1 (1971–2004)	−1.07***			
	(0.26)			
Period dummy 2 (2005–2009)	0.41			0.84**
	(0.30)			(0.35)
Period dummy 3 (2010–)	0.99***			1.16***
	(0.31)			(0.35)
National security	−0.07			
	(0.42)			
Threats to life	0.29			
	(0.27)			
Constant	–	−1.44***	−1.47***	−1.89***
		(0.25)	(0.28)	(0.30)
N	252	252	252	252
Predicted	–	70%	73%	73%
−2 log likelihood	–	296.56	296.51	287.52
AIC	–	304.56	306.50	297.52

Notes: Standard errors in parentheses. ***$p < 0.01$, **$p < 0.05$, *$p < 0.1$. The −2 log likelihood for random effects models is a quasi-log likelihood derived from Laplace approximation using R's *glmer* function (Bates 2010). FE = fixed effects; RE = random effects; AIC = Akaike information criterion.

legislation (H1), the use of adjectives (H3), national security (H8) or a threat to the immigrant's life (H9). First, the age of legislation result suggests that a court ruling against the government is no less likely with well-known legislation. Further, that adjectives and adverbs make no significant difference to case outcomes supports the argument that these parts of speech have lesser impact on power delegation because of their offering a central tendency of meaning. Furthermore, there is no significant evidence that case facts have any systematic effect on judges' rulings. Human rights (H2) has a relatively low *p*-value in the bivariate regression (<0.1), but it does not present sufficient statistical significance to reject the null hypothesis. Counsel cited the *Human Rights Act* in nearly half of all cases analysed since 2000 (when it came into force), but there is little evidence that this submission strategy made any systematic difference. Moreover, besides this Act, no other human rights instruments, such as the *Refugees Convention*, appears to have made a statistically significant difference to case outcomes. Clearly, human rights law is important, but the argument that such laws are sufficient to improve the chances of a win for an immigrant is not sustainable (H2). When included in multivariate analyses, this variable loses even its single-starred *p*-value.

It is indeterminacies in legislation (H4–H6) and the reorganisation of lower courts (H7) that present statistical significances in the bivariate analyses. The exception to this is the second period dummy (2005–09). Model 1 follows up on these bivariate analyses with a fixed effects multivariate model that contains just the language variables. This model is designed to assess whether the language variables continue to be statistically significant in multivariate analysis. Indeterminate modal verbs (H5) lose their statistical significance in this model, with a *p*-value of <0.1. However, the model nonetheless offers good predictive power (70%). Model 2 is the same as Model 1 but with random intercepts for each senior presiding judge. There were 70 different judges that presided in a position of seniority over the 252 cases. Twenty of these judges led their courts in five or more cases, including Lords Denning and Bingham, who have been recognised as major leaders of British jurisprudence. Despite the small sample sizes for each judge, Model 2 is needed to assess the importance of judicial leadership in affecting case outcomes (H10). The fixed effects coefficients in Model 2 retain much the same statistical significances of Model 1, albeit with marginally inflated standard errors and with 'enabling verbs' losing its statistical significance. However, crucially, the difference in explanatory power (measured by error variance, or s^2) between Model 1 and Model 2 is 0.05, suggesting that including random intercepts only very slightly changes model fit. Furthermore, a likelihood ratio test of the differences between Models 1 and 2 yields a χ^2 of 0.05 ($p = 0.82$) with one degree of freedom. This is not statistically significant. There is therefore little evidence to reject the null for H10.

Model 3 provides the most substantively and statistically significant results. It includes the two most important linguistic variables (conjunctions and indeterminate modal verbs), along with the period dummies that capture reforms to immigration tribunals. All coefficients and the constant are statistically significant. This is evidence for rejecting the nulls in H4–H5 and H7. Model 3 also returns the lowest AIC (Akaike information criterion) (297.52) of any model, and correctly predicted the outcome in 73% of cases. As expected, cases contesting enabling language were more frequently brought to appeal after the 2005 tribunal reforms. Specifically, 37 out of 48 cases contesting enabling language came after 2005, and these cases contained higher than average enabling parts of speech per section. Hence, if 'enabling' is included in a multivariate model with the period dummies, it loses its statistical significance. Indeterminate modal verbs in Model 3 gain three-starred significance without the presence of enabling verbs, suggesting a minor suppression effect in Models 1 and 2, albeit that there was insufficient evidence of intercollinearity to justify a composite 'modal*enabling' factor.

A variant of Model 3 run with random intercepts for senior judges (not recorded in Table 4.4) provides no difference in model fit. This is because the period dummies capture the variances that would otherwise be partially explained by different judges and courts, and the period dummies are far more theoretically and statistically significant than the random intercepts. A model containing just the conditional and modal variables with random effects for judges and courts (also not recorded in Table 4.4) provides no significant improvement in model fit either: for judges, $s^2 = 0.2$, $\chi^2 = 1.12$, $p = 0.29$; and for courts, $s^2 = 0.05$, $\chi^2 = 0.82$, $p = 0.36$. With explanatory differences between fixed and random effects models so close to zero, there is little evidence of intra-class variation by judges (H10) or courts.

The model with the greatest leverage over the data is the fixed effects model (Model 3). Interaction terms have not been reported for any model. This is because the most powerful models contain variables for language and period dummies. The latter cannot be combined and, as discussed earlier, there are no grounds for aggregating the linguistic variables into an aggregate factor. Indeed, it is more interesting to see how individual parts of speech operate independently of each other.

The log odds in Table 4.4 tell us the direction and relative strengths of coefficients, but odds ratios are more intuitive (see Table 4.5).

Table 4.5 demonstrates that conditional language increased the likelihood of a pro-immigrant ruling by 14 times. Indeterminate modal verbs increased the likelihood of a pro-immigrant ruling by a maximum of 10 times. The maximum density of conditional language recorded was five parts per section, meaning that in sections with five conjunctions, there was a 14 times greater likelihood of an immigrant winning on appeal. Modal verbs reached a maximum density of two parts per section; where a section contained two uses of 'may' or 'might', the chances of an immigrant winning on appeal jumped by 10 times. These odds ratios provide evidence for rejecting the null in favour of the legal model presented in this chapter.

Table 4.5: Odds ratios for Model 3

Variable	Odds ratio	2.5%	97.5%
Conditional	13.92	5.57	37.45
Modal	10.06	2.75	40.76
PD2 (2005–09)	2.32	1.17	4.66
PD3 (2010–)	3.19	1.61	6.45

Conclusion

An adapted legal model of judicialisation is supported by the evidence presented. The result in over two thirds of the cases studied can be predicted from the language of law and the administration of courts. Rapid increases in government losses on appeal after 1995 coincide with similarly rapid increases in the enactment of indeterminate legislation. This updating of the legal model is not incompatible with attitudinal or strategic theories. Individual judges may pursue their own preferences, and will be conscious of their strategic constraints, but, either way, opportunities to rule against the government came when Parliament used indeterminate language.

As Arthur Dyevre (2010: 311) puts it:

> many strategic accounts of judicial decision-making implicitly assume that 'legal' variables do have some impact on judicial outcomes. Indeed, if constitutional rigidity or the threat of legislative override has an effect on judicial conduct, the reason must be that changes in constitutional

language and clear expressions of legislative will have an impact on the courts.

Previous research on judicial politics has not considered changes in legislative language with sufficient historical breadth. The aim was to fill this gap in the literature. Longitudinal measurement of four linguistic features and analysis of their impact sheds light on the spurs to judicialisation. More data and research are needed on the preferences of British judges, but nuances to the individualist focuses of attitudinal and strategic models are also to be encouraged. As argued by Hönnige (2011), the judicialisation hypotheses need to consider inter-institutional coordination, and the theoretical framework provided by Schmidt's (2008) 'discursive institutionalism' is ideally placed for this endeavour.

As regards the broader thesis of this book, indeterminacy in immigration law undermines its effectiveness. Judges have had to determine the contents, scope and timing of policy, against the wishes of government. This means that one of the most controversial policy issues has been adapted by unelected judges because politicians have been unable, and unwilling, to express their policies in determinate language. The findings therefore link to wider questions about how legislation should be conceptualised in the 21st century. Where H.L.A Hart (1961) described law as an accessible guide to legitimate action, indeterminate legislation presents a new concept: a scaffolding, without clear guidance for what or when actions will be valid. This new concept of law suggests a surrender of political will to changeable circumstances. This further implies that *ex ante* mandates for action are being replaced with *ex post* justifications for action. It is politics by forgiveness, rather than consent. The practical implication for legislators is to consider the opportunity costs. By promulgating legislation that omits key information, time can be saved and flexibility can be gained for policy implementation. However, it is likely that judges will impose clarity on indeterminate law through their rulings. This can impair policy effectiveness and diminish authority. If the calculation is made that indeterminate legislation is nevertheless the most efficient and effective legal instrument, then this decision should come with the expectation of an increased role for the courts.

Furthermore, the sticks with which judges allegedly beat the government – such as human rights law or concern for the life of an immigrant – show no significant correlation with case results. By reacting to change in the language of legislation, judges are acting appropriately. The primary normative implication is that castigating judges, or threatening to clip their wings, is inappropriate. Should the legislature be encouraged to set more determinable limits on power? Or, is the concept of law in need of revision to manage immigration? Either way, the government should expect and welcome scrutiny. It will either come *ex ante* from the legislature or *ex post* in court.

FIVE

Homelessness: how Parliament's language affects local government duties

Mr Jan Luba QC, for the Appellant, and Mr Andrew Arden QC, for the Respondent in this appeal, both agree that amendments to s 193 of the *Housing Act 1996*, made by the *Homelessness Act 2002*, are not happily drafted.

Lord Justice May in Griffiths v St Helen's Metropolitan Borough Council *[2006] EWCA Civ 160 para 1*

... semantic nightmare.

Sheriff Sinclair's appraisal of the composite legal definition of 'becoming homeless intentionally', quoted in Luba and Davies 2010: 502

Introduction

The preceding quotes point to the complexities of homelessness legislation. This chapter looks to homelessness law and policy for the following interconnected reasons. Local authorities have a duty to house certain individuals, which is imposed by parliamentary legislation. So, homelessness law is an important form of coordinative discourse between state institutions. However, unlike immigration law, homelessness law establishes more duties than powers. It allows us to see how accountability for policy decisions is affected by indeterminate legislation. This chapter therefore looks to the second prong of policy feasibility. Where the previous chapter focused on delegation, this chapter looks to accountability. In addition to which, this chapter analyses coordination between different levels of government: national and local. Chapter Four concerned the powers of central government as delegated by the national Parliament. However, coordinating across different levels and among multiple local authorities adds another degree of complexity. Also, this chapter interrogates the effects of adjectives where Chapter Four demonstrated a more substantial effect from conditional conjunctions. Data come from local government housing decisions in England and Wales. Northern Ireland and Scotland are omitted from consideration as their local government laws are entirely separate and can less easily be compared. The aim of this chapter is to provide evidence taken from another level of government that language is a variable for explaining policy effectiveness.

The specific question for this chapter is as follows: what effect does legislative language have on the accountability of policy delivery? Presenting a difference-in-differences (DD) analysis of a natural experiment, it is demonstrated that the adjectives 'vulnerable' and 'likely' had a strong and statistically significant effect on the delivery of homelessness policy in England after 2002. With all 22 Welsh local authorities as the control group, the 22 most similar English local authorities were identified using propensity score matching. These formed the treatment group as their law was identical to Wales', save for the addition of adjectives. The headline findings are that the inclusion of these words in English homelessness law led to a statistically significant drop in the rate of priority need acceptance. Where the average acceptance rate for England and Wales between 1997 and 2014 was 16 individuals per 10,000, in England, after the word 'vulnerable' was added, the acceptance rate averaged at just three per 10,000, a difference of 81%. Given that local authorities in England have populations of up to half a million people, there were a lot of individuals who missed on priority need recognition simply because they claimed in England rather than Wales. Other findings show that the words 'vulnerable' and 'likely' affected the recognition rate of individuals fleeing violence or threats of violence in England. The word 'likely' was only used with regard to those fleeing violence, who were predominantly women escaping domestic violence. It will also be shown that English local authorities had less volatile shifts in recognition rates year on year as compared to their Welsh counterparts. This suggests that English authorities were better able to manage their housing caseload, despite unpredictable demand- and supply-side pressures. This means, straightforwardly, that English local authorities were better able to shirk their duties to house, as compared to Welsh local authorities, and even as compared to themselves before the change in the language of law. Evidence from new panel data is presented. These data cover 728 local authority-years, and were used to test four hypotheses under eight model specifications. Findings show that indeterminate policy language significantly affected the accountability of policy delivery, even when controlling for political, financial and socio-economic variables.

A natural experiment presented itself when both England and Wales adopted substantively identical secondary legislation within a year of each other. The only notable differences between *The Homeless Persons (Priority Need) (Wales) Order 2001* and *The Homelessness (Priority Need for Accommodation) (England) Order 2002* (besides their names and dates) is the addition of the words 'vulnerable' and 'likely' in the latter. This means that in England, the duty of local authorities to house those recognised as eligible, and in priority need, was (and still is) subject to housing officers' assessments of an applicant's vulnerability and/or likelihood of being subject to violence. These indeterminate words qualified in England the exact same categories of priority individuals adopted in Wales, that is, children of 16 or 17 years of age, young people under 21, those coming out of an institutionalised lifestyle (such as prison or the military) and those fleeing violence or threats of violence. By adding adjectives, the English law turned a logical connection to a statistical, or analogical, association. In Wales, homelessness duties depend on simple 'if *A*, then *B*' logical connections – as in 'if newly released from prison, an individual is in priority need for housing'. In England, the determination of duty depends on unexpressed contextual information – as in 'if newly released from prison, and vulnerable as compared to other ex-convicts, then an individual is in priority need for housing'. The English construction yields significantly more discretion to housing officers, and it allows them to shirk their duty with little chance of accountability. It would be difficult at any time to prove that a housing officer was flat wrong in deciding that an individual was not, in fact, vulnerable.

A DD methodology can be used because both English and Welsh local authorities had to comply with identical duties to house those in 'priority need' before the 2001/02 Orders were brought into law. Hence, it is possible to compare the recognition of priority need in both England and Wales before and after the Orders. Section 2 of the *Housing (Homeless Persons) Act 1977* and section 189(1)(c) of the *Housing Act 1996* covered both nations, and included the qualifying adjective 'vulnerable' with regard to priority need assessments for elderly individuals and those suffering with a mental or physical illness. So, the concept of vulnerability, as a qualification of recognising priority need, was not new in 2001/02 for either England or Wales. However, the 1996 Act also had priority need categories that were not qualified by the adjective, namely, with regard to pregnant women, claimants with dependent children and those fleeing an emergency (such as a flood). It is therefore possible to compare the recognition rate of priority need both before and after the secondary legislation of 2001/02. England had the treatment effect of the inclusion of vulnerable for all four of the new priority need categories, where Wales had the exact same categories with no 'vulnerable' qualification. The England Order also included 'likely' solely with regard to individuals fleeing violence or threats of violence. These differences create four trend lines: two for each country before and after the introduction of the 2001/02 Orders. These four trends lines allow for a DD analysis. Before launching into this analysis, a brief history of local government housing provision is provided. Particular focus is placed on the meaning of 'homelessness', as well as the powers and duties of local authorities.

Local government powers and duties to manage homelessness

The constitution of local government in England and Wales derives, primarily, from statute law. As such, the powers and duties of local government are malleable, and indeterminacies in their language cannot be resolved by reference to any higher law. However, there are elements of local government constitutionalism that approach entrenched status. For instance, as a result of local government enjoying some democratic legitimacy, courts have made it clear that none but the most explicit legislation can infringe their powers to act on behalf of their electors. In addition, since 1997, the UK has been a signatory to the Council of Europe's *Charter of Local Self-Government*. This commits the UK government to local democracy and subsidiarity (decision-making at the lowest possible level). However, the Charter is not enforced by a Europe-wide court in the same way as the *European Convention on Human Rights*. Instead, the Charter depends on being enacted by member states and enforced by domestic courts. Much of the content of the Charter was, indeed, enacted by Parliament with the *Local Government Act 2000*; thus, one can say that the powers and duties of local government have pseudo-constitutional status. However, the *Local Government Act 2000* relies on indeterminate language, as can be seen from section 2 of that Act:

> (1) Every local authority are to have power to do anything which they consider is likely to achieve any one or more of the following objects – (a) the promotion or improvement of the economic well-being of their area, (b) the promotion or improvement of the social well-being of their area, and (c) the promotion or improvement of the environmental well-being of their area.

Despite these broadly framed powers, in many policy spaces, it has been demonstrated that local governments no longer enjoy discretion. Instead, they must deliver central government policies, with only minimal deviations permitted. This subordinated role should be seen in the wider context of 'New Public Management' reforms to bureaucracy and service delivery during the 1980s and 1990s. These reforms saw an increasing concentration of policy power in central government, as well as steps taken to improve the efficiency and accountability of delivery at the periphery (Hood 1991). A difficulty has been that the central direction of policy has not been achieved through clearly stated commands. As David Feldman (2004: 253) argued just after the *Local Government Act 2000* took hold:

> the government's determination to change the role of local government away from that of service provider, aroused significant opposition (and non-compliance) from local authorities, especially but not only those controlled by the Labour Party. The territory was increasingly 'juridified' with both the creation of a vast complex of statutory constraints and duties, much poorly drafted, and the development of a significant body of case law in which the courts, with some reluctance, took on the role of umpire.

This chapter focuses on the provision by local government of social housing to those identified as homeless. This is partly because, after immigration, homelessness has been the second-largest source of judicial review caseload at the Administrative Court for over two decades.[31] Clearly, there are problems for litigants and judges in making sense of homelessness law. It is law that raises complex questions of legal, territorial and fiscal jurisdiction, all of which play out in the standard contexts of scarce resources and excess demand. Jurisdictional complexity can be seen from the fact that there are 345 different authorities responsible for housing allocations in England and Wales. These include non-metropolitan boroughs, unitary authorities, metropolitan districts, London boroughs and unitary authorities in Wales. The number and structure of these bodies responsible for housing have changed several times over the course of the 20th and 21st centuries, although essential features were established by the *Local Government Act 1972*.

In addition to which, multiple agencies and departments, working under different legislation, have responsibility for managing homelessness. These include housing authorities, social services, the Department for Communities and Local Government, the Home Office and the Treasury. Furthermore, in every two-tier local government (such as Oxford City Council and Oxfordshire County Council), the district level deals with housing allocations while the county level (or equivalent) deals with social services. Therefore, in cases concerning children that are threatened with homelessness, there is an uneasy overlap in jurisdiction, as well as legal overlap of the *Children Act 1989* and the *Housing Act 1996*.[32] On top of this, central government has a prominent role – from the Treasury providing credit to local authorities to build new houses (Fahey and Norris 2010), to the Home Office creating new offences such as defining begging as 'anti-social behaviour' (Laurie 2004). There is therefore difficulty in providing 'joined-up' and strategic action to manage homelessness (Roche 2004). As a result, coordination between institutions depends on a logic of communication to be effective.

The cause of increased indeterminacy in homelessness policy can best be explained by a brief examination of its history. Not only have there been difficulties in coordinating institutions and actors, but there have also been substantive changes in policy that have complicated its delivery. The provision of housing as a welfare service dates back

---

[31] The Law Commission (1994) *Administrative Law: Judicial Review and Statutory Appeals* (LAW COM.No.226), p 12. The House of Commons Parliamentary Papers (2003/04) *Department for Constitutional Affairs. Judicial Statistics England and Wales for the Year 2003* (Cm 6251), p 20.

[32] See, for instance, *Holmes-Moorhouse v Richmond-upon-Thames London Borough Council* [2009] UKHL 7.

to a Royal Commission established by Lord Salisbury in 1883. A notable turning point in terms of legislation came nearly 40 years later, in 1919, when local authorities were given powers and subsidies from central government to build social housing. The *Housing and Town Planning Act 1919* was a post-war addition to Lloyd George's nascent welfare state. By seeking to protect and improve lives through state intervention, the 1919 Act adopted a different approach to the self-improvement doctrine of the Poor Laws that had existed in one form or another since Tudor England (Elton 1953). That said, the Poor Laws remained on the statute roll until 1948,[33] and the 1919 Act was not specifically concerned with homelessness, but instead provided further powers to house the 'working classes'. An important condition imposed on housing allocations was that applicants had to show evidence of being deserving of a home.

New Treasury loans to support house building produced dramatic results. Estates such as Becontree in Essex emerged as the world's biggest when 170,000 new homes were built there to relieve London's slums. Demand for these houses was high and the government empowered local authorities with wide discretion to discriminate between candidates, albeit with a requirement that 'reasonable preference' be given to particularly needy applicants. These were identified in section 113 of the *Housing Act 1957*:

> (1) A local authority shall, in relation to all the houses and dwellings in respect of which they are required to keep a Housing Revenue Account, observe the requirements specified in the following provisions of this section. (2) The local authority shall secure that in the selection of their tenants a reasonable preference is given to persons who are occupying insanitary or overcrowded houses, have large families or are living under unsatisfactory housing conditions.

Despite this 'reasonable preference', the guiding principle of housing allocations was on the basis of desert rather than need. This approach persisted until it was reversed with the *Housing (Homeless Persons) Act 1977*. From this point, central government took greater control over the provision of social housing and restricted local authorities' discretion (Fitzpatrick and Stephens 1999). In particular, Parliament established that individuals with 'priority need' were to be granted

[33] The Poor Laws were abolished by the *National Assistance Act 1948*.

an automatic right to social housing. Priority need for housing was defined in section 2 of the 1977 Act:

> (1) For the purposes of this Act a homeless person or a person threatened with homelessness has a priority need for accommodation when the housing authority are satisfied that he is within one of the following categories:– (a) he has dependent children who are residing with him or who might reasonably be expected to reside with him; (b) he is homeless or threatened with homelessness as a result of any emergency such as flood, fire or any other disaster; (c) he or any person who resides or might reasonably be expected to reside with him is vulnerable as a result of old age, mental illness or handicap or physical disability or other special reason. (2) For the purposes of this Act a homeless person or a person threatened with homelessness who is a pregnant woman or resides or might reasonably be expected to reside with a pregnant woman has a priority need for accommodation. (3) The Secretary of State may by order, made after appropriate consultations, – (a) specify further categories of persons as having a priority need for accommodation, and (b) amend or repeal any part of subsection (1) or (2) above.

This language contains multiple indeterminacies. For instance, the adjective 'vulnerable' made its first appearance in homelessness law. In addition to which is the elastic qualifier 'special', as in 'vulnerable as a result … [of any] other special reason'. There are also 14 uses of the conjunction 'or', as well as a single use of 'and'. The uses of 'or' set up 14 forking paths, where the law's meaning can be altered, and to cap it all, the 'Secretary of State may by order … amend or repeal any part of subsection (1) or (2)'. Central government was empowered by Parliament to change all categories of priority need at will. Given the difficulties in coordinating action on homelessness, this indeterminate policy language intuitively made coordination more difficult.

This brings us to the current law on homelessness, which is enshrined in two statutes: the *Housing Act 1996, Part VII* and the *Homelessness Act 2002*. According to these statutes, local authorities owe their 'main housing duty'[34] to those who are: (1) eligible, in terms of not being subject to immigration control; (2) in 'priority need';

[34] Section 193(2) 1996 Act.

and (3) homeless or threatened with homelessness unintentionally. These three criteria emerged from further changes to housing policy pursued in the 1980s and 1990s. There was, in particular, a desire to end the perception that certain individuals could 'jump the queue' for housing by having children. In response was the 1996 Act, which established that those defined as 'unintentionally homeless' and with a priority need were owed temporary accommodation for at least two years. After this temporary provision expired, the duty to house disappears, although local authorities then have the power to provide permanent accommodation. The aim with the 1996 Act was to ensure that permanent housing allocations were kept for more deserving tenants. Despite policy changes from the 1977 Act, central government's coordinating role was maintained. Authorities had new duties, not only to provide housing, but also to provide advice and assistance to those making a claim for social housing (Luba and Davies 2010: 684). In addition, each local authority was required by sections 161–5 to draw up a single housing register that would avoid the fast-tracking of those perceived to be in 'need' over those perceived to be more deserving.

New Labour brought in significant changes with the 2002 Act, although much of the legal substance, and, in particular, central government's coordinating role, remained. First, the requirement of a single housing register was removed by the 2002 Act,[35] which also reinstated the idea that reasonable preference must return to those who had become homeless or threatened with homelessness unintentionally.[36] In addition, the Welsh Assembly and the Secretary of State added new categories of 'priority need' under Regulations, which form the basis of this chapter's empirical analysis. The 2002 Act retained considerable central government oversight of housing policy as it obliged authorities to conduct regular reviews and draw up a 'homelessness strategy'.[37] These strategies were meant to weave housing policy into the broader anti-social behaviour policy agenda of the time (Fitzpatrick and Jones 2005). The 2002 Act also sought to create greater choice to those applying for social housing so as to create more 'sustainable communities' (DETR, 2000), although in many housing authorities, choice was and is constrained by limited housing stock (Laurie 2004). Therefore, the 2002 Act retained much of the allocation according to desert ideology of the 1996 Act. Furthermore,

[35] Section 14 2002 Act.

[36] Section 16(3) 2002 Act.

[37] Section 1 2002 Act.

in the aftermath of the English riots in the summer of 2011, Ed Miliband committed the Labour Party Conference to a policy for allocating social housing to those that contribute to the community through work or volunteering. On top of which, the Coalition government's *Localism Act 2011* included a similar policy, signalling a cross-party commitment to desert over need in the allocation of social housing that endured until 2015.

The history of homelessness law paints a picture of fluctuating ideological priorities, framed by increased central government control. Volatile changes to policy are evident from indeterminacies in the legislation. However, even more fundamental indeterminacies exist in law. Most important is the concept of homelessness itself. Homelessness is defined not straightforwardly as rooflessness, in the sense of an individual who sleeps rough. According to statute, a person is homeless if they do not have accommodation that it would be 'reasonable … to continue to occupy'.[38] Reasonableness, in turn, depends on the 'suitability' of the accommodation, which is defined according to parameters that can be amended by the Secretary of State[39]; key considerations are overcrowding and hygiene. An even more complex concept is being 'threatened with homelessness'. This is where accommodation that it is reasonable for an individual to occupy is, for some reason, under threat from either the individual concerned or another party. An individual becomes intentionally threatened with homelessness if they fail to keep up with their rent payments, for instance. Meanwhile, an individual unintentionally becomes threatened with homelessness if domestic violence escalates, thereby making the accommodation unsuitable. Determining homelessness relies heavily on the judgement of housing officers, as one can see from section 177(2) of the *Housing Act 1996*:

> In determining whether it would be, or would have been, reasonable for a person to continue to occupy accommodation, regard may be had to the general circumstances prevailing in relation to housing in the district of the local housing authority to whom he has applied for accommodation or for assistance in obtaining accommodation.

[38] *Housing Act 1996* s 175(3).

[39] *Housing Act 1996* s 210.

It is important to note the wide discretion gifted by Parliament to central government, local authorities and the judiciary to establish workable interpretations for 'homelessness'. This is part of the reason why housing has been dubbed 'the wobbly pillar under the welfare state' (Torgersen, quoted in Fahey and Norris, 2010).

Theory and hypotheses

So, what effect does legislative language have on accountability for policy delivery? Specifically, can including or omitting individual words make a significant difference? I will demonstrate that just individual adjectives can fundamentally alter and undermine the intended effects of a policy. While indeterminate language in legislation offers various practical advantages in tackling complex policies, it creates potentials for bureaucratic drift, moral hazard and, ultimately, unaccountable governance (Strøm et al 2003). I am therefore refining the argument that longer laws generally curtail executive and bureaucratic discretion, as argued by Huber and Shipan (2002). It will be shown that if legislative length is increased through indeterminate parts of speech, such as adjectives, then bureaucratic drift will increase. Here, bureaucratic drift means the deviation of policy delivery from the intent of the legislature (McCubbins et al 1987). Key to this case is the fact that no meaning was given to the word 'vulnerable' by Parliament. Its meaning was finally settled by the UK Supreme Court in the 2015 case of *Hotak and Others v London Borough of Southwark and Another*.[40] As with Chapter Four, evidence again suggests that Parliament undermined its own sovereignty through the use of vague commandments, and judges reasserted a clear logic of communication.

I will describe the theory for this chapter from the abstract idea to its concrete hypotheses. The base theoretical point is that language is the primary mechanism of rule-bound and accountable governance. In particular, coordinative discourse between institutions is a variable that affects how agents behave in response to instructions from their principals, although it is important to reiterate that legislative language is not a fully independent variable. Legislative language operates at a meso-level, linking macroscopic social forces that generated the language to bureaucratic decisions to act on it at the micro-level. Nonetheless, variations in language can have an effect that is observably independent of the forces that created it. Indeed, it is not unusual

[40] [2015] UKSC 30.

for words to take on a life of their own, potentially some distance removed from their intended meanings. Due to these difficulties in identifying the direction of causation, this chapter takes a cue from the 'identification revolution' in political science. A natural experiment allows us to observe an assigned treatment, keeping most other variables constant. This chapter therefore offers important additions to the theoretical and empirical strategies of Chapter Four.

The treatment observed in English law is the addition of adjectives that were omitted in the otherwise identical Welsh laws. However, why are adjectives so impactful on the interpretation of homelessness legislation? In Chapter Four, we saw that conjunctions had the greatest impact on immigration policy, so why the switch in importance from conjunctions to adjectives? All these parts of speech are important for determining policy. However, generally, a theory as to their differences can be posed as follows: conjunctions determine a policy's consequences, whereas adjectives determine its concepts. It is the difference between what law does and what it is. Politically, this difference has the following significance. A power to act is enhanced by multiple forking paths created by conjunctions. A duty to act would similarly be extended if multiple forking paths were added by conditional conjunctions. However, adjectives allow a duty holder to deny the existence of a duty in a given case: 'I deny *x* is "vulnerable", and therefore I have no duty to act'. Adjectives do not operate to extend powers because the concepts of law will more quickly be clarified by judges. Constraining legal action is also more likely to be successful in response to a power than a duty because it is easier to identify and prove when a power has been misused than when a duty has been denied. Specifically, for a policy space like homelessness, a key battle is determining what it means to be homeless and in need. These sorts of definitional questions are far more easily settled in immigration disputes. None of which is to say that other forms of indeterminacy are unimportant to homelessness law. However, adjectives are especially impactful on policy outcomes.

In homelessness legislation, indeterminacy has not progressed in a neat or linear pattern. Nonetheless, an upward trend in the use of indeterminate parts of speech can be observed in Figure 5.1. This graph displays the total numbers of indeterminate parts of speech from every law pertaining to homelessness enacted between 1900 and 2017. This covers 3,635 sections of legislation, from section 1 of the *Housing of the Working Classes Act 1900* to section 13 of the *Homelessness Reduction Act 2017*. Totals are aggregated into five-year

Figure 5.1: Changes to the language of homelessness legislation, 1900–2017

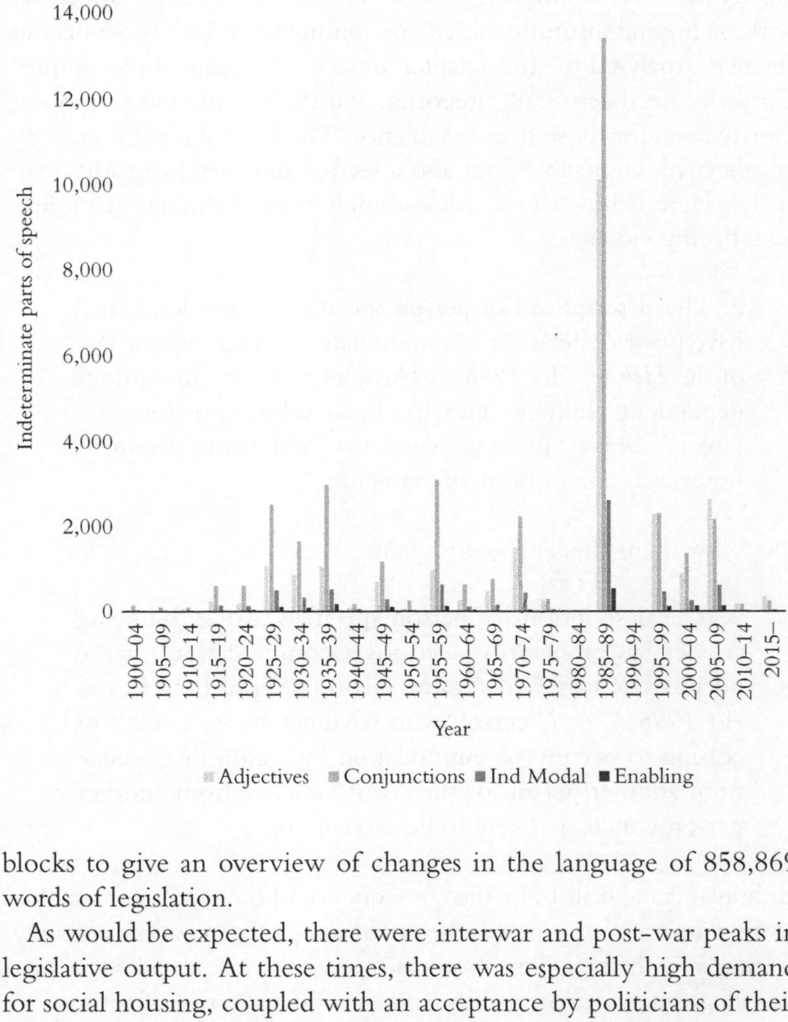

blocks to give an overview of changes in the language of 858,869 words of legislation.

As would be expected, there were interwar and post-war peaks in legislative output. At these times, there was especially high demand for social housing, coupled with an acceptance by politicians of their responsibility to house those affected by the world wars. However, by far the largest output of legislation came in the late 1980s. Legislation enacted from 1985 to 1989 contained 13,426 conjunctions, for instance. That is more than the total number of conjunctions enacted from 1900 to 1960. However, adjectives are the primary concern of this chapter. These also saw vastly increased enactment in the late 1980s, followed by a brief hiatus, before increasing again from the late 1990s through to 2010.

Of particular interest to this chapter are Orders in Council created under the authority of legislation. One for England was created by the Secretary of State, and another for Wales was created by the Welsh Assembly. As mentioned, both established identical categories of priority need: for children aged 16 or 17; for young people under 21; for those leaving institutionalised environments; and for those fleeing violence. Analysed for this chapter are both the general recognition of priority need across all categories, and the specific recognition of priority need for those fleeing violence. The latter includes not only the adjective 'vulnerable', but also a second indeterminate adjective: 'likely'. Here is how the Welsh Assembly framed the duty to house those fleeing violence:

> 2. The descriptions of person specified in articles 3 to 7 have priority need for accommodation under section 189 of the *Housing Act 1996*.... [Article] 5. A person without dependent children who has been subject to domestic violence or is at risk of such violence, or if he or she returns home is at risk of domestic violence.

The following is England's equivalent:

> 2. The descriptions of person specified in the following articles have a priority need for accommodation for the purposes of Part 7 [including section 189] of the *Housing Act 1996*.... 6. A person who is vulnerable as a result of ceasing to occupy accommodation by reason of violence from another person or threats of violence from another person which are likely to be carried out.

For bureaucratic drift to be the consequence of the word 'vulnerable', we must assume that a local authority housing officer wants to comply minimally with their duty. Minimalist compliance provides the best pay-off given resource scarcity and insufficient revenue autonomy. A maximalist application of the duty would entail housing officers ignoring the adjective 'vulnerable' and recognising all applicants that present with evidence of a priority characteristic. This approach would subject the authority entirely to unpredictable demand-side pressures, as is the case for Welsh authorities. While one could argue that 'fleeing violence and being vulnerable' is a tautology, this does not mean that the word 'vulnerable' is inoperative in law. The words 'vulnerable' and 'likely' both enable housing officers to ration supply. Ignoring the chance to filter claimants according to their relative vulnerability would be unpredictable and expensive for English local authorities.

Also, given the small constituency and low participation rate of the homeless, there are high costs to maximalist compliance for local politicians in their vote-, office- and policy-seeking (Strøm 1990).

The following hypotheses are derived from the theory:

> H1: Local authorities applying the word 'vulnerable' to priority need assessments recognise fewer cases as meeting their duty to house.
>
> H2: Local authorities applying the words 'vulnerable' and 'likely' to cases of priority need for those fleeing violence, or threats of violence, recognise fewer cases as meeting their duty to house.
>
> H3: The volatility of duty recognition (year-on-year change in the rate of recognition) is lower in local authorities applying the word 'vulnerable' to priority need assessments.
>
> H4: The volatility of duty recognition for those fleeing violence, or threats of violence, is lower in local authorities applying the words 'vulnerable' and 'likely' to priority need assessments.

The potential flaws with the thesis and hypotheses are, first, assuming minimalist compliance. That this would be a rational response to indeterminate legislation downplays ideological and sociological forces that also affect housing officers. I would not deny the importance of these variables, but argue that the material constraints placed on local authorities encourage, but do not compel, local politicians and civil servants to take advantage of indeterminacies in law to comply minimally with their duties. The second possible flaw in the argument is connected to this point: if the meaning of law is indeterminate, then the minimal level of compliance is also indeterminate. Would the logic of the argument not lead to the conclusion that zero compliance would be possible, and rational, by the inclusion of indeterminate adjectives? The very word 'compliance' is misplaced if a duty is indeterminate. It is impossible to comply with a non-existent, or entirely contestable, duty. My response is that, yes, complete non-compliance is possible. However, persistent non-compliance would itself be risk-laden for local authorities: non-compliance would increase the risks of litigation and the successful judicial review of decisions. This would incur both material costs and reputational harm. Nonetheless, it is impossible to determine precisely what the minimal legal compliance with a duty would be for a local authority. This calculation depends on demand for housing and local differences in the meaning of 'vulnerable'. The threshold for acknowledging an individual's vulnerability will be higher in regions with higher demand for housing. However, this is the point: by shedding the responsibility to define what 'vulnerable' means, Parliament has allowed housing officers to define the law themselves by assessing local needs. The Welsh Assembly has granted no such flexibility to its local authorities. What is not clear is just how far English local authorities are able to use indeterminate words to shirk their duty to house. All else being equal, if fewer individuals are recognised as being in priority need after the 2002 Order in England, it would signal an ineffective policy. The aim of the 2002 Order was to make more generous the recognition of priority need, not more restrictive recognition. So, we can park any ideological or economic arguments, and focus on whether the policy worked as intended.

Another criticism could be that the findings are trite: arguing that Parliament's use of language affects policy delivery is, being blunt, obvious. Parliament would not include words without intended effects, as stated by Lord Rooker in the debate on the 2002 England Order: 'The key test in relation to those categories [of priority need] is whether applicants are vulnerable: that will be for local housing authorities to decide in individual cases'.

A reasonable fear of the 'identification revolution' in political science is that by using natural experiments, we obsess over minutiae and confirm what is obvious. However, there is, in fact, little known as to the significance of including or omitting individual words from law. In particular, operationalising and observing the impact of specific parts of speech remains a prominent research domain. Exploiting a natural experiment to assess the impact of adjectives in legislation is timely and important.

On the specific causal mechanism linking the use of adjectives to bureaucratic drift, one could argue conversely to my thesis that adjectives reduce drift. It could be argued that enabling local contextual variation to be recognised in legislative language enables local authorities to manage their resources better, and allows for more, not less, predictable policy implementation. This is essentially the expectation outlined in H3 and H4. Without the words 'vulnerable' and 'likely', local authorities would be entirely beholden to demand-side variation and would have restricted means of year-on-year budgeting and the modelling of local housing needs. While I would accept that the inclusion of the words 'vulnerable' and 'likely' does enable more controlled and managed policy delivery, it is less predictable for claimants as to whether they will qualify for housing. Therefore, with regard to bureaucratic drift, it allows local authorities to downplay their statutory duties. The unpredictability created by the use of adjectives is hence placed on service users and taken off service providers. Given that the point of enshrining the priority need categories in law was to facilitate the housing of those most in need, it is a threat to policy objectives if housing officers enjoy wide discretion over recognising the vulnerability of applicants.

Methodology and data

Causal inference in political science is typically frustrated by the ambiguity of expected effects from a treatment. However, using a DD approach offers key advantages in identifying and isolating the impact of legislative language without having to control for the innumerable factors that created the language. The utility of DD was notably demonstrated in Card and Krueger's (1994) study of the effects of minimum wage laws on employment rates in New Jersey and Pennsylvania. They showed that when New Jersey introduced a higher minimum wage in 1992, it had no significant impact on employment. This was concluded by analysing 410 fast-food restaurants in the state and the neighbouring state of Pennsylvania. Their DD approach compared the treatment (New Jersey) to the control (Pennsylvania) both before and after the treatment was administered. To support their claim that the treatment had no effect, they needed to observe parallel trends for New Jersey and Pennsylvania continuing in a parallel fashion after the treatment. This was observed and the null hypothesis could not be rejected. If, conversely, New Jersey had experienced a change in the unemployment rate after receiving the treatment, its rate of change would have converged or diverged from Pennsylvania's and the null could, with trepidation, have been rejected. Therefore, the comparison groups had to be similar, such that they had near-parallel employment trajectories before changes to the minimum wage were introduced. The macroeconomic and demographic similarities of the two states were key to the research design. Also, pre-treatment trends may be similar, but in DD analysis, the researcher has to be aware of other policy and contextual changes that occur at the same time as any treatment. A natural experiment is ultimately an observational study, and the researcher does not have the sort of control enjoyed in a laboratory experiment.

Despite these methodological limitations, the DD approach is well-suited to my research question. There was a shift in policy in two countries where the only difference between England and Wales was individual words. This allows us to focus closely on the impact of those words on policy delivery. Specifically, the DD equation for testing H1 and H2 is as follows:

$$\sigma_{it} = \sum_{j=1}^{4} \alpha_j + \beta_1 + \beta_2 (POSTLAW) + \beta_3 (ENG) + \beta_4 (POSTLAW.ENG) + \varepsilon_{it}$$

The model estimates deviation of local authority *i*'s rate of recognising priority need from the mean (σ) at time *t*. There are four intercepts across the y axis (denoted by α) because the DD method compares the treatment and control groups both before and after the treatment is administered, making for the comparison of four lines. There are also, therefore, four regression coefficients to be estimated (denoted by β). The variable *POSTLAW* is a dummy that captures whether in England or Wales, time *t* is after the passing of the Priority Need Orders. The variable *ENG* is a fixed effects dummy for all local authorities in England, both before and after treatment. The DD parameter of interest is *POSTLAW.ENG*, which assesses the trajectory of the treatment group – England after 2002. To have any confidence in rejecting the null, we would need deviation of this coefficient to have occurred, with a very low probability of such deviation happening by chance alone. Other variables were added to the analyses so as to control for political, financial and socio-economic differences between local authorities.

The DD equation for testing H3 and H4 is as follows:

$$z_{it} = \sum_{j=1}^{4} \alpha_j + \delta_1 + \delta_2 (POSTLAW) + \delta_3 (ENG) + \delta_4 (POSTLAW.ENG) + \varepsilon_{it}$$

Here, the dependent variable is the Delta of the z-score. This estimates the change in the extent of deviation of local authority *i* from the mean at time *t*, when compared to the deviation at $t-1$. This model is similar to that used by Matthew Slaughter (2001) to test the impact of trade liberalisation on income convergence across countries.

Before the DD analysis could be conducted, it was necessary to select cases for comparison. England and Wales have many significant differences in their institutions, law, politics, finance and socio-economics. These differences can frustrate comparative analysis. It is not necessary for the treatment and control groups to be identical in DD analysis, but it is important that they be as similar as possible, such that they have near-parallel pre-treatment trajectories in priority need recognition. However, it would also not be acceptable to select local authorities to study on the dependent variable (rates of priority need acceptance). As such, similarities had to be found on predictors of demand for housing. These data come from local labour market information on unemployment, weekly income and population density. Demand for housing from homeless claimants is highest in local authorities with high population densities and high weekly wages, but low rates of employment. In other words, rich, urban or suburban areas with high barriers to labour market entry see the greatest demand for housing from homeless claimants. Of course, there are many other explanatory variables that could have been used to predict demand for housing, but these three are good predictors and have the distinct advantage of having complete data sets for the period under consideration in England and Wales, provided by the Office for National Statistics.[41]

Using propensity score matching (PSM), I identified 22 English local authorities that are most similar to the 22 Welsh local authorities on these local labour market variables. Data were analysed from all 323 local authorities responsible for housing in England for three separate years – 1999, 2004 and 2009 – making a data matrix of 969 local authority-years for England, to compare against 66 local authority-years for the 22 local authorities in Wales. Using the MatchIt function in R (Ho et al 2011), the following English local authorities were identified as the most similar to Wales on the explanatory variables of interest: Bedford, Boston, Calderdale, Carlisle, Chiltern, Darlington, Doncaster, Dover, Durham, Fenland, Great Yarmouth, Hartlepool, Lancaster, North-East Lincolnshire, Northumberland, Pendle, Redcar and Cleveland, Rother, Scarborough, Tendring, Torridge, and Wakefield. These were compared with all of the local authorities in Wales: Blaenau Gwent, Bridgend, Caerphilly, Cardiff, Carmarthenshire, Ceredigion, Conwy, Denbighshire, Flintshire, Gwynedd, Isle of Anglesey, Merthyr Tydfil, Monmothshire, Neath Port Talbot, Newport, Pembrokeshire, Powys, Rhondda Cynon Taf, Swansea, Torfaen, Vale of Glamorgan and Wrexham.

Some of these authorities changed their institutional make-up between 1997 and 2014. Most notably, in England in 2009, some

---

41 See: https://www.nomisweb.co.uk

previously two-tier authorities were merged into unitary authorities, thereby increasing their powers and budgets. Of the authorities studied for this chapter, this specifically affected Bedford, Durham and Northumberland. All of Welsh local government is organised around unitary authorities, whereas in England, it is typically the lower-tier authority that deals with housing matters. Despite these institutional differences between England and Wales, duties for housing the homeless are, and were, essentially identical. Major differences do exist with regard to the resources available for the authorities. Cash availability was, and is, greater per head in Wales than in England. This is an important difference between the two countries, but it is worth recalling that the treatment and control groups need not be perfectly identical, just as New Jersey is not identical to Pennsylvania. The key to DD analysis is minimising pre-treatment differences, and this has been achieved with PSM.

Having identified the 44 local authorities for analysis, data were collected on each for their recognition of priority need. In addition to which, data were collected on each local authority's politics, finance and socio-economics. Comprehensive data on priority need recognition was provided by the Welsh government from 1997 to 2014. For England, data was not in the public domain, but was freely given on request to the Department for Communities and Local Government. Comprehensive data on priority need decisions in England only go back to 1999. These data provided both the total number of priority need acceptances (TPN) and the disaggregated figure for those recognised as in priority need for fleeing violence or threats of violence (TFV). From these data, it was also possible to calculate the change in acceptance in year t as compared to $t - 1$ (DPN/DFV – with 'D' for Delta). All data on recognition of priority need are measured as the number of individuals recognised per 10,000 of the local authority population. The reason for not measuring the proportion of priority need acceptances from the total number of applicants is that the models would be predicting the number of applicants as well as the rate of priority need recognition. The dependent variable measures the rate of recognition, rather than the nature of demand.

In addition to measuring the rate of recognition at time t, I also included a time-lag dummy (LAG) to test for a single-year lag to policy implementation. There is no legal reason for observing any delay in applying the Priority Need Orders as both came into force immediately. However, there may have been delays in establishing infrastructure and assigning resources to comply with the new duties.

Other variables included for analysis can be grouped as political, financial and socio-economic. For political variables, every year in which a local authority was run by a Conservative administration was coded (CON). The Conservative Party generally supports more restricted access to public services, being in favour of individual self-reliance and fiscal security for government. We may therefore expect Conservative-led local authorities to have more restrictive rates of recognition of priority need. However, there are two caveats to this: first, a Conservative government authored the *Housing Act 1996*, so the party's policies are not averse to acknowledging priority need; and, second, the 'Conservative Party' is not a fully independent variable, and their impact on outcomes begs the question of why some local electorates are more likely to vote Conservative in the first place. Nonetheless, CON is a useful variable to consider in conjunction with other variables that assess the potential effects of different parties' ideologies. The other political measure coded the coherence of local authority leadership, Conservative or otherwise (COH). A local authority is scored as 1 if it is run by a single party and 0 if it has no overall party control. A plausible theory is that a volatile party system and/or multi-party governance inhibit long-term policy coherence. This will typically be to the advantage of service users as duty compliance is the policy path of lesser resistance. A single party of any description could better develop coherent housing strategies that will more likely rely on substantive restrictions to achieve long-term housing goals.

For financial variables, I analysed the effect of the Revenue Support Grant (RSG) and the change in this central government funding year on year (RSGD – with 'D' for Delta). RSG replaced the rate support grant in the early 1990s. It was distributed as a formula grant to local authorities to supplement local tax revenue. More generous central government funding (high RSG) and lesser volatility of allocation (low RSGD) could explain the more generous recognition of priority need applications. Conversely, where local authorities face insecure finances, it likely places pressure on housing officers to restrict provision.

The socio-economic variables measure unemployment (UNE), local mean weekly income (INC) and population density (DEN). These variables consider the demand side rather than the supply side for housing. If a region experiences changes in these variables, it is to be expected that it will affect demand for housing and could therefore affect the recognition of priority need. It is necessary to control for these demand-side variables, as well as the political and financial variables on the supply side, so as to isolate the significance of changes in legislative language. It must be noted that several explanatory variables intercorrelate, and could not all be included in a single model without multicollinearity. Therefore, variables were included in multivariate models as interaction terms, or not at all, if there was no significant correlation found for a variable in bivariate OLS (ordinary least squares) regression. Table 5.1 provides descriptive statistics for all variables.

Diagnostics

The same assumptions that apply to OLS regressions, also apply to DD analysis. DD analysis is parametric, relying on the assumptions of a normal distribution of errors, the conditional independence of cause and effect, stationarity in time series, and no multicollinearity between explanatory variables. First, with regards to normality, the universe of data on all 44 local authorities was used to avoid possible biases that could have been introduced by random or stratified sampling techniques. Nonetheless, heteroscedasticity-robust standard errors are reported, in recognition that different local authorities will likely have different degrees of error variance. Second, with regard to endogeneity, the conditional independence of cause and effect is theoretically plausible, in that the recognition of individuals as in priority need will not cause the adoption of new language in policy, at least within the time frame of the data analysed. Of course, it is possible, even probable, that implementing homelessness policy will inform the language used in future policymaking, so complete independence of cause and effect cannot be guaranteed. Some variables were not considered for inclusion in the models because of the likelihood of voiding the conditional independence assumption. For instance, crime rates could not be used as a predictor of changes in the recognition rate for fleeing violence. This would be akin to using violence to predict those recognised as fleeing violence. It would mean having the same term on either side of the equation. Furthermore, with regards to endogeneity, it is important to consider why England and Wales adopted the different language in the first place. The language is not just causative, but symptomatic of the Welsh government's insistence that local authorities strictly apply their duty to recognise priority need. According to a recent report (BBC 2016), Wales is leading the way on homelessness provision in the UK. There is clearly a stronger policy commitment in Wales than across the border. Of course, the different origins of the language matter, but it is only with PSM and

Table 5.1: Descriptive statistics for all variables

Variables	**Control – Wales 1997–2014**						**Treatment – England 1999–2014**					
Dependent variables	**Min**	**Mean**	**Med**	**Max**	**SD**	**N**	**Min**	**Mean**	**Med**	**Max**	**SD**	**N**
Total/10,000 in priority need (TPN)	2.18	19.49	17.40	61.07	10.80	396	0	11.41	8.91	42.35	8.86	332
Total/10,000 recognised as fleeing violence (TFV)	0	2.36	1.92	13.54	2.12	396	0	0.46	0	8.77	0.90	332
Annual increase in recognition of priority need (DPN)	–32.90	0.09	–0.01	27.68	6.62	374	–19.96	–0.58	–0.41	11.89	4.30	310
Annual increase in recognition of fleeing violence (DFV)	–7.96	0.04	0	6.58	1.44	374	–8.77	–0.06	0	2.58	0.76	310
Control variables												
Conservative-run authority, 0/1 (CON)	0	0.03	0	1	0.17	396	0	0.26	0	1	0.44	332
Ideological coherence, 0/1 (COH)	0	0.57	1	1	0.5	396	0	0.48	0	1	0.50	332
Revenue support grant, real terms/capita (RSG)	460	894	909	1,368	203	396	0	123	48	670	179	266
% change in RSG on previous year (RSGD)	–6.88	3.73	3.79	12.01	3.89	374	–100	3.55	–2.17	460.98	47.49	244
Unemployment, % working age (UNE)	2.32	6.51	6.20	14.70	2.11	396	2.10	6.50	6.10	14.60	2.20	332
Income, median weekly (INC)	244	390	396	582	66	396	270	416	411	743	77	332
Population density per hectare (DEN)	0.24	4.02	3.06	23.70	4.55	396	0.57	4.06	3.82	9.79	2.57	332

DD that we can observe just how far the language of legislation affects bureaucratic drift, which is ultimately the aim here.

Third, autocorrelation in time series is likely in England given that local authorities can better manage their caseload year on year. Hence, decisions at time t can influence decisions at $t + 1$. However, the reason for this lack of stationarity is primarily due to the changes in policy language. So, there should be stationarity in the data before 2002 in England, if not after 2002. Finally, testing for multicollinearity (using variance inflation factors, for instance) is not possible because parallel trend lines included in the DD model ought, by definition, to covary. So, the key is to analyse correlations between explanatory variables before specifying models. This was done and guided model specification. With DD analysis, a common robustness test of the parallel trend assumption is analysing, in isolation, some pre-treatment data and then applying a 'placebo' treatment to several years before the treatment. The problem in this instance is a lack of data going back sufficiently before the 2002 treatment. The 'Table 773' data on priority need decisions in England supplied by the Department for Communities and Local Government (DCLG) only go back as far as 1999.

Therefore, despite caution taken to specify models, it must be clearly stated that a relative paucity of data means that null hypotheses can only very tentatively be rejected. There is strong evidence to suggest a significant post-treatment effect of the words 'vulnerable' and 'likely', but it will not do to exaggerate this finding. More research in different policy domains will be required to improve the robustness of these findings.

Results and discussion

Before presenting the results of OLS and DD analyses, Figures 5.2–5.4 present data on the frequency of priority need recognition in time series.

Figure 5.2 describes similar levels of priority need recognition in England and Wales before the introduction of the Priority Need Orders. After the Orders, trends diverged. Wales experienced an initial spike in recognition of priority need, while England saw a more modest increase followed by a precipitous decline. It is interesting to note that at the end of the period under observation, both countries had returned to parallel trends, although significantly further apart than they had been at the beginning of the period. In 2014, the mean rate

Figure 5.2: Total priority need (TPN) recognitions in England and Wales, 1997–2014

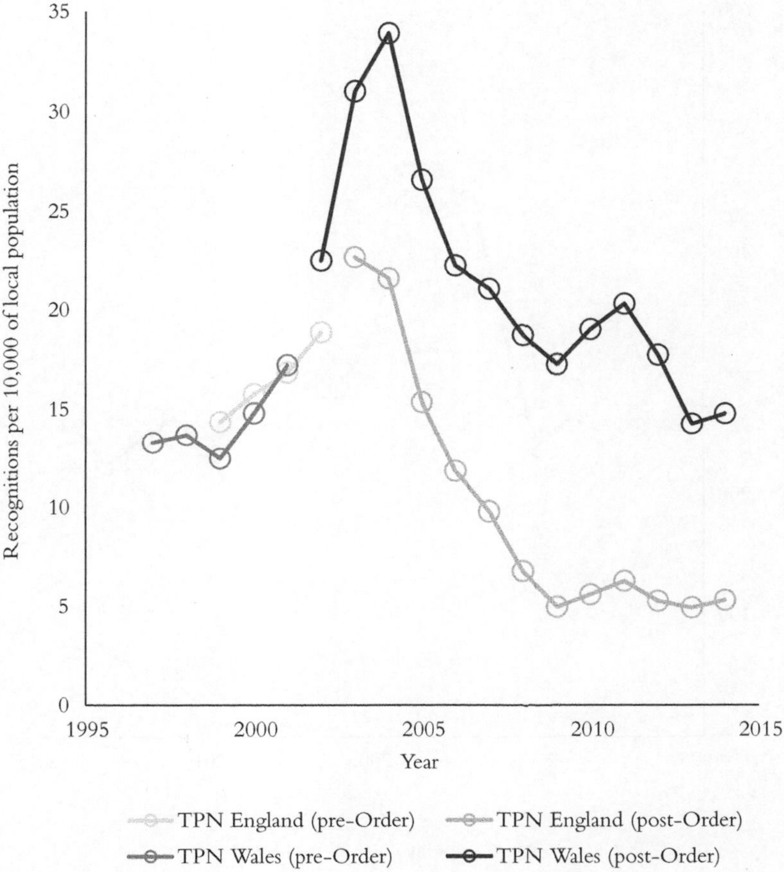

of priority need recognition in England was five people per 10,000 of the local population, whereas in Wales, it was three times as many, at 15. Translated into real terms, Figure 5.3 assesses two representative and comparable local authorities in England and Wales.

Figure 5.3 displays the absolute numbers of individuals recognised as in priority need in two authorities. Caerphilly experienced a more haphazard rate of recognition, suggesting that the recognition rate was determined by demand-side forces beyond the authority's control. In Calderdale, by contrast, there was a smooth decrease in the number recognised as in priority need after an initial post-Order spike in recognitions. This suggests that the housing officers were somewhat better able to manage demand and delimit supply as the 2002 Order bedded in. Being precise, in 2014, Calderdale Metropolitan Borough

Figure 5.3: Absolute numbers of priority need recognitions for Caerphilly and Calderdale, 1997–2014

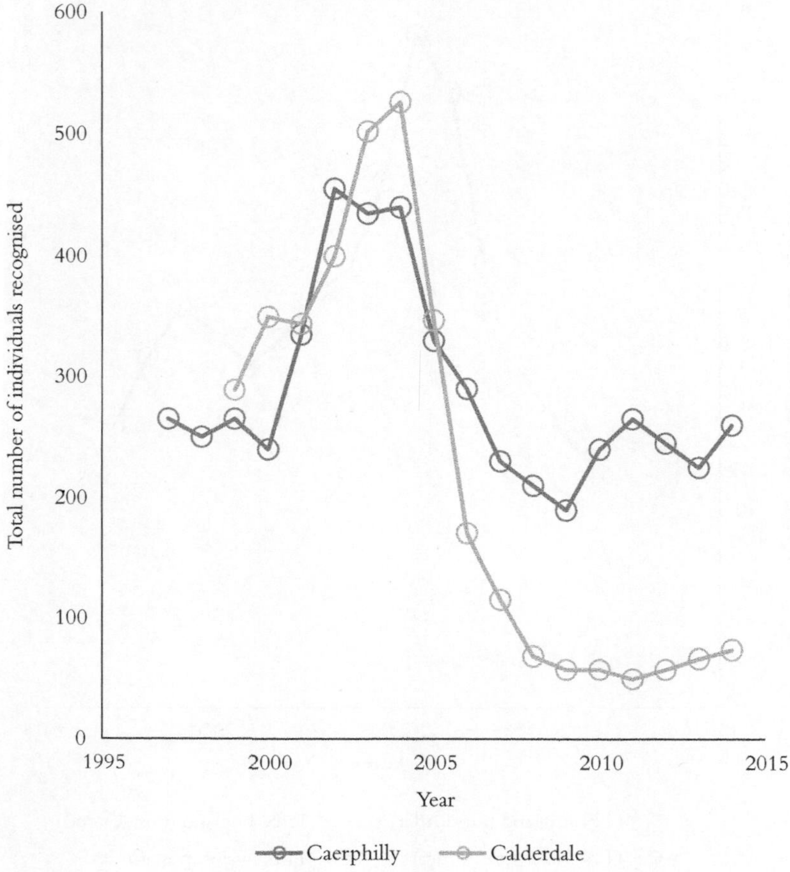

Council recognised 74 individuals as being in priority need, whereas Caerphilly County Borough Council recognised 260 individuals. Caerphilly had a population of 179,900 in 2014, to Calderdale's 207,400. So, as a proportion of its population, the recognition rate was much higher in Caerphilly.

Figure 5.4 appears to display less of a pre-treatment parallel trend between the countries than was seen in Figure 5.2. However, the y-axis scale is in a significantly smaller range than in Figure 5.2. Both England and Wales ranged between 0.5 and 2.36 per 10,000 individuals recognised as in priority need for fleeing violence before the Orders. After the Orders, this range spread to 0.17–4.26 per 10,000. The deviation is especially striking because evidence suggests that there had been no decrease in recorded domestic violence in

Figure 5.4: Total priority need recognitions for those fleeing violence (TFV) in England and Wales, 1997–2014

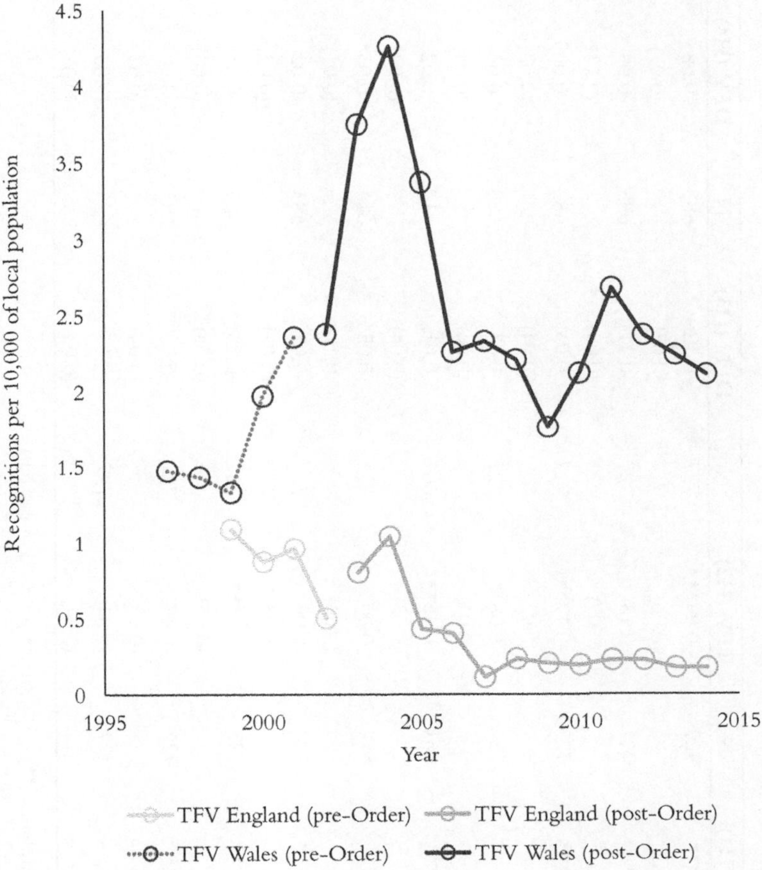

England or Wales over the period (Woodhouse and Demsey 2016). So, why England significantly decreased the recognition of priority need for those fleeing violence cannot be explained on the demand side, and a strong case is emerging for the impact of legislative language on bureaucratic drift.

Tables 5.2 and 5.3 display the results of the bivariate OLS regressions and DD analyses, respectively. All variables were standardised into *z* scores, with means of 0 and standard deviations of 1. This allows for the most effective comparison of regression coefficients. Results from the bivariate regressions were used to inform model specification in the multivariate DD analyses.

Table 5.2 displays statistically significant correlations between almost all of the explanatory variables and the total number of

Table 5.2: OLS bivariate regression results for all variables

	Variable	TPN (H1)	N	TFV (H2)	N	DPN (H3)	N	DFV (H4)	N
Linguistic/legal	ENG	–0.75***	727	–0.98***	727	–0.12	683	–0.08	683
		(0.07)		(0.06)		(0.07)		(0.07)	
	POSTLAW	0.16*	727	0.18	727	–0.21	683	–0.09	683
		(0.08)		(0.09)		(0.09)		(0.13)	
Political	CON	–0.15***	727	–0.17***	727	0.03	683	0.009	683
		(0.03)		(0.02)		(0.04)		(0.03)	
	COH	–0.02	727	0.08**	727	0.03	683	0.03	683
		(0.04)		(0.04)		(0.04)		(0.04)	
Financial	RSG	0.33***	661	0.45***	661	0.01	617	0.02	617
		(0.03)		(0.03)		(0.04)		(0.04)	
	RSGD	–0.03	614	0.003	614	0.05	614	0.03**	614
		(0.03)		(0.04)		(0.1)		(0.01)	
Socio-economic	UNE	–0.21***	727	–0.04	727	–0.03	683	–0.02	683
		(0.03)		(0.03)		(0.03)		(0.03)	
	INC	–0.2***	727	–0.1***	727	–0.13***	683	–0.03	683
		(0.03)		(0.03)		(0.04)		(0.03)	
	DEN	0.07**	727	0.07	727	–0.0007	683	–0.009	683
		(0.03)		(0.03)		(0.04)		(0.03)	
Time	LAG	0.03	727	0.04	727	–0.13***	683	–0.03	683
		(0.03)		(0.04)		(0.03)		(0.05)	

Notes: Heteroscedasticity-robust standard errors in parentheses. *** $p < 0.01$; ** $p < 0.05$; * $p < 0.01$.

applicants recognised as in priority need (TPN), with 'statistically significant' defined here as $p < 0.05$. The exceptions that display no significant correlation are the introduction of Orders in England and Wales (POSTLAW), political coherence (COH), changes to central government funding (RSGD) and the time lag of one year (LAG). The most substantively significant correlations are between TPN and the jurisdiction of an English local authority (ENG) and the provision of central government funding (RSG). It is important to note that English local authorities are significantly less well funded by the RSG than their Welsh counterparts, meaning that the variables ENG and RSG intercorrelate. It is therefore notable that ENG has a stronger coefficient (–0.75) than RSG (0.33) because they cannot both be included in multivariate analyses.

Significant correlations were also revealed from the total number recognised as in priority need for fleeing violence (TFV). Again, ENG provides the most substantive and statistically significant correlation (–0.98). The analyses of the changes in year-on-year recognition (DPN and DFV) reveal fewer correlations. The exceptions are with regard to weekly income (INC) and the time lag (LAG), which correlate with the changing recognition of priority need (DPN). Also, changes to central government funding (RSGD) correlates with changes in the recognition of priority need for those fleeing violence (DFV). *Prima facie*, there is little evidence to reject the null in favour of H3 and H4 on the basis of the OLS regressions.

The coefficients of greatest interest in Table 5.3 are the DD parameters (*POSTLAW.ENG*). For all of the models, bar Models 5, 7 and 8, these coefficients are statistically and substantively significant. The addition of the word 'vulnerable' is modelled as causing a drop of 1.19 standard deviations from the mean in Model 1. In real terms, this is a deviation from a mean priority need recognition of 16 individuals per 10,000 to an acceptance rate of three per 10,000, a drop of 81%. Given that the mean population for the 22 English local authorities between 1999 and 2014 was 141,498, Model 1 expects a recognition rate of 226 individuals to drop to just 42; that is 145 individuals per authority not housed on account of their priority need. Given that there are 323 such authorities in England, there could have been as many as 50,000 individuals who were not recognised as being in priority need after the Order came into force. This evidence allows for a tentative rejection of the null in favour of H1.

Model 2 adds unemployment (UNE) to the model specification, being the only variable with statistical and substantive significance in the bivariate analyses that also does not correlate with ENG. Model 2

Table 5.3: Difference-in-differences analysis

Variable	Model 1 TPN (H1)	Model 2 TPN (H1)	Model 3 TFV (H2)	Model 4 TFV (H2)	Model 5 DPN (H3)	Model 6 DPN (H3)	Model 7 DFV (H4)	Model 8 DFV (H4)
DD parameter	–1.19***	–1.05***	–0.86***	–0.86***	–0.28*	–0.61***	0.13	0.12
	(0.16)	(0.16)	(0.17)	(0.17)	(0.22)	(0.17)	(0.27)	(0.28)
ENG	0.2**	0.08	–0.3*	–0.3*	0.13	0.42**	–0.19	–0.19
	(0.09)	(0.14)	(0.16)	(0.16)	(0.2)	(0.19)	(0.26)	(0.27)
POSTLAW	0.71***	0.66***	0.54***	0.66***	–0.09	0.25	–0.13	–0.12
	–0.11	(0.11)	(0.14)	(0.15)	(0.14)	(0.18)	(0.27)	(0.16)
RSGD								0.03**
								(0.01)
UNE		–0.18***						
		(0.03)						
INC				–0.08***		–0.25***		
				(0.03)		(0.09)		
INC*ENG						0.24***		
						(0.1)		
Intercept	–0.21**	–0.2**	0.03	–0.07	0.13	–0.17	0.15	0.14
	(0.1)	(0.09)	(0.12)	(0.13)	(0.12)	(0.15)	(0.14)	(0.14)
Adjusted R^2	0.2	0.23	0.27	0.28	0.007	0.02	0.001	0.002
N	728	728	728	728	684	684	684	615

Notes: Heteroscedasticity-robust standard errors in parentheses. ***$p < 0.01$; **$p < 0.05$; *$p < 0.01$.

has a marginally higher R^2 than Model 1, and the model shows that when controlling for another variable, the DD parameter retains its statistical significance. Models 3 and 4 similarly suggest that when disaggregating the priority need data, the same pattern emerges in priority need recognition for those fleeing violence or threats of violence. This gives some support for rejecting the null in favour of H2.

Models 5 and 6 suggest that including the word 'vulnerable' did decrease the variability of priority need acceptances year on year. This is evidence in support of rejecting the null for H3. Model 6, in particular, includes an interaction term for weekly incomes in England (INC*ENG) as these variables correlate positively. Again, controlling for socio-economic variables does not remove the importance of language on the effectiveness of policy.

Models 7 and 8 do not provide evidence for rejecting the null in favour of H4. It is likely that year-on-year variance in the numbers fleeing violence is too small to register a statistically significant difference. The mean number of individuals seeking recognition of a priority need when fleeing violence was just seven for the English local authorities studied. As such, it is important to note that H4 must be rejected in favour of the null.

Model fit is greatest for Models 2 and 4. Model 6 presents strong statistical significance but, with an R^2 of just 0.02, model fit is low. None of the models present high R^2, but this is unsurprising given that multiple lines are being modelled simultaneously.

Conclusion

There is strong evidence to suggest that the use of indeterminate adjectives in legislation created opportunities for bureaucratic drift. As such, there is reason and evidence to conclude that legislative language substantially affected the accountability of policy delivery in local government. It had been the intention of Parliament to recognise more individuals as being in priority need for housing, but in England, after the 2002 Order, there were significantly fewer individuals recognised than was the case in Wales, or even in England before the Order came into force. The words 'vulnerable' and 'likely' appear to have created such indeterminacy that litigants sought judicial clarification. In 2015, the UK Supreme Court finally provided an authoritative meaning for the word 'vulnerable'. This is best summarised in Lord Neuberger's ruling at paragraphs 39 and 40:

> when assessing whether or not an applicant is vulnerable, an authority must, as Arden LJ said in para 6 of her judgment in the *Johnson* case, 'pay close attention to the particular circumstances of the' applicant. Indeed, as Ms Thompson … rightly said the issue of vulnerability must be determined not so much by reference to each of the applicant's problems, but by reference to them when taken together.…
>
> Arden LJ was not right to go on to say that the authority must, or even can, 'tak[e] into account its own burden of homeless persons and finite resources' when assessing whether an applicant is vulnerable … an authority's duty under Part VII of the 1996 Act is not to be influenced or affected by the resources available to the authority … the fact that the authority may be very short of money and/or available accommodation cannot in any way affect whether an applicant is in priority need.

Especially notable in his ruling is where Lord Neuberger confronts the discretion of local bureaucrats: 'In so far as a balancing exercise between housing the homeless and conserving local authority resources is appropriate, it has been carried out by Parliament when enacting Part VII'. In other words, the effect of Parliament's language may have given the impression that local housing officers could use their discretion in determining what 'vulnerable' means in accordance with local conditions when, in fact, the intention of Parliament was, according to the court, to enable enhanced analysis of an individual's circumstances, and not use words like 'vulnerable' as licence to shirk duties.

This is how the courts made sense of Parliament's language. In reality, the sovereign's language was indeterminate and had no explicit 'logic of communication'. This logic was provided by judges. In all likelihood, the government instructed Parliament to use indeterminate language so as to enable greater post-promulgation flexibility in policy delivery. This approach to the rule of law puts greater emphasis on the rulers than the law. It is an executive-centred policy approach that poses a significant risk to democratic accountability. How can agents of the legislature know of their powers and duties if those power and duties are indeterminate? Despite the advantages of flexible policy implementation, the use of indeterminate language undermines the purpose of crafting legislation as a secure record of sovereign intent.

Besides clarity in the law, there are alternative means available to improve executive accountability. Local authorities have, in particular, undergone significant reforms with the intention of improving their accountability to local voters. The *Local Government Act 2000* obliged local authorities to adopt a separated executive cabinet and to describe their powers in a local constitution. These reforms will only be partially successful in securing accountability if Parliament continues to deny fiscal autonomy to local government, and provides only semi-authoritative instructions on policy.

Anticipating the effects of legislative language is especially important to policymakers seeking to achieve complex social objectives. While this book is framed in 21st-century British social policy, the implications of the findings are pertinent to all democratic legislatures. Legislators set out complex objectives in the cybernetic language of legislation. A temptation for policymakers can be to forgo the rigours of closed, algorithmic clarity of language in order to take advantage of commonly used language. This allows for post-legislative bargaining on policy specifics. The risk to this approach comes when discretion and adaptability are only partly intended. With housing policy, central government has long sought to be more than merely an onlooker in providing shelter for those in need. The desire to balance the local and central direction of a policy can lead to a messy game of chicken where powers and duties are asserted or denied on both sides. The incentive for duty shirking is especially high for local agents faced with resource scarcity and limited control over revenues. These local policy agents are best incentivised to constrain the scope of a duty by taking advantage of linguistic indeterminacy. This is a phenomenon that is not confined to Britain, nor is it anything new. However, the specific effects of individual words on policy delivery have not previously been established in research on this scale. That as many as 50,000 people could have been denied priority access to housing simply because of a single adjective shows the potential impact that language can have on policy.

SIX

How Parliament's language affects individual rights

> Equality … requires government not to treat people unequally without justification. The notion of equal worth is thus a fundamental precept of our constitution. It gains its ultimate justification from a notion of the way individuals should be treated in a democracy. It is constitutive of democracy.
>
> *Jowell 1994:* 7

> The Commission [for Equality and Human Rights] shall exercise its functions under this Part with a view to encouraging and supporting the development of a society in which – (a) people's ability to achieve their potential is not limited by prejudice or discrimination, (b) there is respect for and protection of each individual's human rights, (c) there is respect for the dignity and worth of each individual, (d) each individual has an equal opportunity to participate in society, and (e) there is mutual respect between groups based on understanding and valuing of diversity and on shared respect for equality and human rights.
>
> Equality Act 2006, *section 3*

Introduction

How is the provision of rights affected by indeterminate legislation? This chapter will describe how indeterminacies in anti-discrimination and equality laws have undermined the effectiveness of policy. Specifically, rights are increasingly couched in language that allows their interpretations to be stretched, narrowed and entirely reimagined. Effects have included the only partial realisation of policy goals. In addition to which has been reliance, in the face of indeterminacy, on well-worn practices. In other words, despite the desire to effect ambitious policy change with regards to equality, indeterminacies in law have enabled only modest changes and have encouraged the courts to take a safe, conservative approach to interpreting the content of rights. Drawing on the opening quotes, the Commission for Equality and Human Rights is tasked with 'encouraging and supporting the development of a society in which people's ability to achieve their potential is not limited by prejudice or discrimination'. Given the indeterminacy of this language, the default approach to rights is to rely on notions of equality that are well established, as being in Jeffrey Jowell's words, 'constitutive of democracy'. There is a desire to achieve significant change in the provision of rights, but this is frustrated by the unclear exposition of what rights exist and how they may be enjoyed.

This chapter therefore looks to the third primary goal of policy: the establishment of individual rights. These are legally backed claims to autonomy and dignity. However, beyond this thin definition, rights are notoriously difficult to define in substance and to enjoy in practice, which is why analysing the impact of language can help isolate the particular roots of confusion and frustrated change. As compared to the preceding two chapters, this chapter looks to communicative discourse as well as coordinative discourse (Schmidt 2008: 310), in that rights are communicated to citizens as well as being protected through coordinated state power. Analysing communicative discourse between the state and citizens will allow us to see how citizens deal with indeterminate messages. This, in turn, allows assessment of the desirability of indeterminate policy, as well as considering its feasibility (Pollitt and Bouckaert 2004). Desirability is measured as the coherence and legitimacy of policy. Findings suggest that language affects both significantly. Evidence is taken from looking at the life cycle of two anti-discrimination laws: from their promulgation to their being succeeded by other laws. Specifically, the chapter offers detailed process tracing analysis of the *Race Relations Act 1976 (Amendment) Regulations 2003*[42] and the *Employment Equality (Religion or Belief) Regulations 2003*.[43] These regulations were selected for a 'method of difference' comparison as they are similar in substance but differ linguistically, and have had different policy effects as a result.

---

[42] SI 2003/1626.

[43] SI 2003/1660.

Theory and research design

The theoretical focus of the chapter therefore differs from the preceding chapters. Not only is the analysis focused on communication between the state and society, but it also looks to the effects of indeterminate modal and enabling verbs on the indeterminacy of legislation. Preceding chapters considered how conjunctions have allowed powers to be stretched, while adjectives allowed duties to be constrained. Now we look to how indeterminate modal and enabling verbs have allowed the 'interpretative space' to be repositioned (Lester and Piore 2004: 264). The modal verbs 'may' or 'might' can, in conjunction with the enabling verbs 'make' or 'amend', allow the government to create new legal language. This repositions the interpretative space in the sense that wholly new policy terrain is staked out, with new indeterminacies to be resolved. Of course, it is possible for the government to use secondary legislation to clarify the meaning of primary law, for example, adjectives could be given a narrow, or contextually specific, definition. However, secondary legislation that clarifies the parent legislation is the exception, not the norm. For one thing, it is not possible for secondary legislation to remove indeterminacies in primary law entirely. If there is any perceived mismatch between primary and secondary legislation, the former prevails regardless of how plainly worded the latter may be. Second, the use of secondary legislation is a cheap and easy way to change policy. With governments facing increased demands for policy change, it is not in their interests to use secondary legislation just to narrow the interpretative space; better to move that space into new policy terrain.

A further theoretical addition of this chapter is the focus on multinational government. Much of the anti-discrimination law in the UK comes from European Union (EU) law. Where the preceding chapters looked to central and local government, respectively, this chapter looks at the communication of meaning from supranational government to citizens via Parliament. All EU law has (at the time of writing) direct effect[44] and supremacy[45] over UK law. It therefore does not need to be enacted by the British Parliament to have any legal purchase. However, most regulations and directives from the EU are domesticated by UK legislation. One of the principal complaints of Eurosceptics was the perceived diminution of Parliament's sovereignty

[44] *NV Algemene Transporten Expeditie Onderneming van Gend en Loos v Nederlandse Administratis der Belastingen* Case 26/62 [1963] ECR 1.

[45] *Flaminio Costa v ENEL* Case 6/64 [1964] ECR 585.

as EU institutions could change British laws. This level of access was achieved by use of a 'Henry VIIIth clause' in section 2(2) of the *European Communities Act 1972*:

> (2) at any time after its passing Her Majesty may by Order in Council, and any designated Minister or department may by regulations, make provision – (a) for the purpose of implementing any Community obligation of the United Kingdom, or enabling any such obligation to be implemented, or of enabling any rights enjoyed or to be enjoyed by the United Kingdom under or by virtue of the Treaties to be exercised; or (b) for the purpose of dealing with matters arising out of or related to any such obligation or rights or the coming into force, or the operation from time to time, of subsection (1) above; and in the exercise of any statutory power or duty, including any power to give directions or to legislate by means of orders, rules, regulations or other subordinate instrument, the person entrusted with the power or duty may have regard to the objects of the Communities and to any such obligation or rights as aforesaid.

The conjunction of 'may' and 'make' are critical to this extraordinary grant of power from Parliament to government: 'Her Majesty may … make provision'. The provision is by Order in Council, which is a form of subordinate law. This grant of power is known as a Henry VIIIth clause because secondary legislation can be used to change primary legislation. It was that great Tudor monarch's tendency to use executive orders to frustrate Parliament that is alluded to. As the House of Lords Constitution Committee has argued, these powers are not used to remove policy confusion: 'Delegated powers in primary legislation have increasingly been drafted in broad and poorly-defined language that has permitted successive governments to use delegated legislation to address issues of policy and principle, rather than points of an administrative or technical nature' (House of Lords Select Committee on the Constitution 2016: 7).

As described in the introduction, a logic of communication depends on programmes of action being derived from philosophies. What the Lords have here described is a process of changing policy and principle on the hoof. Not only is the language 'poorly-defined', but it lacks anchoring to broader ideas. This is, as described, a process of repositioning the interpretative space. Repositioning affects the operation of institutions, which, by their essence, are there to control and delimit the possible range of policy interpretations. Three policy outcomes are most likely from this. First, policies change but cause high disapproval from those affected. This will be because the reasons for change are not anchored by any clear principles. Second, policy change is achieved but is limited as institutions assert established norms of interpretation to make sense of indeterminate law. Institutions, such as courts, will integrate the new policy language with old ideas of what is deemed appropriate (March and Olsen 1989). Third, policies do not change at all. Change is arrested by the lack of any clear plan of action, making the *status quo* the path of least resistance. The primary hypothesis of this chapter links the second and third outcomes:

> H1: Secondary legislation containing indeterminate parts of speech will fail to achieve comprehensive policy change.

In other words, indeterminacy in anti-discrimination law achieves only limited change or no change at all to rights provision. Here, 'comprehensive' means the adaptation of policy substance and procedures to effect change from the *status quo ante*. Well-worn policy language will be the fallback, used instead of new, but unusable, policy language. This is a qualitative hypothesis, which is untestable with statistical methods. However, it is an important claim to test and justifies the use of qualitative methods in this chapter.

Indeterminate language leads to incomplete implementation primarily because litigants, their lawyers and the courts will seek a secure interpretation of policy language. Judges ultimately decide on the meaning of laws disputed in court. Where a literal interpretation of legislation is impossible, judges resort to several methods in order to reach a stable meaning. These methods are typically used in parallel, rather than in series, and have been described collectively as a 'global method' of construction (Bennion 2008, 2009). First, judges will seek to avoid any interpretation that causes a grievous injustice or an absurd outcome (Cross et al 1995). This is known as 'the golden rule'. Second, judges will try to guess what Parliament had wanted to achieve from the law. This is called 'the mischief rule' and has even encouraged judges to read transcripts of Hansard to find clues as to what was intended.[46] Having done all of this, the judges will also aim to integrate legislation with principles of common law, or axioms of international law, such as those that derive from EU law and

[46] *Pepper (Inspector of Taxes) v Hart* [1992] UKHL 3.

the *European Convention on Human Rights*. Judges will also consider academic analyses of indeterminate language. There is no single correct method of statutory interpretation, which is why multiple levels of judicial appeal are available. The essential point here is that the greater the indeterminacy in law, the greater the need for judges to reassert norms of interpretation. The safest interpretation will therefore typically be a conservative interpretation. In other words, that which conserves what is widely understood, rather than seeing through major change.

To test these claims, the research design of this chapter also differs from that used in preceding chapters. Specifically, this chapter presents evidence from process tracing, rather than correlation analysis. The impact of language within two laws is traced from their promulgation to their being superseded. Furthermore, rather than analysing primary legislation, this chapter analyses two comparable pieces of secondary legislation. The *Race Regulations* and *Religion or Belief Regulations* were selected because they deal with similar a subject matter but have different degrees of linguistic indeterminacy. This makes them useful comparators. They have also had a limited life cycle, from promulgation in 2003 to being largely supplanted by the *Equality Acts* of 2006 and 2010. Within this limited time frame, we can observe how the indeterminacies in these regulations were normalised as institutions groped for workable interpretations. We can also see how this process of interpretation was marginally more difficult, and therefore more conservatively pursued, with regard to the marginally more indeterminate *Religion or Belief Regulations*. Data are taken from all 31 cases that disputed the two sets of regulations, from the Employment Tribunal up to the Supreme Court, between 2003 and 2010. Twenty cases disputed the marginally more indeterminate *Religion or Belief Regulations*, and a further 11 disputed the *Race Regulations*. Nearly double the caseload, from an admittedly small number of cases, sought to clarify indeterminacies in the *Religion or Belief Regulations*. However, first, some historical context is offered, with a description of developments in this field of law.

Developments in anti-discrimination and equality law

Anti-discrimination and equality legislation have shown marked changes in their language. However, before delving further, it is worth understanding the distinction between the two components.

In simple terms, anti-discrimination law may be defined as negative, and equality law as positive, in that anti-discrimination is freedom from discriminating treatment, whereas equality is the right to equal treatment. However, the utility of this definition is limited as positive and negative components are not mutually exclusive (Koch 2005). Nevertheless, for the purposes of this chapter, the distinction will suffice. Anti-discrimination and equality legislation are of considerable interest, first, because these laws have wide variances in their language, with most modern laws relying on indeterminate parts of speech. In keeping with the narrative proposed in Chapter Three, this indeterminacy is a result of high ambition to achieve 'equal concern and respect' between citizens (Dworkin 1977). Yet, this ambition is frustrated by uncertainty as to what degrees of equality can be achieved, or are even desirable. Hence, the law is framed in language that can be adapted. Second, anti-discrimination and equality legislation does not just seek to establish means for resolving 'boundary disputes' between citizens, it also seeks to establish means to resolve 'rights disputes' (Robertson 2010). This is where the fight is not merely over resources, but over concepts of justice. Such concepts are not easily framed in plain language. Third, anti-discrimination and equality legislation also create tensions with policies that intentionally discriminate, for instance, an increased portion of public spending decisions hinges on a deliberate choice between more and less deserving recipients. Fourth, rights claims can clash, such as occurred, for instance, in the 2016 case of *Lee v McArthur & Ors*.[47] In this case, Christian bakers refused to ice a cake with a gay rights message but lost their appeal and were found to have illegally discriminated. Finally, anti-discrimination and equality legislation can be used by citizens to augment their public or private law suits. For instance, in July 2010, two asylum seekers successfully appealed against a deportation order as they would not be treated equally as homosexuals in their home countries of Iran and Cameroon.[48] In private law, employees can rely on anti-discrimination law to support their claims of unfair dismissal. Given these factors, it is little surprise that legal change in this field comes with indeterminacies.

A means of resolving indeterminacies in law is by drawing on well-worn definitions. In the UK, principles of equality undergird the rule of law, such as was most forcefully recognised by A.V. Dicey's (1915) classic account: the rule of law, he argued, applied equally to all regardless of rank. This may be described as formal equality, and there

[47] [2016] NICA 29.

[48] *HJ (Iran) v Secretary of State for the Home Department (Rev 1)* [2010] UKSC 31.

are also principles of equity and procedural fairness that have long existed in English and British law, albeit that the common law also has a long tradition of discriminating between categories of claimant in the apportionment of property, trusts, contracts and so on. Therefore, it was via statute law that significant developments in anti-discrimination and equality were advanced.

These developments began in the interwar period. Rights of women were enhanced after female suffrage was partially granted in the *Representation of the People Act 1918*. For instance, the *Sex Disqualification (Removal) Act 1919* removed legal impediments from women seeking to serve in public office. Furthermore, during the 1920s, legislation guaranteed greater equality between the sexes as regards property, voting and divorce. Early 20th-century legislation also promoted a modicum of inter-faith equality with the *Roman Catholic Relief Act 1926*. Also, with fairly unsurprising timing, the rights of disabled citizens were improved by the *Disabled Persons (Employment) Act 1944*. It was not until the 1960s when race discrimination was first tackled through the *Race Relations Acts* of 1965 and 1968. These were followed in the 1970s by the *Equal Pay Act*, the *Sex Discrimination Act* and another *Race Relations Act*. The latter established the Commission for Racial Equality (CRE) as a non-departmental public body to oversee the implementation of anti-discrimination policies. Little happened in the 1980s, save for the enactment of a 10-section long *Sex Discrimination Act* in 1986. The 1990s saw enhanced provision for disabled people with the *Disability Discrimination Act 1995* and the *Disability Rights Commission Act 1999*. The principal outcome of these late 20th-century laws was that statutory duties were placed on employers, contractors, service providers and public authorities not to discriminate directly.

Anti-discrimination legislation in the 20th century achieved much, but there was a lack of intersectionality, meaning that there was little overlap between different anti-discrimination policies and little consistency between anti-discrimination laws. For instance, those individuals that held more than one protected status could fall between two or more stools. This concept of intersectionality was developed by Kimberlé Crenshaw (1989). She criticised 'single-axis' frameworks as assuming that, for example, women are white, black people are men and black women are forgotten by both camps. This problem was extended by inconsistencies between laws. Not only were there textual indeterminacies, but also inter-textual puzzles. For instance, Lord Justice Mummery opened his reasoning in the 2010 Court of

Appeal case of *Aylott v Stockton-On-Tees Borough Council*[49] by describing problems with disability discrimination legislation:

> This appeal is about how the *Disability Discrimination Act 1995* … should be interpreted in law and applied in practice. The course of the proceedings demonstrates that problems persist, even after 15 years' experience of the legislation. The problems are not solved by attempting to work from other discrimination legislation and the authorities on how that should be construed. Many of the problems are different in practice. Important features of the 1995 Act have no equivalent in sex discrimination and race discrimination law.

For the EU, anti-discrimination law was developed by the Treaty of Amsterdam through the amendment of Article 234 of the EU Treaty. Article 234 had offered protection against discrimination on the grounds of nationality. The new Articles 13 and 29 added protections in education, employment, health care, housing and immigration (Bell 2009). Mark Bell (2002) described these changes as amounting to a shift from a trade-based market integration model, towards a social citizenship model for the EU. Article 13 was implemented by the *Race Directive*[50] and the *Framework Directive*.[51] Both of these were domesticated into UK law by secondary legislation, including the *Race* and *Religion or Belief Regulations*. These regulations added offences of indirect discrimination, harassment and victimisation to the law.

In the UK, policy was further developed by the move to equality legislation with the *Equality Acts* of 2006 and 2010. Where anti-discrimination law relies on complaints from individuals, equality law creates a positive requirement that public and private bodies promote equality within 'social reality' (Schiek and Chege 2009). Public and private bodies must follow procedures to minimise discrimination and encourage equality. These requirements are strict, as one can see from an early case brought under the 2010 Act. The then Secretary of State for Education, Michael Gove, lost a judicial review case brought against his decision to stop planned capital expenditure on school

[49] [2010] EWCA Civ 910 at para 1.

[50] 2000/43/EC.

[51] 2000/78/EC.

buildings.[52] Gove was not found to be discriminating in his decision, but was found to be not sufficiently considering the implications of his decision on people of different genders, races and disabilities. The move to equality legislation had made the UK among the EU's more progressive upholders of rights. Indeed, the EU has not itself gone as far as the UK in enacting equality law, which is described as the 'fourth generation' of anti-discrimination legislation. Indeed, it was non-governmental organisations (NGOs) from the UK and The Netherlands that pushed for anti-discrimination law through the EU's institutions (Schiek and Chege 2009: 3–6).

Equality legislation was intended to resolve the issue of intersectionality described earlier. For example, the issue of intersectionality is contained primarily in section 14 of the *Equality Act 2010*. This section legislates for 'combined discrimination' and 'dual characteristics'. It was also intended for the *Equality Acts* to add new protected characteristics, such as age, that had been neglected by previous anti-discrimination laws.[53] They were also designed to quicken the pace of social change in the UK, which had been shown to be sluggish in institutions such as the Metropolitan Police.[54] However, these ambitions were framed by indeterminate legislation. For example, sections 158–159 call for 'positive action' to be taken, relying on the following indeterminate language:

> 159 (1) This section applies if a person (P) reasonably thinks that – (a) persons who share a protected characteristic suffer a disadvantage connected to the characteristic, or (b) participation in an activity by persons who share a protected characteristic is disproportionately low.
>
> Part 5 (work) does not prohibit P from taking action within subsection (3) with the aim of enabling or encouraging persons who share the protected characteristic to – overcome or minimise that disadvantage, or participate in that activity.

[52] *Luton Borough Council & Nottingham City Council & Ors, R (on the application of) v Secretary of State for Education* [2011] EWHC 217.

[53] Section 4 of the *Equality Act 2010* lists all protected characteristics: 'The following characteristics are protected characteristics – age; disability; gender reassignment; marriage and civil partnership; pregnancy and maternity; race; religion or belief; sex; sexual orientation'.

[54] This was the conclusion of the Stephen Lawrence Inquiry, which reported in February 1999 that parts of the Metropolitan Police remained 'institutionally racist'.

> That action is treating a person (A) more favourably in connection with recruitment or promotion than another person (B) because A has the protected characteristic but B does not.

This language contains adjectives, adverbs and conjunctions. In addition to which are indeterminate verbs such as 'enable', 'encourage', 'overcome' and 'minimise'. These sorts of verbs were not isolated in previous chapters, but can be studied in greater detail in this process-tracing chapter. The sovereign Parliament has not determinately assigned meaning to the act of suffering 'a disadvantage connected to [a] characteristic'. In the absence of plain meaning, it will be up to private citizens and judges to interpret the law.

Discourse analysis method and results

Discourse analyses were conducted for all 870 sections of primary legislation pertaining to anti-discrimination and equality enacted since 1900. This analysis begins with section 1 of the *Employment of Women Act 1907* and ends with section 2 of the *Lords Spiritual (Women) Act 2015*. In addition to which, 832 regulations from secondary legislation were analysed from 1987 to 2010. The starting date of 1987 was chosen as being the earliest year for which secondary legislation is available on Parliament's digital repository (legislation.gov.uk). The year 2010 was chosen as the finishing date because it marks the end point of this chapter's process-tracing analysis. Data were taken from 116 statutory instruments, starting with regulation 1 of the *Race Relations (Offshore Employment) Order 1987* and ending with regulation 2 of the *Equality Act 2010 (Amendment) Order 2010*. This makes for a total data set of 1,702 sections and regulations.

These data are not samples. Every section and regulation relevant to anti-discrimination and equality was coded, although secondary regulations that were merely initiating the implementation of legislation were not coded, nor were those that only applied to one of the UK's four nations. This includes all commencement and revocation orders. However, any commencement order that made supplementary amendments was coded. For primary legislation, the same coding program used in previous chapters was applied. For secondary legislation, a different approach was needed. First, it was not necessary to measure the use of indeterminate modal verbs and enabling verbs as it is unusual to further delegate from a delegated statutory instrument.

Second, manual coding was used instead of computer coding. This was done to code each individual regulation simply but accurately. Where computer coding provides comprehensive results, manual coding allows more penetrating analysis of each regulation. To ensure accuracy, 5% of regulations were recoded. Parts of speech were coded according to a simple binary (present = 1; absent = 0), and there was no need for inter-coder reliability tests because there was no interpretation of meanings. As with all previous chapters, the aim here is to analyse meaninglessness, rather than meaning.

Figure 6.1 describes the increased enactment of indeterminate primary legislation. The enactment of adjectives, adverbs and conjunctions saw the greatest increases. The *Disability Discrimination Act 1995*, on its own, contains more adjectives and adverbs than all the laws enacted from 1907 to 1965 combined. The proportion of adjectives per section (not reported in Figure 6.1) has also increased. Where the *Employment of Women Act 1907* had 0.5 adjectives or adverbs per section, the *Special Educational Needs and Disability Act 2001* had 15 adjectives or adverbs per section. Figure 6.1 shows that rates of growth increased significantly under Labour-led governments. These governments were more ideologically committed to tackling discrimination and promoting equality. However, the indeterminacies in the legislation mean that these rights had and have indeterminate potency. As demonstrated by the preceding chapters, adjectives, adverbs and conjunctions can stretch or narrow the range of possible interpretations of legislation. This can allow employers, for example, to deny rights to their employees by taking advantage of indeterminacy in the law.

Enactment of indeterminate modal verbs and enabling verbs has also increased. As argued, these parts of speech allow interpretative space to be repositioned. This can be seen most clearly in the following excerpt from section 158 of the *Disability Discrimination Act 1995*:

> (4) Regulations may make provision as to the circumstances in which treatment is to be taken to be justified, or is to be taken not to be justified, for the purposes of section 3A(1)(b) as it has effect for the interpretation of 'discriminate' in subsection (1).
>
> (5) Regulations under subsection (4) may (in particular) provide for section 3A(3) to apply with prescribed modifications, or not to apply, for those purposes; but treatment of a disabled person cannot be justified under

Figure 6.1: Indeterminate parts of speech enacted in anti-discrimination and equality primary law, 1907–2015

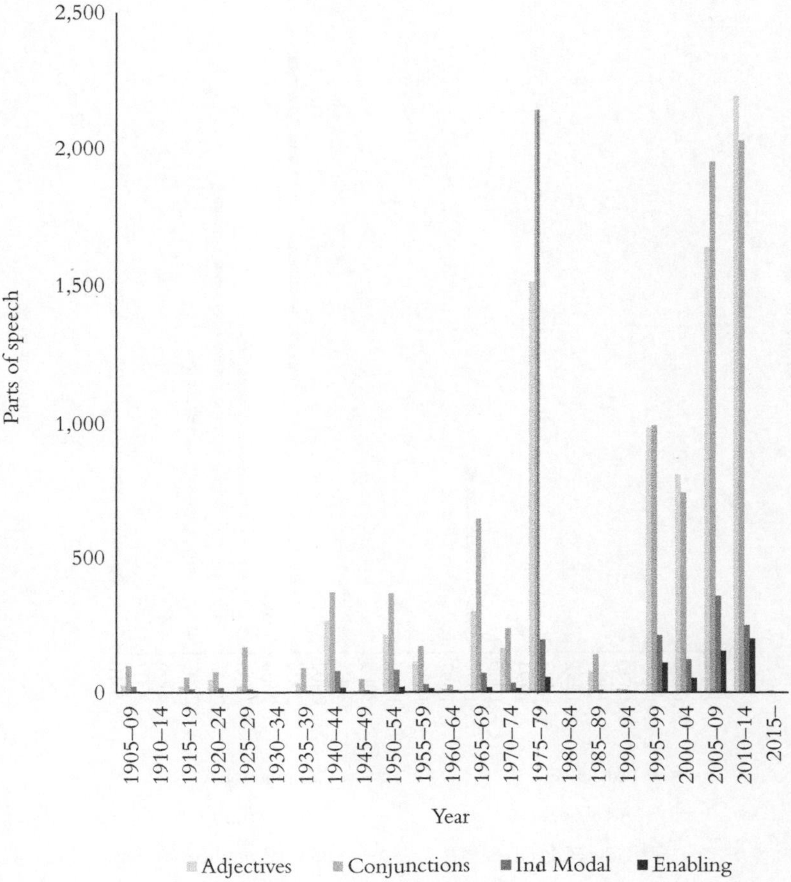

> subsection (4) if it amounts to direct discrimination falling within section 3A(5).

In other words, secondary legislation can be used to vary when discrimination can or cannot be justified, with or without modifications. The law's meaning can be changed by the Secretary of State. Which begs the question: to what extent has secondary legislation changed the interpretability of primary law?

Figure 6.2 describes changes wrought by 116 statutory instruments and their 832 individual regulations. The increases in adjectives and conjunctions in totals, as well as per section proportions, are clear. This means that secondary legislation added more indeterminacy, rather than clarifying primary law. There was rapid growth in indeterminate

Figure 6.2: Indeterminate parts of speech enacted in anti-discrimination and equality secondary law, 1987–2010

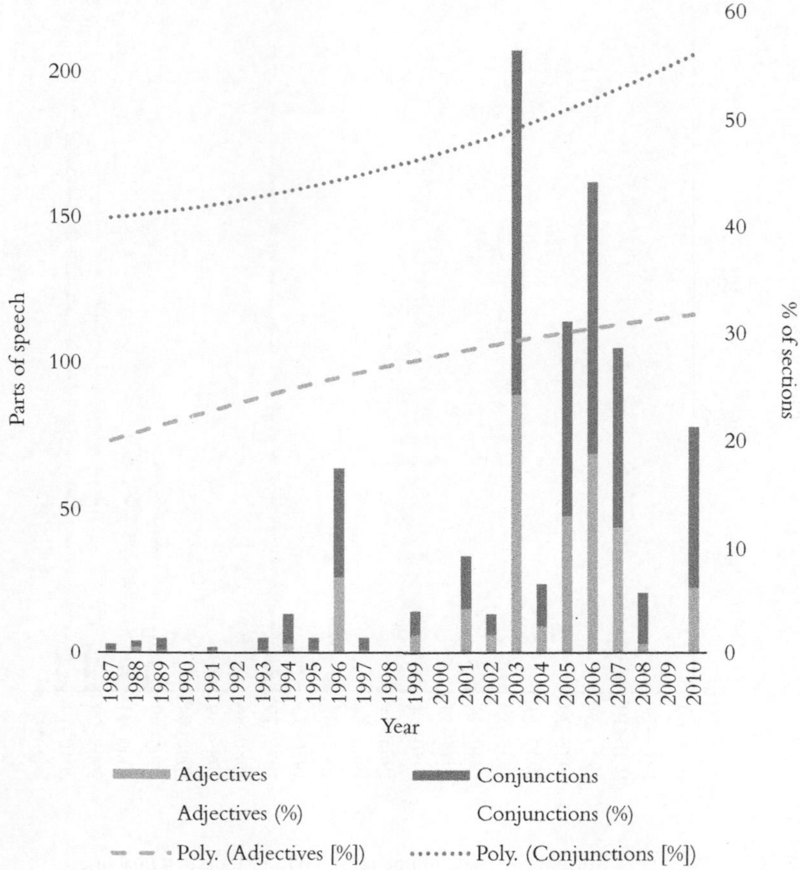

output after 2001. Of all the regulations created between 1987 and 2010, 88% of those relying on adjectives came after 2001, and 85% of all regulations utilising conjunctions came after 2001. Manual coding allowed me to assess other notable features. For instance, specific amendments were made to primary law in 57% of all the regulations coded. Therefore, a majority of regulations (over 400) fundamentally changed primary law. On top of which, 110 new offences were introduced by secondary legislation.

Of the 116 statutory instruments, two were selected for comparison. Vital statistics on the *Race* and *Religion or Belief Regulations* are provided in Table 6.1.

Fifty-two regulations make up the *Race Regulations*, and 39 regulations form the *Religion or Belief Regulations*. Of the 52 *Race Regulations*, 51

Table 6.1: Comparison of the *Race* and *Religion or Belief Regulations*

	Regulations	Adjectives	Conjunctions	Amendments	Offences
Race	52	8	28	51	16
Religion	39	31	33	0	14

(98%) amended primary legislation, but without adding many new adjective phrases (just eight [15%]). There were, however, a majority of regulations reliant on conditional conjunctions (28 [54%]). The *Race Regulations* implemented the *Racial Equality Directive* (2000/43/EC), but did so by amending existing UK legislation (the *Race Relations Acts*), whereas the *Religion or Belief Regulations* made no such amendments because the subject matter was new to UK law. These regulations domesticated the EU *Framework Directive* (2000/78/EC). This new law was communicated in regulations where 31 (79%) relied on adjective phrases and 33 (85%) added conditional conjunctions to the law.

There are, therefore, similarities between the two sets of regulations; both were promulgated in the same year, according to much the same motivations and under the authority of section 2(2) of the *European Communities Act 1972*. However, there are also differences between the two sets of regulations with regards to their content and, crucially, their language. First, the *Race Regulations* extended existing protections by adding new offences of indirect discrimination and harassment. Also, a new defence of discrimination as a 'genuine and determining occupational requirement' was added to law. The *Race Regulations* had a well-established legal foundation but nonetheless aimed at significant change. The explanatory notes for the regulations describe a wide range of situations covered:

> The Directive is concerned with the principle of equal treatment between persons, irrespective of racial or ethnic origin, in the areas of employment (and related matters), social protection, social advantage, education and access to and supply of, goods and services which are available to the public, including housing.

The *Religion or Belief Regulations* created an entirely new area of protection in British law. This protection included offences of direct discrimination, indirect discrimination, harassment and victimisation, as well the defence of a 'genuine and determining occupational requirement'. These two statutory instruments have been compared to assess the impact of their language on policy outcomes, with the results showing further evidence that indeterminate policy undermines effectiveness.

Results

This chapter relies on evidence taken from the LexisLibrary website.[55] All cases pertaining to the *Race* and *Religion or Belief Regulations* were analysed. Analysis covered private and public law cases on the basis that these regulations are public policies that implicate private relations. Results are divided into two sections that consider the feasibility and desirability of policy as affected by legislative language. Feasibility focuses on inter-institutional coordinative discourse. This section considers how indeterminate language affects the delegation and accountability of policy decisions. Desirability focuses on extra-institutional communication with society. This section considers how indeterminate language affects the coherence and legitimacy of policy decisions.

On feasibility

With regard to the inter-institutional coordination of policy, there are four principal points of analysis. These concern the substance of policy, questions of procedure, the superintendence of policy from powerful institutions and the granting of discretion.

First, as regards policy substance, indeterminacies in the *Race* and *Religion or Belief Regulations* created disputes as to who was protected, when and to what extent. For the marginally more indeterminate *Religion or Belief Regulations*, in particular, there were few clear domestic or European law precedents available to flesh out its meaning. As such, judges either fell back on a narrow construction of the legislation or inferred by analogy from related cases. The case of *Hashwani v Jivraj*[56] heard at the UK Supreme Court is exemplary. The dispute centred on an arbitration clause in a joint venture agreement. H and J had been business partners who had agreed that should any disputes need to be resolved, a conciliation panel of three members of the Ismaili community would arbitrate. Their joint venture came

[55] See: https://www.lexisnexis.com/uk/legal/

[56] [2011] UKSC 40.

to an end and H sought to appoint C, who was not from the Ismaili community, to arbitrate over H's claim to $4.4 million. J submitted that the appointment of C breached the arbitration clause of the joint venture agreement. However, H counter-claimed that not employing C in such a way, simply on the grounds of his faith, would constitute illegal discrimination under regulations 6 and 7 of the *Religion or Belief Regulations*:

> 6 (1) It is unlawful for an employer, in relation to employment by him at an establishment in Great Britain, to discriminate against a person – (a) in the arrangements he makes for the purpose of determining to whom he should offer employment; (b) in the terms on which he offers that person employment; or (c) by refusing to offer, or deliberately not offering, him employment.

> 7 (3) This paragraph applies where an employer has an ethos based on religion or belief and, having regard to that ethos and to the nature of the employment or the context in which it is carried out – (a) being of a particular religion or belief is a genuine occupational requirement for the job.

These regulations contain several conjunctions, as well as the adverb 'deliberately' and the adjective 'genuine'. The confusion created by this language was outlined by Lord Clarke SCJ at paragraph 15 of his ruling:

> (i) are arbitrators persons who are under a contract to do work so as to fall within the 2003 Regulations and, if so, do parties who make an arbitration agreement specifying religious qualifications for eligible arbitrators thereby make an arrangement for the purpose of determining to whom they should offer employment or do they agree to offer, or deliberately not to offer, employment within the meaning of the 2003 Regulations? (ii) if so, in the circumstances, did the requirement for all the arbitrators to be members of the Ismaili community constitute a genuine occupational requirement (GOR) which it was proportionate to apply within reg 7(3)? (iii) if not, did the whole arbitration agreement fail or was only the discriminatory provision void?

In the end, the court ruled in favour of J: that being from the Ismaili community was a genuine requirement of an arbitrator. This reversed the decision of the Court of Appeal. The Supreme Court decided not to give fuller effect to the anti-discrimination protections. A similarly cautious result was reached in the cases of *R (Couronne and others) v Crawley Borough Council and others; R (Bontemps and others) v Secretary of State for Work and Pensions*.[57] Two sets of claimants from Mauritius were denied Jobseeker's Allowance or homelessness assistance because they were not 'habitually resident' in the Common Travel Area (United Kingdom, Republic of Ireland, Isle of Man or Channel Islands). The claimants alleged that this was racial discrimination under the *Race Regulations*, and they filed a case for judicial review. In hearing the case, the High Court had no precedent to rely on, so they fell back on the ordinary meaning of the word 'habitually' to resolve the case against the claimants. Parliament had not defined the word adequately, so the courts had to determine its meaning. The courts thereby determined significant policy questions, but generally did so in a manner that constrained the scope of policy.

Although indeterminacies have also led to the courts expanding, rather than constraining, the scope of policy, they only did so, however, when reason or precedent overwhelmingly supported their moves. So, in the case of *Abbey National Plc and another v Chagger*[58] brought under the *Race Regulations*, the Employment Appeal Tribunal (EAT) sought to resolve a drafting anomaly that had omitted 'colour discrimination' from the wording of the regulations, as stated by Underhill J at paragraph 35 of his ruling:

> In our view it is inconceivable that the Directive [*The Race Directive*] is not intended to apply to discrimination which is expressed as being on the ground of colour: for the reasons already given, such discrimination is in practice necessarily an aspect or manifestation of discrimination based on 'racial or ethnic origin'. We have no doubt that the European Court of Justice would not give even the time of day to a submission that a claim of 'colour discrimination' did not attract the operation of the Directive.

Further evidence of judges determining the substance of policy is given in the following with regard to policy desirability. The evidence

[57] [2006] EWHC 1514 (Admin).

[58] [2009] IRLR 86.

presented so far concentrates specifically on how institutions (in this case, courts) sought to coordinate with other institutions (other courts or Parliament) to work out what the law said. Similar problems with coordinative discourse emerged as regards the correct procedures for implementing the Regulations. A central procedural question was determining the burden of proof when applying both the *Race* and *Religion or Belief Regulations*. The same formula was used in both sets of Regulations, as laid out in regulation 41 of the *Race Regulations* and regulation 29 of the *Religion or Belief Regulations*:

> Where, on the hearing of the complaint, the complainant proves facts from which the tribunal could, apart from this regulation, conclude in the absence of an adequate explanation that the respondent … has committed against the complainant an act to which regulation[s] appl[y]; or is … to be treated as having committed against the complainant such an act, the tribunal shall uphold the complaint unless the respondent proves that he did not commit, or as the case may be, is not to be treated as having committed, that act.

Judges had to determine what an 'adequate explanation' would be, and had to navigate several conditional conjunctions, such as in 'has committed … or is … to be treated as having committed'. In the absence of clear language, the courts set the burden of proof and decided when it shifts from claimant to respondent. These decisions had major policy implications, and the judicial resolution, as expected by H1, constrained the potential scope of policy. A precedent was established by a 2005 case, and the courts had to draw on sex discrimination case law in order to clarify the procedural confusion. This fallback material was known as the 'Barton Guidance'.[59] The application of similar burdens of proof to all forms of discrimination law, despite differences in legislation, was approved by the House of Lords so as to maximise procedural consistency.[60] The 2005 case in question, *Wong v Igen Ltd and other appeals*,[61] was a conjoined appeal heard at the Court

[59] *Barton v Investec Securities Ltd* [2003] ICR 1205, [2003] IRLR 332 para 25.

[60] *Rhys-Harper v Relaxion Group plc* [2003] UKHL 33, [2003] ICR 867.

[61] *Wong v Igen Ltd and others (Equal Opportunities Commission and others intervening); Emokpae v Chamberlin Solicitors and another (Equal Opportunities Commission and others intervening); Webster v Brunel University (Equal Opportunities Commission and others intervening)* [2005] EWCA Civ 142.

of Appeal. It involved separate claims of sexual, racial and disability discrimination. The Barton Guidance stressed that the burden of proof was on the claimant to prove that discrimination could be inferred from the facts. The potentiality of 'could' is important as irrefutable proof of discrimination is rare. The burden of proof threshold on the claimant is set fairly low, and having established that one 'could' infer discrimination from the facts, it shifts to the respondent, who must be able to show that discrimination cannot, in fact, be inferred. The Barton Guidance became the standard for resolving such questions. In addition to which, the *Wong* ruling was itself used to resolve other cases studied for this chapter.[62]

Responsibility for the courts to determine key substantive and procedural matters extended to a general superintendence of policy interpretation. There are seven cases of the 31 studied where the judgment was a full or partial reversal of a lower court decision. In all seven of the cases, bar one, the higher court dismissed the claimants' claims of discrimination. The higher courts thereby restricted the scope for bringing a discrimination claim. This cautious superintendence is shown by Mummery LJ at paragraph 198 of his ruling in *British Medical Association v Chaudhary*:

> despite what the majority [on the Tribunals] said about agreeing with one another, it was not possible to extract a single principle from the three opinions of the majority … the reasoning of the majority was inconsistent with binding authorities of the House of Lords and the Court of Justice of the European Communities … and was wrong in law.

The only case where a lower court was overturned, and the claimant's discrimination complaint was upheld, was *Saini v All Saints Haque Centre and others*,[63] brought under the *Religion or Belief Regulations*. The case focused on harassment, and was heard by the EAT. The claimant, Mr Saini, had resigned from the respondent's centre and claimed harassment on the grounds that he was being pressured to justify the dismissal of another colleague, Mr Chandel. Mr Chandel had been dismissed by the board of directors because he was a Hindu. The board was overseen by two men of the Ravidassi faith. The case turned on whether Mr Saini could allege harassment on the grounds of religion, even when it was not his religion that was at issue, but the

---

62 Notably, *Mohmed v West Coast Trains Ltd* [2006] All ER (D) 224 (Nov).

63 [2009] IRLR 74.

religion of his colleague. This case was complicated as 'harassment' is an indeterminate offence that was new to law. It was a concept introduced by statute in section 40 of the *Administration of Justice Act 1970*. Parliament had left its meaning to be determined by judges:

> Punishment for unlawful harassment of debtors.... (1) A person commits an offence if, with the object of coercing another person to pay money ... he – (a) harasses the other with demands for payment which, in respect of their frequency or the manner or occasion of making any such demand, or of any threat or publicity by which any demand is accompanied, are calculated to subject him or members of his family or household to alarm, distress or humiliation.

The courts had to cross-reference different statutes and common law precedents to create a workable rule of law. In this case, the Employment Tribunal (ET) was held to have misdirected itself by constraining the regulations' scope to harassment against one's own religion. Despite these seven cases where lower courts' rulings were corrected, in the vast majority of appeals, the judicial hierarchy was in agreement. What we find, therefore, is that the courts worked harmoniously to assert norms of interpretation. This task was effectively delegated to them by Parliament enacting indeterminate law.

Moving on from delegation, other cases point to problems of accountability for decisions. In the absence of clear instructions, courts may either refuse to take a decision or will defer to another agent of Parliament with greater decision-making capacity, competence or legitimacy (Strøm et al 2003). Two cases of the 31 studied for this chapter saw the courts dismiss claims for discrimination on the grounds that there were insufficient grounds to bring the claim, and that the courts therefore lacked jurisdiction. First was the case of *British Medical Association v Chaudhary*,[64] a case that disputed the *Race Regulations*. In this case, a doctor of Asian origin applied to the British Medical Association (BMA) to support his claim of racial discrimination. His claim was against regulatory bodies that he believed had sabotaged his career goal of becoming a urologist. The BMA refused to represent Mr Chaudhary as they doubted the strength of his claim. His solicitors then instructed the BMA that they would be sued for direct discrimination, indirect discrimination and victimisation. This was on the grounds

[64] [2007] EWCA Civ 788.

that their refusal to support Mr Chaudhary was closed-minded. The ET dismissed the claims for direct discrimination and victimisation, but held that the BMA had indirectly discriminated by not sufficiently considering the racial discrimination suffered by Mr Chaudhary. The BMA was ordered to pay £814,877 in damages.

The BMA appealed, but were dismissed by the EAT. They appealed further to the Court of Appeal, which reversed the judgments of the lower courts and struck out the damages award. The rulings submitted that the Tribunals had 'perversely' analysed the facts and had formed the erroneous inference that Mr Chaudhary's claim to the BMA was dismissed due to a discriminatory policy. However, Mr Chaudhary had impugned the BMA after he had served them notice of litigation. In other words, the indirect discrimination and victimisation claims were based on the refusal of the BMA to change their position after Mr Chaudhary had accused them of discrimination. This is akin to blackmail. The Court of Appeal's restrained approach to the definition of discrimination and victimisation decreased the potential scope of the *Race Regulations*.

The second case was a more straightforward denial of jurisdiction. It was regarding a claim brought under the *Religion or Belief Regulations*. In the case of *Padgett v Board and Trustees of the Tate Gallery*,[65] the EAT followed the reasoning of the ET in denying that it could resolve the case at hand. The case concerned an art installation that was proposed by Mr Padgett to the Tate Gallery. As a Unitarian, he had developed a conceptual 'performance around the themes of contemporary art and religious fundamentalism' that comprised a sugar cube memorial to the founder of the Unitarian Church. The Tate Gallery thanked Mr Padgett for his application but rejected it as inappropriate for their exhibition. Mr Padgett claimed that this decision discriminated against his religion and denied him access to employment. The *Religion or Belief Regulations*, it was argued on behalf of the Tate, were intended for those already in employment or those applying for employment. The Tribunals agreed that Mr Padgett's case could not be considered under either of these headings. The vital point in this and the preceding case is that it was not clear whether the courts had jurisdiction. Regardless of how strong or weak the individual claims were, the courts themselves had to decide when or how to intervene in policy. They opted for the more cautious option.

The cases also show courts deferring to other agents of Parliament, and in the absence of determinate law, the courts were compelled to

[65] [2007] All ER (D) 239 (Dec).

assess the reasonableness of decisions taken in several cases. Judicial assessments of reasonableness are controversial (Mayo 2003). They involve the courts analysing decisions taken by democratically accountable agents, with the potential of replacing those decisions. A core axiom of reasonableness testing is that Parliament would expect its commands to be implemented in a manner that does not defy logic or accepted moral standards.[66] Five of the 31 cases turned on a reasonableness test. In four of the five cases, it was denied that the test could be used, and appeals by barristers to use it were dismissed. Lawyers tried to encourage a more expansive interpretation of indeterminate language, but the courts shut them down. A cautious – norm-conserving – application of the reasonableness test can be seen from the following dictum of Slade J in the only case to use such a test: *Pricewaterhouse Coopers LLP v Popa*.[67] The case disputed the *Race Regulations*:

> [60] In accordance with the guidance given by Lord Neuberger in *Derbyshire*, whilst considering the question primarily from the perspective of the alleged victim, the view that the victim has suffered a detriment must be objectively reasonable in all the circumstances. The ET should focus on the word 'detriment'.

Slade J was seeking a reasonable definition of 'detriment'. The court would not need to perform such a definitional role had 'detriment' been more clearly defined in the regulations. The problem of interpretation can be seen in regulation 29(2): 'Where a relevant relationship has come to an end it is unlawful for the relevant party – (a) to discriminate against another party, on grounds of race or ethnic or national origins, by subjecting him to a detriment'. This is the only mention of detriment in the regulations, apart from regulation 52, which confirms that a detriment is not the same as harassment. The parent Act to these regulations – the *Race Relations Act 1976* – has no further mention of what a detriment is, even in its interpretation section (section 78). Thus, the judges were faced with establishing a standard measure for detriment and opted for a test that imports aspects of reasonableness criteria from common law. In this case, therefore, the use of a reasonableness test was not a means for the judges to extend

[66] As per Lord Diplock in *Council of Civil Service Unions v Minister for the Civil Service* [1983] UKHL 6, [1984] 3 All ER 935 at 951.

[67] UKEAT/0030/10/DA.

the possible interpretations of the law. Rather, it achieved the reverse by anchoring the interpretation of 'detriment' to a well-established rule of construction.

The point is that indeterminate legislation leaves questions begging as to who is accountable for policy decisions. Lawyers urged the courts to determine the reasonableness of decisions because there was significant doubt. Judges, for the most part, declined invitations to rule decisions as unreasonable and instead deferred to the more powerful litigant. Leaving the accountability for decisions with the more powerful of the litigants restricted the potential scope of anti-discrimination rights. A specific difficulty in managing decision-making responsibility can be seen from another case brought under the *Race Regulations*: *Abbey National Plc and another v Chagger*.[68] The EAT refused to apply a reasonableness test and thereby overruled the ET. The reasoning is summarised by Underhill J at paragraph 56 of his ruling:

> [56] … what the tribunal was doing was dismissing the appellant's explanation simply because it involved unfair conduct: it had accordingly fallen into the well-known error, exposed in *Glasgow City Council v Zafar* and *Bahl v Law Society*, of confusing the question whether the employer had acted reasonably with the question whether his explanation, however unreasonably it showed him acting, was true.

Underhill consciously turns to 'well-known' analysis to resolve the case. References to the *Zafar*[69] and *Bahl*[70] cases also show reliance on precedent. A similar resolution was reached in a case disputing the *Religion or Belief Regulations*, which also turned on the *Zafar* precedent.[71] As stated by Elias J:

> [40(4)] The explanation for the less favourable treatment does not have to be a reasonable one; it may be that the employee has treated the Claimant unreasonably. That is a frequent occurrence quite irrespective of the race, sex, religion or sexual orientation of the employee. So the mere

68 [2009] IRLR 86.

69 [1998] 2 All ER 953.

70 [2003] IRLR 641.

71 *Ladele v Islington London Borough Council* [2009] All ER (D) 100.

> fact that the Claimant is treated unreasonably does not suffice to justify an inference of unlawful discrimination to satisfy stage one. As Lord Browne Wilkinson pointed out in *Zafar v Glasgow City Council.*

Two more cases considered the reasonableness test but also overruled its attempted use.[72] There is therefore good evidence for H1 from both the *Race* and *Religion or Belief Regulations*. The indeterminate language in both sets of regulations failed to achieve comprehensive policy change, although it must be noted that evidence here is taken from judicial decisions, and unobserved are the many interpretations of these regulations outside the courtroom. Nonetheless, both public and private organisations will calibrate their policies in response to court rulings. That the courts were tentative in their application of these laws will have had significant effects. The *Religion or Belief Regulations* relied somewhat more heavily on indeterminate language than did the *Race Regulations*. This was largely because of the relative novelty of these protections to UK law. However, the *Race Regulations* also created significant difficulties of interpretation that encouraged a conservative judicial response.

On desirability

Desirability, as discussed in the introduction, is the label given to communicative discourse, that is, language directed at citizens. Less important than whether the language means anything are the social effects of miscommunication. The components of desirability in policy language are its coherence and its legitimate use. There were significant difficulties faced by citizens in knowing their rights because of incoherence and indeterminate legitimacy. As a result, judges restricted the scope of possible interpretations for the legislation.

With regards to the coherence of policy, first to be considered are the categories of individual protected by the two sets of regulations. How 'race' and 'religion or belief' were defined was critical to the laws' comprehensibility. The definition of protected characteristics

72 *Wong v Igen Ltd and others (Equal Opportunities Commission and others intervening); Emokpae v Chamberlin Solicitors and another (Equal Opportunities Commission and others intervening); Webster v Brunel University (Equal Opportunities Commission and others intervening)* [2005] EWCA Civ 142; and *Eweida v British Airways Plc* [2008] All ER (D) 13 (Dec).

for the *Race Regulations* was taken from section 3 of the *Race Relations Act 1976*:

> (1) In this Act, unless the context otherwise requires – 'racial grounds' means any of the following grounds, namely colour, race, nationality or ethnic or national origins; 'racial group' means a group of persons defined by reference to colour, race, nationality or ethnic or national origins, and references to a person's racial group refer to any racial group into which he falls.

It is unclear from this whether the 'grounds' for discrimination describe the thought process of the discriminator or a more objective factual grounding. In addition, it is not clear from where an individual's origins should be inferred. The definition of protected characteristics for the *Religion or Belief Regulations* is similarly indeterminate. As it states in regulation 2: '(1) In these Regulations, "religion or belief" means any religion, religious belief, or similar philosophical belief'. This regulation was amended just three years later by section 77(1) of the *Equality Act 2006* in order to remove 'or similar', and so as to include the lack of religious belief as a belief system that should not be discriminated against. Removing 'or similar' suggests that the government became conscious of this adjective's inability to provide a coherent rule of law. Yet, the meaning of 'philosophical belief' was left open to expansive interpretation by litigants and the judiciary. Two cases interrogated the meaning of religious or philosophical belief. The first drew on several precedents to establish a test for determining which belief systems to protect. In the case of *Nicholson v Grainger PLC and others*,[73] Tim Nicholson had been made redundant by the respondent company in July 2008. He submitted that his dismissal was discriminatory on account of his 'philosophical belief' in an impending climate catastrophe. The employer appealed against an ET ruling that the employee's belief was protected by the *Religion or Belief Regulations*. The EAT dismissed the employers' appeal, contending that, on a strict construction of 'belief', Mr. Nicholson's views were protected. The judge, Mr Justice Burton, developed a formula at paragraph 24 of his judgment. He drew on several precedents:[74]

---

[73] [2009] All ER (D) 59 (Nov).

[74] *Eweida v British Airways plc* [2009] IRLR 78; *Campbell v UK* (1982) 4 EHRR 293; and *R (on the application of Williamson) v Secretary of State for Education and Employment* [2005] 2 All ER 1.

> there must be some limit placed upon the definition of 'philosophical belief' for the purpose of the Regulations.… I shall endeavour to set out the limitations, or criteria, which are to be implied or introduced by reference to the jurisprudence set out above. (i) The belief must be genuinely held. (ii) It must be a belief and not, as in *McClintock v Department of Constitutional Affairs*, an opinion or viewpoint based on the present state of information available. (iii) It must be a belief as to a weighty and substantial aspect of human life and behaviour. (iv) It must attain a certain level of cogency, seriousness, cohesion and importance. (v) It must be worthy of respect in a democratic society, be not incompatible with human dignity and not conflict with the fundamental rights of others.… As it was put in argument, such philosophical belief does not need to amount to an '-ism'.

Burton J created a five-point test to determine what is protected by the *Religion or Belief Regulations*. In doing so, he relied on precedent and the jurisprudence of the European Court of Human Rights. Both litigants to the case demanded this clarification, and the result determined the scope of the legislative framework. Essentially, Mr Justice Burton responded to the litigants' confusion by determining the meaning of 'belief'. This intervention was spurred by Parliament's indeterminacy. In a later case heard before the ET, Mr Power, a former employee of Greater Manchester Police, contested his redundancy. He claimed that the reason for his dismissal was his beliefs in Spiritualism and life after death. The ET allowed the application, and the EAT dismissed an appeal from the Police. Both courts applied Burton J's five-point test and asserted that Mr Power's Spiritualism was cogent and worthy of respect.[75] Again, it was judges who had to determine what had been said by the sovereign Parliament.

These last two cases appear to contradict the hypothesis (H1) as the courts ensured the protection of various beliefs, rather than taking a conservative approach and denying protection. However, the courts had to rely on extant reasoning to determine which beliefs were worthy of protection, and new protections granted in the regulations were only partially implemented. Beyond the definition of belief systems, there were several new grounds created upon which discrimination claims could be brought. These included indirect discrimination, harassment

75 *Power v Greater Manchester Police Authority* [2010] All ER (D) 173 (Oct).

and victimisation. It is worth noting that the *Race Regulations* do not explicitly create a rule against victimisation, although it is part of the wider law against racial discrimination. Focus will lie on indirect discrimination, with evidence showing that the courts substantially restricted its potential scope.

Indirect discrimination is allowed if it can be described as a 'proportionate means of achieving a legitimate aim'. Where direct discrimination on the basis of race or religion can never be justified, in some circumstances, indirect discrimination is defensible. Exactly the same test for indirect discrimination was used in both the *Race* and *Religion or Belief Regulations*. It is a test that draws on the proportionality jurisprudence of the European Court of Justice and the European Court of Human Rights. A proportionality test entails analogic reasoning, and does not rely on a logic of communication. Authority is delegated to judges to balance competing claims. It allows judges to determine what a proportionate act of discrimination might be, and, more importantly, to define legitimate policy aims. However, a legitimate aim will be more difficult for the judges to determine than proportionate means. This is because such policy decisions, either in a private organisation or from a public authority, are best taken by those familiar with a policy space. Therefore, one would expect judges to avoid delegitimising an aim, and instead defer to other decision-makers. The vital point is that protection against indirect discrimination is indeterminate, and therefore dominated by context and discretion rather than explicit authorisation.

The evidence taken from the cases of both the *Race* and *Religion or Belief Regulations* is precisely that. In none of the cases surveyed for this chapter did the courts overrule a policy aim as illegitimate. There is nonetheless evidence of counsel for the complainants attempting to establish the illegitimacy of aims. Such challenges only came under the *Religion or Belief Regulations* in cases where religious views clashed with sexual orientations. The case of *Ladele v Islington London Borough Council* concerned whether the marriage registrar of the respondent council could opt out of officiating civil partnerships on account of her Christian views on marriage.[76] The ET held that she had been indirectly discriminated against by the council. The EAT and the Court of Appeal overruled this judgment on the grounds that the aim of promoting civil partnerships was enshrined in primary legislation and must therefore be considered a legitimate aim. The dispute centred

[76] At the EAT: [2009] IRLR 154. At the Court of Appeal: [2010] LGR 690.

on what precisely the aim was, as Lord Neuberger MR explained on behalf of the Court of Appeal:

> [20] The ET decided that there had been indirect discrimination against Ms Ladele, because the blanket policy of requiring all registrars to perform civil partnership duties put individuals who held the orthodox Christian belief, that marriage was a union between one man and one woman for life, at a disadvantage when compared with others who did not hold that belief. While it accepted that the promotion of the LGBT [lesbian, gay, bisexual and transgender] community was a legitimate aim, the ET concluded that Islington's treatment of Ms Ladele was not a proportionate means of achieving that aim….
>
> [45] The problem with the ET's analysis is, as the EAT pointed out, that it wrongly identifies Islington's aim, as it overlooks the point that the service which Islington stated that they aimed to provide was not merely one which was effective in terms of practicality and efficiency, but was also one which complied with their overarching policy of being 'an employer and a public authority wholly committed to the promotion of equal opportunities'….
>
> [46] I find it very hard to see how this could be challenged, either as being Islington's actual aim, in the light of the evidence, or as being a legitimate aim, in the light of Islington's Dignity for All policy, current legislation and mainstream thinking.

In none of the 31 cases surveyed was a policy aim deemed to be illegitimate. So, the judges adopted a wide margin of appreciation to the concerns of public and private organisations to determine the legitimacy of their aims. Even more difficult for judges to define is the second half of the proportionality equation: whether a legitimate aim is implemented by proportionate means. Another case where religious and gay rights clashed is illustrative. Once again, the question arose as to whether individuals could opt out of performing certain tasks that lay within their job description. The case was that of *McClintock v Department of Constitutional Affairs* referred to earlier in the dictum of

Burton J.[77] Mr McClintock was a Justice of the Peace (JP) and member of the Family Panel. He claimed that as a Christian, he could not place a child in the adoptive care of a same-sex couple, and he sought a general exception to him administering such arrangements. He was told that section 79 of the *Civil Partnership Act 2004* would not allow any such exceptions to be made, and he therefore resigned. He put in a claim for indirect discrimination on the grounds that the means of implementing the policy were disproportionate. Elias J at the EAT resolved the case by pointing out that a JP could not refuse to apply the law, even if it was against his or her personal beliefs. Such a situation could result in a lack of judges to apply swathes of law:

> [53] Mr Diamond [Counsel for Mr McClintock] made the perfectly cogent point that it seems to be something of a paradox if a magistrate can properly recuse himself from a particular case on the grounds that his public actions or words have created the appearance of bias and yet will not be permitted to do so where the objection to the law may be for entirely the same reasons but have been only privately expressed. We recognise the force of that. However, the apparent paradox dissolves once the purpose of the rules is appreciated. Recusal for apparent bias occurs where the parties have a reasonable suspicion arising from some particular factor, such as the fact that the judge has a financial interest, or exceptionally because he or she has expressed strong views on an issue, that the judge may not be able to conduct the trial fairly and impartially. This is different from a situation where the judge is refusing to apply the law because he has moral objections to it, or thinks that it has been introduced prematurely or has been insufficiently considered. He is then expected to put his personal views to one side – which judges frequently have to do – and there is no reason why the parties should not trust him to be able to do that.

My argument is not that Elias J's decision was right or wrong in terms of the law or morality. My point is that the lack of clarity in the law encouraged caution and reliance on existing principles of law. This was a reasonable response from Elias J to his institutional constraints. It would have been inappropriate for the judge to build new legal

[77] [2008] IRLR 29.

protections on such wobbly pillars as were provided by the *Religion or Belief Regulations*. In the absence of a logic of communication, judges turn to a logic of appropriateness (March and Olsen 1989).

In only one case of the 31 reviewed were the means deemed disproportionate to achieving a legitimate aim. This was *R (Elias) v Secretary of State for Defence* at the Court of Appeal.[78] In this case, a claimant applied for compensation from the Japanese government for her internment in a prisoner of war camp during the Second World War. She and her family were British citizens but had not been born in the UK and were therefore denied compensation. The court ruled that discriminating between British citizens and non-British citizens was a legitimate policy aim, but doing so on the basis of the place of birth was not proportionate, and was therefore unlawful. Specifically, the court decided that the means could not be justified as place of birth (as discussed in the immigration chapter) is not determinative of citizenship under UK law.

With regard to the coherence of policy, judges have had to rely on past precedent to flesh out the meaning of law. The past therefore shaped the future direction of policy. Of course, this sort of 'path dependency' or 'logic of appropriateness' is to be expected, but the extent to which the past informs future developments is enhanced by indeterminate legislation that lacks sufficient clarity to affect substantial change. The final case to be considered demonstrates a somewhat absurd result that the government explicitly did not want. This case moves beyond the internal coherence of law to consider the legitimacy of indeterminate policy. The courts ended up ruling, in part, on what it is to be Jewish.

The case is the *Jewish Free School* (JFS) case that was heard by the Court of Appeal[79] and the Supreme Court.[80] These cases circled around the meaning of both the *Race* and *Religion or Belief Regulations*, but the *Race* regulations ultimately settled the case. The specific question was whether the school's use of a matrilineal test to determine Jewishness, and thereby admittance to the school, discriminated against a young man on the basis of his ethnicity. The following discussion will focus on the reasoning of the Supreme Court that heard the case with a rare nine-judge constitution. JFS is a top-performing comprehensive school, funded by the local authority. It is also described as a voluntary-aided faith school, administered in accordance with Orthodox Judaism.

---

78 [2006] EWCA Civ 1293 CA (Civ).

79 [2009] EWCA Civ 626.

80 [2009] UKSC 15.

The school is oversubscribed, and therefore gave preference to those recognised as Jewish by the Office of the Chief Rabbi of the United Hebrew Congregation of the Commonwealth (OCR). Recognition was accorded to those whose mother was Jewish or whose mother had converted to Orthodox Judaism before their birth. A boy, referred to as M, had applied to the school but was refused admittance. Although his father was Jewish and his mother had converted prior to his birth, she had converted to Masorti Judaism rather than Orthodox Judaism. According to the OCR guidelines, M did not pass the matrilineal test and was therefore not Jewish according to Orthodox standards.

M's father – referred to as E – applied for judicial review at the High Court, claiming that the JFS was discriminating on grounds of ethnicity. The High Court rejected this claim, but the Court of Appeal allowed it on the basis that while the JFS intended to discriminate on religious grounds, it was actually discriminating on ethnic grounds. The JFS appealed to the Supreme Court, where several interveners joined the case in support of the JFS – including The United Synagogue, The Board of Deputies of British Jews and the Secretary of State for Children, Schools and Families. The Equality and Human Rights Commission and the British Humanist Association intervened in support of E.

Three separate conclusions were reached by the nine judges. The Court's majority ruling was given by five justices (Lord Phillips, Lady Hale, Lord Mance, Lord Kerr and Lord Clarke), who held that M had been directly discriminated against on the grounds of his ethnicity. Two justices (Lord Hope and Lord Walker) held instead that indirect discrimination had taken place, and that while the school had a legitimate aim, its means of achieving it was not proportionate. Finally, Lord Rodger and Lord Brown, in their dissenting judgment, held that the school's admissions policy was not discriminatory because the ethnic background of the mother was irrelevant and all that mattered was that she had not converted to Orthodox Judaism. The ruling of the majority was controversial; they were seen to be determining the criteria for recognising an individual as Jewish. What is more, according to some observers, the justices were using recognition criteria that are essentially Christian, rather than Jewish, in that conversion and self-recognition were alleged to have been the only relevant factors in determining one's religion (Mancini 2010). Three very different solutions to the problem were put forward by the Supreme Court, and this was the only case of the 31 studied for this chapter where any dissenting opinions were offered.

The key question to resolve is: were the judges motivated by a desire to clarify the meaning of the legislation? Arguably, they were. Even if the court's decision was contentious, and one might even say wrong in the interests of social justice, it was not wrong in terms of the legislation. The legislation offered several ill-defined categories of protected characteristics. The clearest conclusion of what the law actually said was that an ethnic test was racially discriminatory. This is despite the revered and ancient lineage of the matrilineal test in Judaism. Section 1 of the *Race Relations Act 1976*, as amended by regulations 3–4 of the *Race Regulations*, renders unlawful discrimination on the 'grounds' of 'colour, race, nationality or ethnic or national origins of the person to whom it is applied'. Not only are the 'grounds' not defined, but neither is ethnicity. In terms of 'grounds', the court had to decide whether this referred to the motives for the discriminator to act or the facts upon which he relied. The court opted for the more easily identifiable means, and therefore safer option, of assessing what facts formed the grounds for discrimination. The JFS had based its admission decisions on the fact of the matrilineal test and its conformity with the OCR's religious guidance. In the case of M, that entailed an assessment of the origins of M's ethnicity via his mother. Therefore, the grounds of the decision not to admit M were based on facts relating to his ethnic origins, and not only on his religion, as was the professed policy of the school.

Barristers for the JFS defined ethnicity according to precedent set out in *Mandla v Dowell Lee*.[81] This defined ethnicity according to seven tests of membership. However, the majority on the Supreme Court ruled that this was a definition of an ethnic group, not ethnic origins. According to the *Mandla* ruling, M was not a member of the Orthodox Jewish ethnic group, but his ethnic origins were Jewish on account of his mother's conversion. By distinguishing the *Mandla* ruling, the court had to resolve not just what constituted membership of an ethnic group, but also admittance to that group of new members. In other words, the court had to define the legal status of the origins of ethnicity, which constitutes an anthropological question of some complexity.

A further complication was that UK law offers no proportionality defence to a charge of direct discrimination. Had the court determined, as per Lords Hope and Walker, that the JFS had indirectly discriminated, then a proportionality test could have been used in favour of the school. The majority of the Court decided that the

[81] [1983] 1 All ER 1062.

school's admissions policy discriminated directly because its aim was to distinguish between individuals from different religions but this, in fact, led to ethnic discrimination. The Court was unable to use proportionality review because they had opted for a narrow definition of ethnic discrimination, being based on an individual's descent or lineage. The judges were adopting a construction of the legislation that was appropriate by constraining its possible interpretations, even if the result was questionable. This result was that judges muscled their way into determining what it is to be Jewish in UK law. This decision was, of course, controversial given the delicately interlinking religious and ethnic markers of Judaism. The ruling has implications for Jewish schools, as well as other faith schools.

Parliament provided several tools for tackling discrimination. The law was flexible in order to resolve this multilayered problem. However, in the absence of clear conceptual definitions of ethnicity, the courts felt compelled to follow the more cautious route of declaring direct discrimination. This was done instead of the judges using their own analysis of proportionality to come up with a solution for JFS. It is worth highlighting that the judges were fully aware of the difficulties they faced. Their responsibility to resolve the indeterminacies was not relished. As Lord Phillips put it at paragraphs 8 and 9 of his ruling:

> [8] While the court has appreciated the high standard of the advocacy addressed to it, it has not welcomed being required to resolve this dispute. [9] … there may well be a defect in our law of discrimination. In contrast to the law in many countries, where English law forbids direct discrimination it provides no defence of justification. It is not easy to envisage justification for discriminating against a minority racial group. Such discrimination is almost inevitably the result of irrational prejudice or ill-will. But it is possible to envisage circumstances where giving preference to a minority racial group will be justified. Giving preference to cater for the special needs of a minority will not normally involve any prejudice or ill-will towards the majority.… Nothing that I say in this judgment should be read as giving rise to criticism on moral grounds of the admissions policy of JFS in particular or the policies of Jewish faith schools in general, let alone as suggesting that these policies are 'racist' as that word is generally understood.

This statement shows how unwilling Lord Phillips was to find the admissions policy as being discriminatory, and it could have been resolved by allowing a proportionality test. One could argue that the *JFS* case is therefore evidence against the hypothesis (H1) because it is a case where the law was too determinate, and what was required was greater indeterminacy to allow the courts to adopt a flexible test of proportionality. However, such a conclusion would make two mistakes: first, by linking a proportionality test with indeterminacy; and, second, by suggesting that the dispute in *JFS* was created by the law being too determinate, whereas it was, in fact, too arbitrary. On the first point, a proportionality test is founded on a careful and justified balance of rights that can be defended through careful reasoning. It is therefore the opposite of indeterminate as it seeks the best possible resolution to a clash of rights. This requires clear law with well-established procedural rules to be workable. On the second point, the issue in *JFS* was that the law of direct discrimination was arbitrary, but this does not make it determinate. Arbitrariness means that the law applies even where it is inappropriate, and will thereby create uncertainty in the law (Endicott 2011). This is a consequence of there being no clear logic of communication that links broad principles to specific programmes of action. In this case, the law of direct discrimination was based on categories of religion and ethnicity that had not been defined by Parliament or the government, so it was not clear who or what was to be protected by the law. The task of establishing conceptual clarity in the law, and providing some missing logic, had been tacitly delegated to the courts by Parliament. Therefore, even if one concludes that the result in *JFS* was wrong, the focus of criticism should be the legislation rather than the judges. The legitimacy of the *Race* and *Religion or Belief Regulations* is in doubt, in that it is not clear how individual policy decisions link to authorised statements of Parliament's will. The disconnect between sovereign power and policy action has encouraged the courts to adopt a broadly cautious approach that resolves disputes according to principles of law that do enjoy the backing of sovereign authority.

Conclusion

This chapter has considered the impact of indeterminate auxiliary modal verbs, as well as supranational laws, on the determinacy of domestic statutes. Evidence suggests that regulations brought in since 1987 have not clarified the law on discrimination and equality, but have made it more difficult to determine policy in this field. For two particular sets of regulations – the *Race* and *Religion or Belief Regulations* – case law suggests significant difficulties in establishing workable coordinative discourse between institutions, as well as communicative discourse with the general public. These difficulties have, in turn, undermined ambitions to delegate to, and hold to account, agents responsible for administering policies. These difficulties have also undermined the coherence of the law, and therefore its perceived, and real, legitimacy. The feasibility and desirability of indeterminate law has been scrutinised. However, again, a tart conclusion that indeterminate law is morally reprehensible cannot be sustained. Indeterminate law undermines the effectiveness of policy administration, but it could well be described as the understandable consequence of complex and demanding policy change, pursued under difficult circumstances.

It may also be tempting to conclude that EU Directives needed to be more carefully incorporated into British law so as to prevent judges fulfilling a significant political function. However, such a conclusion cannot be drawn from the current chapter. The Directives were carefully incorporated by assimilating the language of the EU Directives with existing UK anti-discrimination and equality laws. It may be the case that some EU Directives are poorly incorporated into the UK, but that is not the subject of this book and to assert it here would be speculative. As in the other chapters, the aim was not to assert any criticism that law ought to be better drafted; rather, the aim is to demonstrate that law has become increasingly indeterminate – for better or worse – and that this is much of the reason why non-political agents of Parliament have seen their policy role enhanced. It is also worth stressing that we have not observed the many cases where anti-discrimination and equality laws have achieved significant reforms to public and private relationships and that have not led to legal action. Looking at how effective laws are from cases that disputed them could be compared to judging car safety by only analysing crashes. However, the point is that the regulations were simply incomplete. To be workable, they needed more detailed definitions, and these were provided by the courts as the last resort. Without these judicial clarifications, the law would have been administered haphazardly, leaving significant unanswered questions as to its legitimacy. It is hard to criticise the political will to stamp out discrimination, or to work for greater equality. However, it is also hard to deny that as a consequence of various forces, politicians have not made their voices clear and have required citizens to use courts to attain some clarification.

Part Three: Fixing the code

SEVEN

Constitutional language: lessons from beyond Westminster

> The State shall organize a democratic planning system to support national development, which shall provide solidity, dynamism, competitiveness, continuity and equity to economic growth for the political, social and cultural independence and democratization of the nation.
>
> *Article 26 of the Mexican constitution*

> … the state shall be under a primary duty … to promote an increase in people's social and economic well-being and quality of life, especially those of the most disadvantaged persons. To promote social justice, ensure equal opportunity and carry out the necessary corrections to inequalities … by making every effort to ensure the efficiency of the public sector.
>
> *Article 81 of the Portuguese constitution*

Introduction

Previous chapters have demonstrated how indeterminate legislation can affect policy effectiveness. These chapters in Part Two begged the question: what, if anything, can be done by policymakers to ensure a logic of communication? A typical solution to resolving indeterminacy in one law is to interpret it by reference to another. In most democracies, this is facilitated with a constitution that forms a repository of principles and procedures for clarifying subordinate laws. The UK lacks any codified or entrenched constitutional law. However, this chapter will interrogate the effects of indeterminacies in constitutional laws. If constitutional law is itself indeterminate, subordinate laws can be even more difficult to reconcile to any logic of communication. For a constitution to solve those problems identified in preceding chapters, its meaning has to be plain.

The provisions quoted at the opening of this chapter come, first, from the constitution with the most adjectives and adverbs of any Organisation for Economic Co-operation and Development (OECD) country – that is, Mexico's constitution, with 6,419 adjectives and adverbs – and, second, from the constitution with the greatest proportion of adjectives and adverbs to all other words – that is, Portugal's constitution, where 10.32% of all words are adjectives or adverbs. With these particular provisions, Mexican and Portuguese constitution designers were attempting to manage economic development. This is difficult to achieve with plain language, and reflects ambitions to pursue social-democratic solutions to economic inequalities. Yet, the language is highly indeterminate. Acting on these provisions will create the difficulties of delegation, accountability, coherence and legitimacy identified in the chapters of Part Two. How, for instance, is a Mexican citizen to know if their state has worked towards 'solidity, dynamism, competitiveness, continuity and equity' in the economy? Any one of these five adjectives could allow power to be stretched, or duties to be shirked.

So, the specific question for this chapter is as follows. If 'a long constitution is a (positively) bad constitution' (Tsebelis and Nardi 2016), what specific textual elements cause the most damage? Tsebelis and Nardi argued that 'substantive restrictions' contained in longer constitutions create rigidities, and thereby spur demand for amendments when new coalitions reject those restrictions. As a consequence of substantive restrictions, Tsebelis and Nardi demonstrated that longer constitutions are correlated with lower levels of gross domestic product (GDP) per capita and higher levels of corruption. Their evidence is compelling, but further compels the following question: is it just the substance of long constitutions that is '(positively) bad', or can the language used have an impact as well? Longer constitutions are a product not only of more detail, but also of other elements of 'garrulity' (Voigt 2009; Bjørnskov and Voigt 2014; Tsebelis and Nardi 2016: 459). Most notable of which, I will argue, are the use of noun-qualifying adjectives and adverbs. This chapter will demonstrate: (1) that these indeterminate parts of speech are increasingly used in constitutional language; (2) that they are more difficult to interpret; and (3) that they therefore give greater influence to elites with sufficient resources to impose their preferred interpretations. As such, besides substantive restrictions, it is important to consider the effects of under-substantiated restrictions. These under-substantiated restrictions empower elites to determine the meaning of words in their own interest. These interpretations create new substantive restrictions. Elites are thereby able, with relative ease, to reposition the 'interpretative space' (Lester and Piore 2004). Also, as Tsebelis and Nardi argued, new substantive restrictions create ideological rigidities and increase the demands for change. Findings in this chapter suggest that indeterminate constitutions contribute to the deleterious effects associated with wordy constitutions in terms of both poor economic performance and corruption.

This chapter therefore brings together the works of Tsebelis and Nardi (2016) on the dangers of wordy constitutions with the analysis of the 'Comparative Constitutions Project' on the interpretability of constitutions (Melton et al 2013). Furthermore, I have expanded and updated the research design of Tsebelis and Nardi, and drilled down into the specific semantic elements that have had the greatest effects on governance. By again applying computer-assisted natural language processing (NLP) technology, it was possible to analyse the parts of speech used in 644,422 words from 33 OECD constitutions. The aim of this chapter is to observe textual differences in constitutions and to model their effects.

Unforeseen events, ideological realignments and globalisation all militate against predictable policymaking (Lindblom 1959). The response, especially in the democratic world, has been to future-proof constitutions. Clear exposition of principles is increasingly rejected in favour of loose constitutional language that can enable discretion and adaptability. Henry Maine (1861) described a shift in law during the 19th century 'from status to contract'. What indeterminate parts of speech achieve is the capacity for those with status to reinterpret the social contract. It is not a contract that is of equal benefit to citizen and state, but significantly to the advantage of the state and powerful citizens. Prominent examples include the 'elastic clause' (Art 1(8)) of the US constitution. This clause allows Congress to pursue federal policies to the extent they believe is 'necessary and proper'. Just these two adjectives and a conjunction have enabled a variety of interpretations and have encouraged fierce legal and extra-legal battles. The key nuance to Tsebelis and Nardi is therefore that language is important in addition to word length. Even a relatively short text (such as the US's taciturn 7,762-word constitution) can create vast quantities of verbiage in contextual, subtextual and inter-textual elaborations. In other words, scholars would need to read vastly more than the constitution itself to be able to understand and interpret the US constitution, and this is especially the case with *prima facie* indeterminate parts of speech, such as adjectives or adverbs. Much is made of the importance of institutional and contextual variables in the study of constitutions, but more attention is needed on the textual variables that open up interpretation to extra-textual elements. Language is the medium through which institutions share, pool and exert authority. This medium is an important explanatory variable in many of the policy debates of our age (Schmidt 2008; Hönnige 2011; Williams 2017a, 2017b).

As with Tsebelis and Nardi, my case selection draws on OECD countries. This chapter therefore offers global comparisons, allowing us to put the UK's struggles with indeterminacy into a broader context. The OECD members are culturally and historically diverse, but have shared commitments to democracy and open trade. These differences and commonalities allow for comparisons to be made and inferences to be drawn as to the effects of different styles of constitutional language. As with Tsebelis and Nardi, Israel and the UK have been omitted from the analysis as neither has a codified constitution. Included here, but missing from Tsebelis and Nardi, is Chile. This sole South American member joined the OECD in 2010 and thereby fell outside the 2000–06 time frame for the earlier work. This chapter presents several binary regressions graphically, as well as recreating the multivariate regressions run by Tsebelis and Nardi. The binary regressions display strong correlations between the proportion of adjectives and adverbs in a constitution and its interpretability. It will also be shown that the number of adjectives and adverbs in a constitution correlates even better with macroeconomic performance and corruption than does word length alone. The findings therefore suggest that the machine reading of textual elements offers important insights for constitutional engineering.

Theory and hypotheses

Examples are needed to describe the argument. Already mentioned are the three famous words – 'necessary and proper' – that have elasticated the US constitution's First Article. There have been wildly different visions of 'federalism' (the contraction and expansion of federal government power) resulting from these three words. Limited federal power in the early 20th century (the 'Lochner' era) gave way to rapid 'New Deal' expansion, pushed by Franklin Delano Roosevelt (FDR) and helped by the US Supreme Court case of *West Coast Hotel Co. v. Parrish* in 1937.[82] Great Society social reforms of the 1960s then created a period of 'regulated federalism', before a long phase of 'new federalism' was inaugurated under the Nixon administration, again seeing significant federal retrenchment (Kettl 1980). The point is that assessing constitutional language on the basis of how many words there are can overlook the variable effects of different words. Some parts of speech are *prima facie* indeterminate, and must be clarified by extensive and ongoing interpretation. Just three words in the US constitution were able to sustain fundamentally divergent policy goals.

Another short constitution muddled by indeterminate language is Iceland's. The island nation sustains its government on just 4,089 constitutional words. However, its freedom of expression provision is both wordy and reliant on indeterminate language:

> Freedom of expression may only be restricted by law in the interests of public order or the security of the State, for the protection of health or morals, or for the protection of the rights or reputation of others, if such restrictions are deemed necessary and in agreement with democratic traditions.
>
> *Article 73*

Three linguistic features are especially likely to undermine plainness here: adjectives and adverbs, conditional conjunctions, and indeterminate modal verbs. Adjectives allow those wishing to restrict freedom of expression to determine the meanings of 'necessary' and 'democratic' narrowly. Conditional conjunctions here ensure that any determination of the law depends on circumstance, so as to protect 'health *or* morals, *or* for the protection of the rights *or* reputations of others, *if* such restrictions are deemed necessary *and* in agreement with democratic traditions'. Finally, the modal verb 'may' offers a looser grip than alternative verbs such as 'will' or 'shall' would provide, as in 'Freedom of expression may only be restricted ...'.

Iceland's freedom of expression provision contrasts starkly to that of Poland's: 'The freedom to express opinions, to acquire and to disseminate information shall be ensured to everyone' (Article 54). Poland's constitution is, at 19,602 words, nearly five times longer than Iceland's. However, its protection of free speech is far less elastic and liable to elite domination. It had been the ambition of Iceland to become a haven of free speech (Vallance 2010), but the European

82 300 U.S. 379 (1937).

Court of Human Rights became a notable critic of the country's record in this regard (Arnarsdóttir 2015).

Constitutions are increasingly drafted with indeterminate language. This yields greater discretion to policymakers to manage complex social demands. All legal provisions need interpreting and can be dominated by powerful agents. However, plainness of exposition empowers citizen interpreters, whereas indeterminacy can allow the powerful to trade in constitutional language and raise the costs of its interpretation. For instance, it was necessary for some Icelandic citizens to take an appeal to the European Court of Human Rights so that their preferred interpretation of free speech law could be adopted. Indeterminacy also makes it more likely that ideological interpretations will become entrenched and difficult to change. For example, an ideological coalition defined 'necessary and proper' to mean limited government for one generation of Americans. Then, with much difficulty, a new coalition came and redefined the words to sanction expanded government. These battles over the definition and redefinition of words create instabilities, similar to those formed by plainly worded 'substantive restrictions'. The specific addition to Tsebelis and Nardi's argument is the point that both substantive and indeterminate restrictions create legal rigidity: the former through limitations on action; and the latter through elite interpretations of words that, in turn, create limitations on action. The least restrictive constitutional language is that which provides for a limited range of substantive restrictions, and does so with plain, and easily comprehensible, language. Any reader who has had a contract to sign – such as with a landlord or telephone company – will likely have realised that both the length of the contract and its use of indeterminate language signalled an asymmetry of power.

Difficulties in interpreting a constitutional text are crucial to this theory. From these difficulties arise subsidiary effects on society and economics. Of course, as was described in previous chapters, difficulties of interpretation were themselves caused by various social and political forces that affected the drafting and ratification processes. Constitutional language derives from choices made by actors to cement, or augment, their own status (Elster 1995). In addition to which, constitution drafters will seek to address popular concerns and redress past policy failings. Furthermore, this drafting takes place within a context of demanding international norms, such as the expected protections of human rights (Levitsky and Way 2006). Given all these forces acting on a constitutional text, it is tempting to dismiss its language as ephemeral and more a matter for legal scholarship.

However, even constitutions derived from similar contexts have wide variances in their language. Constitutions in formerly fascist regimes, for instance, employ markedly different language. This is despite the contents being cut from a similar liberal-democratic cloth. Austria's 41,366-word constitution is nearly four times the length of Italy's 11,708-word constitution. However, Italy's contains more adjectives and adverbs (10% of all words) than Austria's (9%). Italy's constitution also utilises more conditional conjunctions (5%, to Austria's 3%) and more indeterminate modal verbs (0.88%, to Austria's 0.31%). The interpretability of these texts is likely to be different as a result.

Interpretability of a constitutional text is, as Melton et al (2013) demonstrated, a latent variable, meaning that interpretability cannot be observed directly. The textual and contextual components of interpretability are too many and varied. What can be measured are the inter-coder reliability scores of academics and students who have read the constitutions and offered their interpretations. Melton et al (2013) have such reliability scores for all the world's major constitutions, and these data are used in this chapter to test whether specific parts of speech are correlated with greater or lesser reliability scores. The specific theory presented here is that adjectives and adverbs (as compared to conditional conjunctions and indeterminate modal verbs) have the greatest impact on reliability scores, and thereby have the greatest policy effects. The reasoning focuses on sentence structure and methods of interpretation. Adjectives and adverbs primarily influence the subject of a sentence. They qualify the interpretation of nouns and verbs, and determine how the subject of a sentence clause – be it the government, the legislature or a citizen – will interpret the powers, duties and rights enumerated. Even when adjectives or adverbs qualify the object of a sentence, they place the onus on the subject to offer a viable interpretation. These parts of speech also tend towards rigidity. Once interpreted authoritatively, their meaning can be difficult to reinterpret. What, for instance, a '*free* citizen' is has been subject to waves of reinterpretation by different generations, across various contexts and by different constellations of elites. However, once given a central tendency of meaning, qualifications like 'free' require a 'critical juncture' before a fundamentally different interpretation will be accepted (Collier and Collier 2002). This process of crystallisation in the interpretation of adjectives and adverbs was identified in Chapter Four in relation to immigration law. Hence, as with excessively long constitutions, under-substantiated restrictions also create rigidity.

Conditional conjunctions, alternatively, focus on the object of sentences, and, of course, the modality of 'may' focuses on the verb of a sentence. These parts of speech can also be indeterminate and capable of authoritative interpretation. However, they rely far more on contextual variables that may be beyond the control of the subject of a sentence. These parts of speech are, therefore, less prone to rigidity when compared to adjectives and adverbs, with rigidity, here, meaning difficulty in amending or reinterpreting a provision that has become fixed. So, in agreement with Tsebelis and Nardi, I contend that rigidity in the constitutional text is damaging to economic growth and facilitates corruption. Rigidity favours those with no incentives to change the *status quo*. These individuals will be better placed to frustrate policy change if: (1) there are many substantive restrictions; or (2) there are under-substantiated restrictions that have been subject to authoritative interpretation (Tsebelis 2002). A middle way between these extremes creates the most effective constitution because unrestrictive and plain language empowers citizens, rather than state elites.

There are four linked hypotheses derived from this theory. The first is historical:

> H1: Modern constitutions contain more adjectives and adverbs than older constitutions.

Newer constitutions are written to address more varied demands for social policies than would have been expected in the 19th or early 20th centuries. The so-called 'new constitutionalism' caters for extensive and complex powers and liberties across a range of policy spaces (Hirschl 2004, 2006). It is increasingly difficult to distil these various policy demands into plain language. As such:

> H2: Constitutions with a higher proportion of adjectives and adverbs are less interpretable (have lower inter-coder reliability scores).

Of all the linguistic elements, adjectives and adverbs are expected to create the greatest indeterminacy. This can be presented formally by adapting equations used by Melton et al (2013: 12). First:

$$I_{jk} = \alpha_0 + \alpha_t T_{jk} + \alpha_c C_k + v_k + u_k \quad (1)$$

Here, *I* denotes the interpretability of constitutions (*j*) in different countries (*k*), *T* denotes the textual attributes of the constitution, and *C* captures the characteristics of each country. To flesh out the textual attributes (*T*), I have added three parts of speech that are particularly impactful on the interpretability of texts:

$$T_{jk} = \alpha + \beta_1 ADJ_{jk} + \beta_2 CON_{jk} + \beta_3 MOD_{jk} + \varepsilon_{jk} \qquad (2)$$

Adjectives and adverbs (*ADJ*), conditional conjunctions (*CON*), and indeterminate modal verbs (*MOD*) are expected to affect interpretability. However, in particular, adjectives and adverbs are expected to offer a significant linear correlation with interpretability. This, in turn, requires the next two steps in Melton et al's formal analysis:

$$R_{ij} = \beta_0 + \beta_p P_{ij} + \beta_n I_j + u_j + r_{ij} \qquad (3)$$

Here, *R* denotes the reliability scores of different coders. This score is a linear function of the coding process (*P*) and the interpretability of the text (*I*) across *i* iterated measurements of *j* constitutions, with *u* and *r* as residuals for the constitution and the coding, respectively. Melton et al then substitute the *I* in equation 3 with the formula in equation 1:

$$R_{ijk} = \gamma + \beta_p P_{ijk} + \gamma_t T_{jk} + \gamma_c C_k + \varepsilon_{ijk} \qquad (4)$$

This, in turn, allows me to substitute the *T* in equation 4 with a coefficient capturing the most impactful textual attribute – adjectives and adverbs:

$$R_{ijk} = \gamma + \beta_p P_{ijk} + \gamma_{adj} ADJ_{jk} + \gamma_c C_k + \varepsilon_{ijk} \qquad (5)$$

As argued, lesser interpretability (and hence lower reliability scores) is of benefit to a narrower section of elites. This, in turn, closes down the broader social utility of a constitution and can create rigidities that inhibit economic performance. Hence, beyond the institutions responsible for economic performance are the effects of inter-institutional language (Persson and Tabellini 2003; Blume et al 2009):

> H3: Constitutions with a high proportion of adjectives and adverbs are more rigid (have a lower predicted probability of amendment).

These first three hypotheses focus on the constitutions in themselves. In other words, these hypotheses look to how constitutions have changed and the effects of these changes on interpretability and rigidity. I then turn to consider the wider policy effects. For this analysis, it is more fruitful to consider not the proportion of adjectives and adverbs, but the logged total numbers of these parts of speech. This is because policy effects are magnified by a larger number of substantive and under-substantiated restrictions. Totals are logged, as was done by Tsebelis and Nardi for total word length. Logged totals are used on the assumption that each additional adjective or adverb is more impactful in smaller overall word counts.

> H4: Constitutions with a high logged total number of adjectives and adverbs are associated with lower levels of GDP per capita.

Also, elite capacity to determine meaning will likely be self-serving:

> H5: Constitutions with a high logged total number of adjectives and adverbs are associated with higher levels of corruption.

Of course, there is a possibility of reverse causation in H5: more corrupt political cultures may draft a constitution with a greater number of restrictions couched in indeterminate language. Furthermore, indeterminate constitutional language may be fully endogenous to corrupt political culture, where corruption is both cause and effect of indeterminacy in social discourse. A 'logic of communication' between institutions depends on a shared set of cultural and linguistic norms that will more likely be absent from a country with a weak or non-existent public sphere (Schmidt 2008). Despite these difficulties in establishing causation, I argue that textual variables sustain some important independent effects on economic and political outcomes.

Research design

Data from 33 OECD countries (all bar Israel and the UK)[83] have been collected from the Comparative Constitutions Project and the World Bank. All these countries have, by dint of their OECD membership, similar commitments to the rule of law and judicial independence. Such commitments are essential if textual variables are to count at all. If mere lip service is paid to constitutional language, one could not expect changes in language to have any impact. So, it is essential that these 33 nations all be committed to constitutional democracy. From these nations' constitutions, all 644,422 words ('tokens') were analysed using the Natural Language Toolkit (NLTK) program used for previous chapters.

The inter-coder reliability scores from Melton et al's (2013) study of constitutional interpretability were also collected for each of the 33 countries in order to test H2. Also, for H3 and H4, the correlations run by Tsebelis and Nardi (2016: 476) were repeated with updated data. To update these regression analyses, I included Chile and the latest version of the Swedish constitution, which was significantly amended in 2009 and 2012. For New Zealand, I used the official version available on the University of Richmond's 'Constitution Finder' website.[84] This is because the Comparative Constitutions Project has a longer, non-canonical version of New Zealand's constitution that includes addenda and treaties. I also used the latest available economic data from the World Bank. For instance, data on GDP per capita were averaged from 2007 to 2015. Tsebelis and Nardi noted that their analysis cuts off before the 2007 financial crisis so as to avoid unrepresentative data. My data covers the financial crisis and some of its aftermath. My data may not be representative of longer-term trends, but they have sufficient breadth to give a good indication of each economy's relative performance.

[83] Australia (AUL), Austria (AUS), Belgium (BEL), Canada (CAN), Chile (CHL), Czech Republic (CZR), Denmark (DEN), Estonia (EST), Finland (FIN), France (FRN), Germany (GDR), Greece (GRC), Hungary (HUN), Iceland (ICE), Ireland (IRE), Italy (ITA), Japan (JPN), Latvia (LAT), Luxembourg (LUX), Mexico (MEX), Netherlands (NTH), New Zealand (NEW), Norway (NOR), Poland (POL), Portugal (POR), Slovakia (SLO), Slovenia (SLV), South Korea (KOR), Spain (SPN), Sweden (SWD), Switzerland (SWZ), Turkey (TUR), and the USA (USA).

[84] http://con nder.richmond.edu (accessed 6 January 2017) is now retired. The text may now be accessed at www.legislation.govt.nz/act/public/1986/0114/latest/096be8ed80762277.pdf

Table 7.1: Descriptive statistics

Frame	Description	Min	Mean	Median	Max	SD
Constitutional	Constitutional interpretability (inter-coder reliability score from Melton et al) [REL]	65.49	77.13	77.45	92.13	6.70
	Predicted probability that a constitutional amendment will *not* occur (from Tsebelis and Nardi) [RIGID]	0.001	0.54	0.54	0.999	0.36
	Constitution age (years since 1789) [YEAR]	0	150.73	164	222	61.40
	Constitution length (in log words) [LOGLEN]	8.16	9.62	9.63	11.05	0.73
	Constitutional devolution to sub-national government [LEVELS]	0	0.88	1	1	0.33
	Constitutions with common law origin [LAWCOM]	0	0.15	0	1	0.36
Textual	Adjectives and adverbs as % of all constitutional words [ADJ]	3.95	8.05	8.32	10.32	1.39
	Total number of adjectives (in log words) [LOGADJS]	4.93	7.04	7.06	8.77	0.80
	Conditional conjunctions, including 'if'/'or'/'and', excluding 'not', as % of all words [CON]	2.89	4.42	4.45	5.77	0.67
	Indeterminate modal verbs ('may'/'might') as % of all words [MOD]	0.31	0.72	0.72	1.65	0.27
	Sum of all indeterminate parts of speech as % of all words [ADD]	8.82	13.19	13.29	16.02	1.53
Economic	Log of GDP per capita PPP, averaged 2007–15 (World Bank) [LOGGDP]	9.67	10.45	10.50	11.41	0.37
	% of labour force with a secondary education, 2015 (World Bank) [EDUSEC]	20.30	46.91	45.10	72.90	12.41
	Total natural resources rent as % of GDP, 2015 (World Bank) [NATRES]	0.00	1.04	0.29	12.20	2.31
	Trade as % of GDP, 2015 (World Bank) [TRADE]	28.00	106.67	85.99	391.50	68.41
	Foreign direct investment as % of GDP (World Bank) [FDI]	–3.63	4.10	2.08	33.86	6.69
	Gross savings as % of GDP, 2015 or latest available (World Bank) [SAVE]	9.97	26.37	24.88	53.95	8.95
Political	Transparency International Corruption Perceptions Index inverted, 2015–16 [CORRINV]	10	31.61	28	70	15.79

All variables and their operationalisations are summarised in Table 7.1.

Results

First to be considered is H1 – whether constitutions are increasingly reliant on adjectives and adverbs. Figure 7.1 presents the linear relationship between the age of a constitution (measured in years since 1789) and the proportion of all constitutional words that are adjectives or adverbs.

Figure 7.1 presents evidence to reject the null hypothesis in favour of H1. The trend line ($y = 6.21 + 0.01x$, $R^2 = 0.29$, $p = 0.001$★★★) describes a steady increase in the use of adjectives and adverbs in constitutional language. The R^2 is nonetheless low, with notable outlying constitutions, such as Portugal's. This constitution has both youthfulness (it was promulgated in 1976) and an unusually high reliance on adjectives and adverbs (10.32% of all words). Despite outliers, the trend presents a low probability (0.001) of having emerged by chance alone. This trend therefore suggests a change in

Figure 7.1: Relationship of constitution age and proportion of adjectives

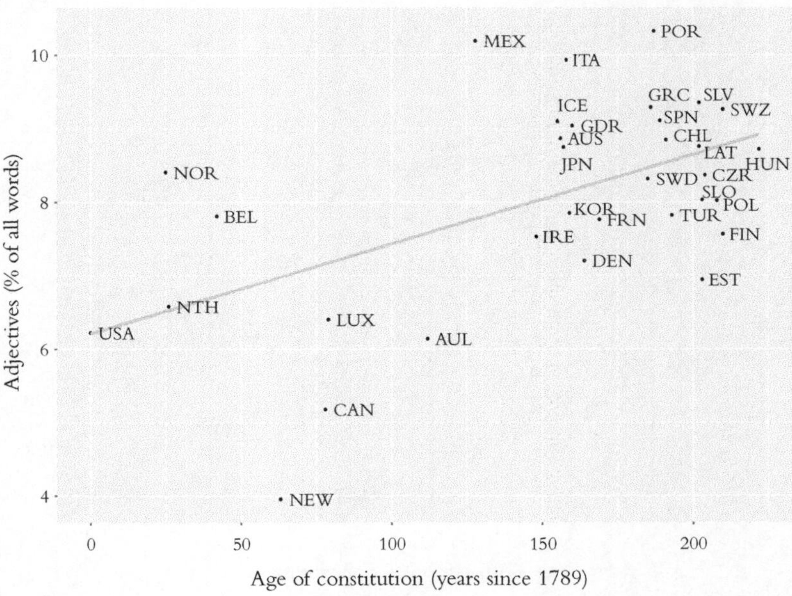

constitutionalism. The genre of constitutional language has changed, from plain contractual exposition to more qualified language.

Interestingly, there is no significant correlation between the age of constitutions and the use of conditional conjunctions or indeterminate modal verbs. Increased use of conjunctions would suggest an increasing desire to manage processes, to conjoin disparate principles and to reconcile the constitutional text with its context (if *A* and/or *B* occurs, then do *C*). Increased use of the indeterminate modal verb 'may' would signal an increased reliance on deliberate delegation (the government *may* authorise). That neither conjunctions nor the use of 'may' have increased significantly suggests that modern constitutionalism focuses on substantive, rather than procedural, discretion. Adjectives and adverbs allow the meaning of concepts to be authorised by powerful actors, without relying on specified conditions or the deliberate delegation of discretion.

There is also a strong correlation between the proportion of adjectives and adverbs used and the interpretability of the constitutional language (measured with inter-coder reliability scores from Melton et al), as Figure 7.2 shows.

Figure 7.2 displays a statistically significant trend (y = 95.52 + –2.29x, $R^2 = 0.23$, $p = 0.005$★★★). This is evidence to reject the null

Figure 7.2: Relationship between proportion of adjectives and interpretability

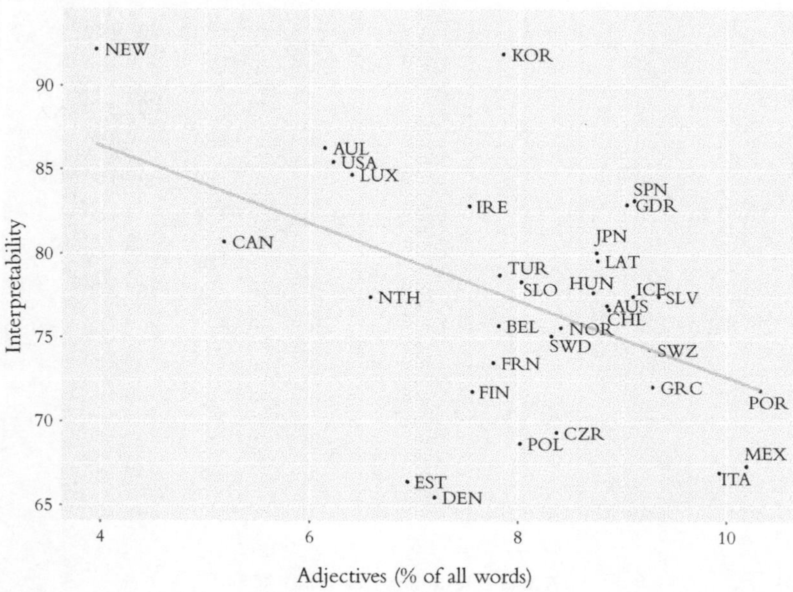

Table 7.2: Interpretability regressed against proportion of adjectives and adverbs, and other variables (bivariate regressions)

Variable	Coefficient	Constant	Multiple R^2
Constitution age	–0.34**	0.67***	0.14
	(0.15)	(0.11)	
Word length (log)	–0.32*	0.6***	0.1
	(0.17)	(0.1)	
Federalism	–0.2	0.61***	0.07
	(0.13)	(0.13)	
Common law	0.37***	0.38***	0.28
	(0.11)	(0.04)	
Proportion of adjectives/adverbs	–0.55***	0.79***	0.23
	(0.18)	(0.12)	
Number of adjectives/adverbs (log)	–0.49**	0.7***	0.16
	(0.2)	(0.12)	
Proportion of conjunctions	0.23	0.31***	0.05
	(0.19)	(0.11)	
Proportion of modal verbs	0.13	0.4***	0.01
	(0.22)	(0.08)	
Additive measure of indeterminacies	–0.38*	0.67***	0.1
	(0.2)	(0.13)	

in favour of H2. Table 7.2 demonstrates, further, that in comparison to other explanatory variables, the presence of adjectives and adverbs yields the largest coefficient, with the strongest statistical significance. All variables were normalised to between 0 and 1 to make for comparable coefficients.

Only the correlation of interpretability (the dependent variable) with common law constitutions presents a higher R^2 than does the proportion of adjectives and adverbs. Just five nations in the sample have common law origins (AUL, CAN, IRE, NEW, USA), so the sample is small. Also, one could expect the coders providing the reliability scores, being based in North America, to have been somewhat more familiar with common law constitutions. However, Melton et al (2013: 401, emphasis in original) address this point head on:

> One would think that the coders, who were primarily graduate students working in North America in the early twenty-first century, would have great difficulty understanding constitutions from different contexts, and that we would observe a bias towards modern constitutions produced in countries with cultural and political traditions

> similar to those of the United States. While we do find that constitutions vary significantly in their level of interpretability, contextual barriers do *not* seem to challenge readers. Constitutions written in bygone eras, in different languages, or in extremely different cultural milieux are no less interpretable by readers than are those written in closer temporal and cultural proximity.

Despite the stronger R^2, common law presents a smaller coefficient (0.37***) than does the proportion of adjectives and adverbs (–0.55***), or the logged number of adjectives and adverbs (–0.49**).

Table 7.3 presents multivariate regression models. These models show that the statistical significance of the proportion of adjectives and adverbs is retained even when controlling for a constitution's word length and the federalisation of the constitution. Statistical significance slips to an unsatisfactory single star ($p < 0.1$) when the age of the constitution is added (Model 4), and loses all significance when common law constitutions are controlled for (Model 5). Given that several of the independent variables correlate with each other, there is a risk of multicollinearity and a suppression effect. Also, as Figures 7.1 and 7.2 show, there is some autocorrelation on the dependent

Table 7.3: Interpretability regressed on proportion of adjectives and adverbs, and other constitutional variables (multivariate regressions)

Variable	**(1)**	**(2)**	**(3)**	**(4)**	**(5)**
Proportion of adjectives	–0.55***	–0.48**	–0.5**	–0.42*	–0.13
	(0.18)	(0.2)	(0.21)	(0.24)	(0.28)
Number of words (log)		–0.13	–0.04	–0.03	–0.09
		(0.18)	(0.21)	(0.21)	(0.21)
Federalism			–0.14	–0.12	–0.11
			(0.15)	(0.15)	(0.14)
Constitution age				–0.12	–0.06
				(0.18)	(0.17)
Common law					0.27
					(0.15)
Constant	0.79***	0.81***	0.89***	0.91***	0.66**
	(0.12)	(0.13)	(0.16)	(0.16)	(0.21)
Multiple R^2	0.23	0.24	0.26	0.28	0.35
Adjusted R^2	0.2	0.19	0.19	0.17	0.23

Notes: N = 33. Standard errors in parentheses. ***$p < 0.01$; **$p < 0.05$; *$p < 0.1$. Variance inflation factors for Model 5: ADJ (1.57); LOGLEN (1.33); LEVELS (1.21); YEAR (1.23); LAWCOM (1.42).

variable, in that constitutions have become somewhat less interpretable with time, although the variance inflation factors for all variables in model 5 do not exceed the threshold of 2 that would signal substantial multicollinearity. Nonetheless, Models 4 and 5 are somewhat over-saturated with variables given a relatively small N size of 33. The key finding, therefore, is Model 2. Even when controlling for differences in word length, the proportion of adjectives has a strong and statistically significant impact on interpretability. This adds nuance to Tsebelis and Nardi's argument that word length is 'positively bad' by considering the differential effect of specific parts of speech. It is evidence to reject the null in favour of H2. Furthermore, Figure 7.3 demonstrates that while there is a correlation between word length and the proportion of adjectives and adverbs used, there are several outliers. This suggests that even short constitutions can be indeterminate and create problems of interpretability.

Some countries deviate significantly from the trend and error margins displayed ($y = 0.02 + 0.83^{\star}x$, $R^2 = 0.19$, $p = 0.011^{\star\star}$). Iceland has one of the shortest constitutions in the OECD (4,613 words) but relies on a high proportion of adjectives and adverbs (9.1%). Conversely, Canada's 19,565-word constitution is one of the longest in the OECD but only 5.2% of those words are adjectives or adverbs.

Figure 7.3: Relationship of constitution length (log words) and proportion of adjectives

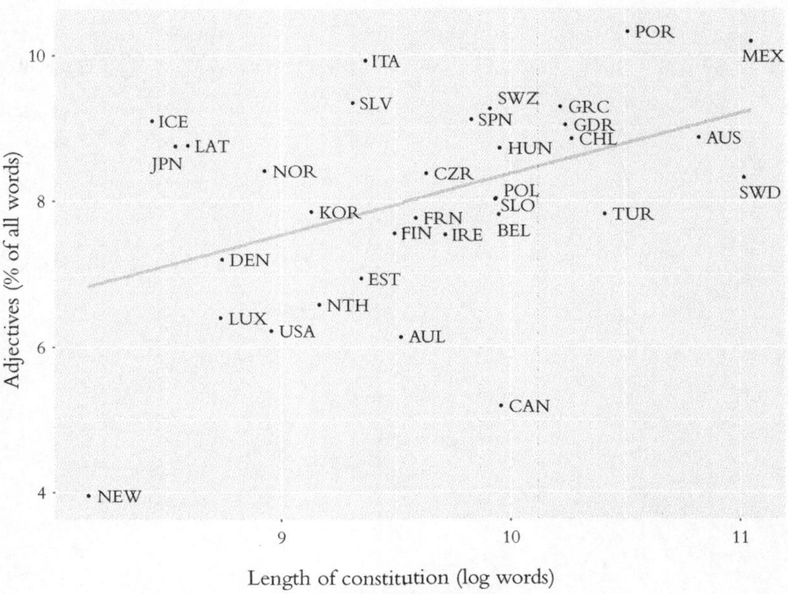

Of course, this means that there are significantly more adjectives in Canada's constitution as compared to Iceland's (1,095 and 420, respectively).

Tsebelis and Nardi (2016: 464) found that the number of times a constitution is amended correlates positively with its rigidity, when word length is controlled for. This was a crucial, yet counter-intuitive, finding. It might reasonably be expected that more rigid constitutions (those more difficult to amend) would be amended less often. However, long constitutions that are difficult to amend are restrictive, which encourages citizens and elites to seek substantial reforms more regularly. Long and rigid constitutions are therefore brittle, rather than strong. However, it is worth noting that even short constitutions can create rigidity, and brittleness, if they contain a high proportion of adjectives and adverbs. Indeed, Canada's constitution is marginally less rigid (having a lower predicted probability of remaining unchanged, at 0.21) than Iceland's much shorter text (0.28). This pattern is borne out for all OECD countries, as shown in Figure 7.4.

Figure 7.4 demonstrates that rigidity is also positively correlated with the proportion of adjectives and adverbs in a constitutional text, albeit with large residuals ($y = -0.19 + 0.09x$, $R^2 = 0.13$, $p = 0.049$★★). This is evidence to reject the null in favour of H3. The reasoning is that adjectives and adverbs qualify not only the powers, duties and

Figure 7.4: Relationship between proportion of adjectives and constitutional rigidity

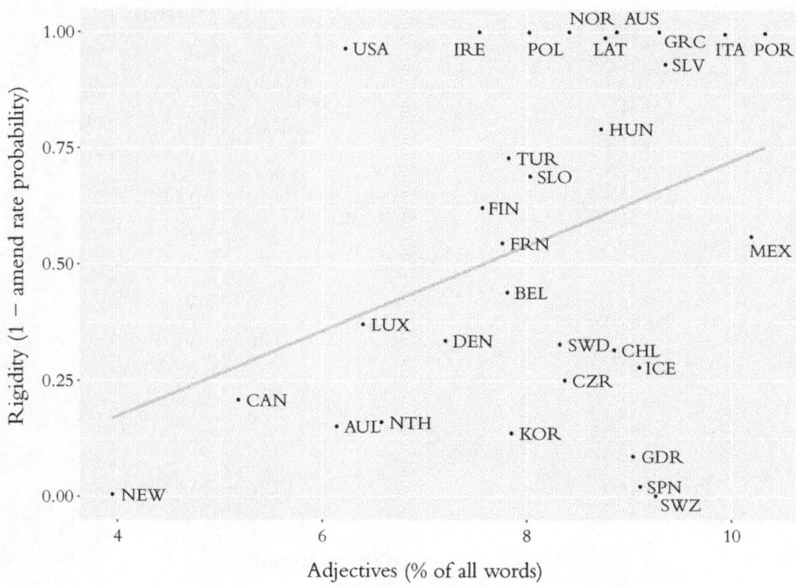

rights contained in a constitution, but also the procedures by which a constitution can be amended. It should be noted that there are wide error margins around the trend line. However, the point of displaying Figure 7.4 is to show that just as long constitutions have more adjectives and adverbs (see Figure 7.3), they are also found in higher proportions in more rigid constitutions.

These findings can be explained as consequences of half-baked ideologies, that is, where principles are only partially formed. Under these circumstances, it is likely that constitution drafters will be garrulous and qualify their language with adjectives and adverbs. This is for lack of certainty as to how their ideology should be expressed. The quotes that opened the chapter demonstrate this point. Portuguese constitutional engineers wanted 'the state … to promote an increase in people's social and economic well-being and quality of life … by making every effort to ensure the efficiency of the public sector'. In other constitutions, ideological substance is omitted, or at least kept to a minimum, in favour of clear procedures for settling disputes. So, for instance, New Zealand's easily amendable constitution does not need regular amending because its language is largely procedural, rather than substantive. It is language that establishes a means for resolving disputes, rather than being language that triggers disputes.

Not displayed in Figure 7.4, but also of note, is the finding that higher proportions of adjectives and adverbs correlate positively with greater constitutional scope, more executive power and more legislative powers (all measures taken from the Comparative Constitutions Project). Also not displayed is the finding that high proportions of adjectives and adverbs in a text are negatively correlated with levels of judicial independence (also taken from the Comparative Constitutions Project). This therefore suggests, as theorised, that adjectives and adverbs in a constitution signal high levels of state authority and weaker civil society. The effects of this asymmetry between state and society can be seen in economic performance, and from here, findings describe the effects of constitutional language, and analysis moves away from considering the texts in themselves. For this analysis, the log number of adjectives and adverbs is used in correlations. The following graphs demonstrate that models based on the number of adjectives and adverbs used have better predictive power than do models based on word length alone. This is true with regard to economic performance and corruption. Economic performance is measured by averaged GDP in purchasing power parity (PPP) between 2007 and 2015. Data are taken from the World Bank. Corruption is measured, as per Tsebelis and Nardi, as the

Figure 7.5: Relationship between constitution length and GDP per capita (PPP mean 2007–15)

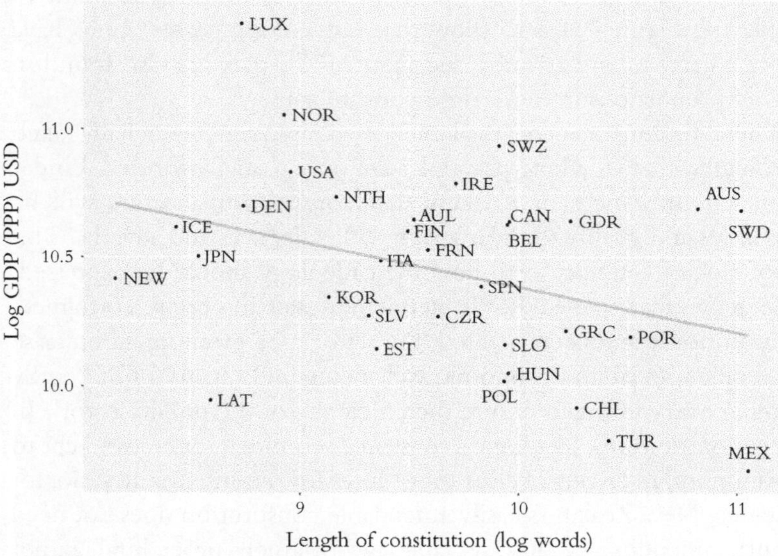

Note: $y = 12.15 + -0.18x$, $R^2 = 0.12$, $p = 0.046$★★.

Figure 7.6: Relationship between number of adjectives and GDP per capita (PPP mean 2007–15)

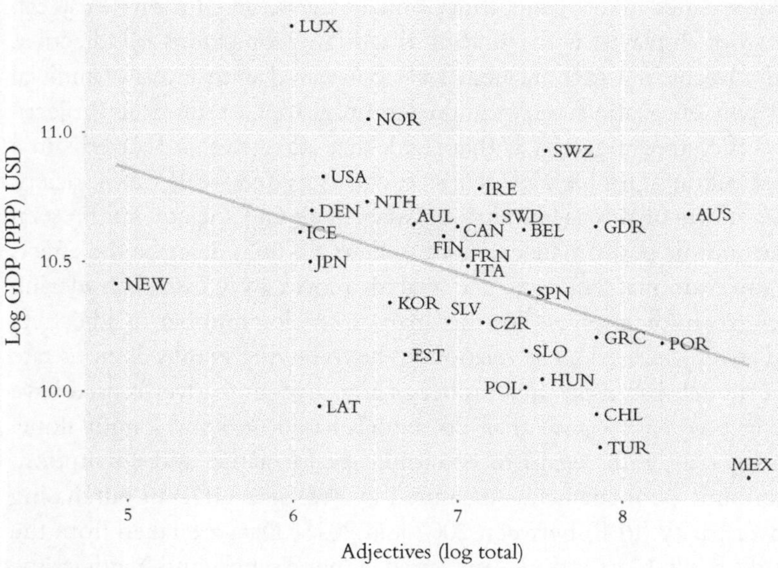

Note: $y = 11.86 + -0.20x$, $R^2 = 0.18$, $p = 0.012$★★.

Figure 7.7: Relationship between constitution length and corruption (CPI 2016)

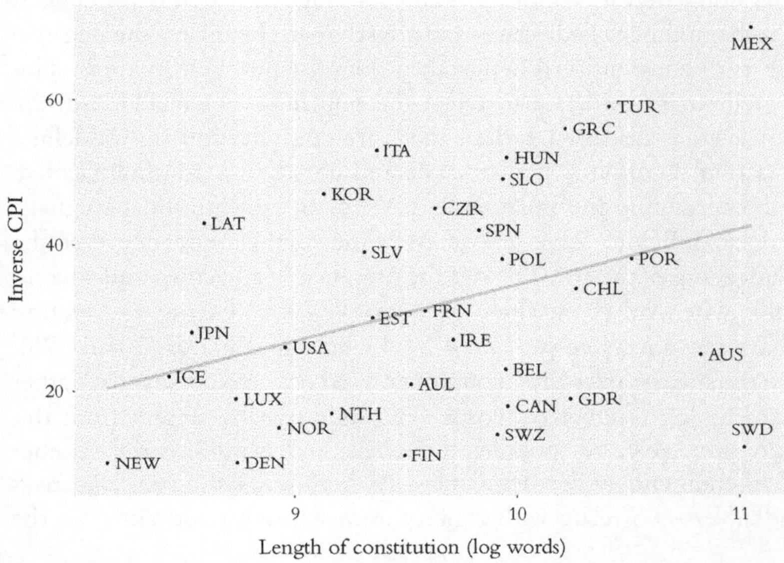

Note: $y = -42.01 + 7.65x$, $R^2 = 0.13$, $p = 0.043$★★.

Figure 7.8: Relationship between number of adjectives and corruption (CPI 2016)

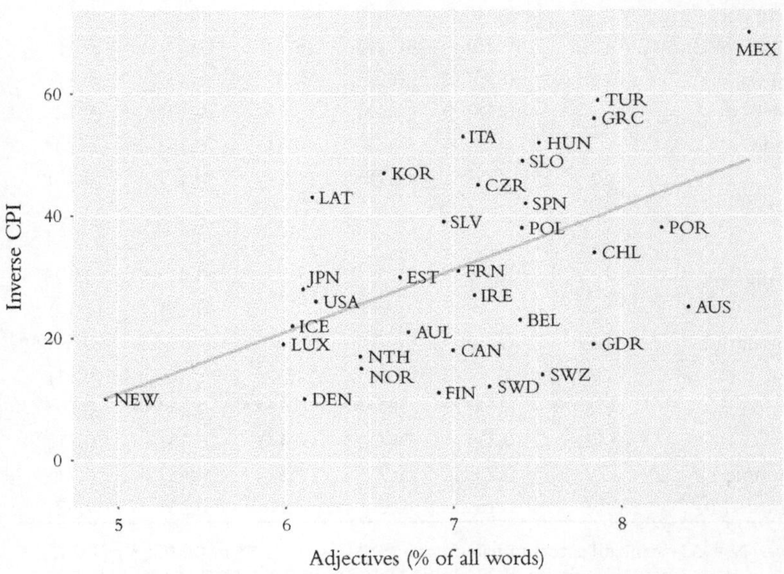

Note: $y = -39.86 + 10.15x$, $R^2 = 0.26$, $p = 0.002$★★★.

inverse of Transparency International's Corruption Perceptions Index (CPI), where high scores mean high perceptions of corruption.

As compared to Figures 7.5 and 7.7, Figures 7.6 and 7.8 suggest that the number of adjectives and adverbs better explains the negative effects of constitutional design than does the number of words. This is preliminary evidence to reject the null in favour of H4 and H5. However, as discussed earlier, there are complications in modelling causation. Economic performance and corruption are multifaceted, and ascertaining the independent effects of constitutional language will be difficult. Table 7.4 offers some further evidence that the relationship between GDP and the presence of adjectives and adverbs holds when other variables are controlled for. This is a recreation of a regression table presented by Tsebelis and Nardi (2016: 475), which here includes the log number of adjectives and adverbs, rather than the log number of words. The only variable absent from this regression table, but present in Tsebelis and Nardi's, is the number of amendments under democracy. As Figure 7.4 showed, adjectives and adverbs correlate with rigidity even without controlling for the

Table 7.4: GDP per capita regressed on proportion of adjectives, constitution length and corruption

Variable	**(1)**	**(2)**	**(3)**	**(4)**	**(5)**	**(6)**
Number of adjectives	–0.44** (0.17)	–0.43** (0.17)	–0.4** (0.16)	–0.4** (0.17)	–0.33** (0.15)	–0.02 (0.13)
Secondary education	–0.17 (0.15)	–0.16 (0.15)	–0.19 (0.14)	–0.19 (0.15)	–0.24* (0.13)	–0.15 (0.1)
Natural resources		–0.13 (0.18)	–0.07 (0.18)	–0.07 (0.19)	–0.11 (0.17)	–0.17 (0.12)
Trade			0.31 (0.18)	0.31 (0.24)	0.19 (0.17)	0.23* (0.13)
FDI				–0.003 (0.25)		
Savings					0.41** (0.15)	0.19 (0.12)
Corruption						–0.52*** (0.11)
Constant	0.78*** (0.12)	0.78*** (0.12)	0.7*** (0.13)	0.7*** (0.14)	0.51*** (0.13)	0.59*** (0.1)
Multiple R^2	0.22	0.23	0.3	0.3	0.45	0.71
Adjusted R^2	0.17	0.15	0.2	0.17	0.35	0.62

Notes: N = 33. Standard errors in parentheses. *** $p < 0.01$; ** $p < 0.05$; * $p < 0.1$. Variance inflation factors for Model 6: LOGADJS (1.40); EDUSEC (1.09); NATRES (1.09); TRADE (1.15); SAVE (1.34); CORRINV (1.63).

number of amendments under democracy. This is not the case with word length (Tsebelis and Nardi 2016: 463). As rigidity correlates with both the number of amendments and the presence of adjectives and adverbs, we can infer that the number of amendments also correlates with the presence of adjectives and adverbs. As such, these should not be included together as explanatory variables in the same model. The number of amendments is not a variable that is needed to test the theory presented here: that adjectives and adverbs affect policy outcomes.

All models, bar Model 6, present statistically significant regression coefficients for the number of adjectives and adverbs. This gives grounds for rejecting the null hypotheses for H4 and H5. Strong findings hold even when other important predictors of economic performance are controlled for. It is only in Model 6 where the *p*-value for adjectives and adverbs creeps above 0.1. Given the strong correlation between the presence of adjectives and adverbs with corruption (see Figure 7.8), there is likely a suppression effect at work here that has affected the *p*-value and the strength of the coefficient, albeit that variance inflation factors for Model 6 do not exceed 2, and thereby suggest no significant multicollinearity.

Clearly, modelling the relationship between textual and contextual elements is complicated by the possibility of endogeneity. Indeed, Tsebelis and Nardi (2016: 475), in their equivalent regression table, also found no significant correlation of word length and GDP when savings and corruption were included. Yet, this evidence suggests that the language of constitutional law has a significant impact on policy outcomes even when controlling for other, rival explanations.

Conclusions

The bottom line is that adjectives and adverbs are '(positively) bad' when used in constitutions. I have specifically argued that constitutional language has changed significantly over time in the world's richest democracies. Besides other textual attributes, such as word length and content, qualifying adjectives and adverbs affect both interpretability and policy outcomes. As such, not only do substantive restrictions in a constitution cause rigidity, but so, too, do under-substantiated restrictions couched in qualified language. Even short constitutions can leave significant latitude to elites. This raises a vital point that word length masks the thousands, even millions, of words of subtext and inter-textual writings that will be encouraged by indeterminacies such as 'necessary and proper'.

There are empirical, moral and policy implications of these findings. The empirical implications are that despite these strong preliminary findings, more research is needed to test links between constitutional language and policy effects. Various research designs besides correlation analysis will likely be fruitful. Qualitative research is well placed to build and test hypotheses regarding the interplay of textual and contextual factors. Natural experiments will also be available in countries with sub-national governments, or when the same country institutes major constitutional reform. Sweden, for instance, significantly increased the length of its constitution in 2009 and 2012 (from 13,635 words to 60,045 words). However, Sweden's newer constitution has a significantly lower proportion of adjectives and adverbs (9.34%, compared to 8.32%). Whether the newer constitution is more empowering of the state or the citizenry is a worthy area of research.

More broadly, research is needed to consider the effects of omitting a clear logic of communication from constitutions. A Polish citizen does not need power or connections to interpret the statement: 'The freedom to express opinions … shall be ensured to everyone'. In Iceland, freedom of expression depends on whether powerful individuals believe that restrictions are 'in the interests of public order or the security of the State, [or] the protection of health or morals, or for the protection of the rights or reputation of others'. The Icelandic version takes language from Article 8 of the *European Convention on Human Rights*, which, in this case, does not provide determinate guidance on when freedom of expression ought to be restricted.

How constitutional engineers should craft solutions to modern times is therefore the moral implication derived from this chapter. By utilising elastic language, the state can potentially address a wider range of citizen demands with greater efficiency. However, broad civic empowerment is traded for efficiency. The longer-term effects of this are, arguably, ineffective for delivering sustained economic growth without corruption. The policy implication of this chapter is therefore that constitutional language is best when kept short and plain. Both substantive restrictions and under-substantiated restrictions create power asymmetries that benefit the state and disempower the citizen. These findings are important for those seeking a codified British constitution. The following chapter scrutinises what efforts have already been taken to codify the ancient practices of British statecraft.

EIGHT

Filling gaps: the Human Rights Act 1998

> The rule of construction which s 3 *Human Rights Act 1998* lays down is quite unlike any previous rule of statutory interpretation. There is no need to identify an ambiguity or absurdity. Compatibility with convention rights is the sole guiding principle. That is the paramount object which the rule seeks to achieve. But the rule is only a rule of interpretation. It does not entitle the judges to act as legislators.
>
> *Lord Hope of Craighead in* R v A (No 2) *2001 UKHL 25 at 108*

> [The *Human Rights Act 1998*] represents an unprecedented transfer of political power from the executive and legislature to the judiciary, and a fundamental re-structuring of our 'political constitution'.
>
> *Ewing 1999: 79*

Introduction

The *Human Rights Act 1998* (HRA) incorporated most of the rights contained in the *European Convention on Human Rights* (ECHR) into UK law. Since it came into force in October 2000, British litigants have been able to pursue their Convention rights through domestic courts. Prior to this, litigants could claim a breach of their Convention rights at the European Court of Human Rights (ECtHR) in Strasbourg. However, this time-consuming and costly process offered limited protection. As such, since the HRA came into force, it has proven a popular tool for litigants and their counsel to take on public and private sector opponents. The aim of this chapter is to assess whether the HRA has worked to correct indeterminacies in other legislation.

In the words of Lord Hope, quoted earlier, the HRA has established a rule of construction 'unlike any' previous rules. Keith Ewing similarly describes the Act as 'unprecedented' and as affecting a 'fundamental re-structuring of our "political constitution"'. A political constitution is one in which the distribution of power in society depends on day-to-day politics, rather than codified principles. The alternative to a political constitution is a legal constitution. The latter is usually promulgated at a critical turning point in a nation's history, and provides if not timeless, then at least durable, principles as to how government works, and to what ends. The HRA was promulgated in the early years of the New Labour government, after 18 years of Conservative government and a period with no major constitutional reform. The late 1990s was not a critical turning point in the nation's history, but it was a time of significant innovation in British constitutionalism.

This chapter assesses the implementation of the HRA. The claims made by Hope and Ewing as to the novelty and impact of the HRA are both analysed critically. Pertinent to the thesis of this book, I ask and answer the following question: has the HRA provided means for agents of Parliament (most notably, judges) to construct a logic of communication? In other words, can the HRA's new rules of construction provide filling material for the various gaps identified in contemporary law? Does this gap-filling achieve a result similar to the national constitutions studied in Chapter Seven? In more technical terms, can confusion created by the text of laws, in context, be resolved by inter-textual references?

The argument presented in this chapter is that the HRA has provided new tools of statutory construction but these are not as innovative as is claimed by Hope and Ewing. To a significant extent, the HRA made explicit what had been implicit: that principles of individual rights underpinned the common law. These principles have, indeed, served to clarify the rule of law where statutory language is indeterminate. However, another key argument for this chapter is that the HRA and ECHR are themselves highly indeterminate. The upshot of which have been difficulties for judges in using the HRA to construct away indeterminacies in other laws. It has also encouraged caution from judges, in the sense of their being unwilling to expand the application of human rights to domestic law, without there being clear justification for doing so. This justification typically takes the form of precedent in common law, or a sufficient statutory basis for action. What we have not seen in the decade or so (2000–10) during which the Act bedded down is evidence of judges using the HRA to change public policies unilaterally. This claim has been made by the government, no doubt frustrated at losing cases relating to, in particular, national security and immigration.

Transcriptions of court cases are used to describe the HRA's development since October 2000. As with Chapter Six (on anti-discrimination and equality law), this chapter utilises a thematic rather than a chronological structure. The themes are those probed throughout the book, with the overarching theme being the effectiveness of policy, as observed through its feasibility (coordination by delegation and accountability) and desirability (communication by coherence and legitimacy). The aim is to demonstrate that neither the feasibility nor the desirability of policy language has been much enhanced by the HRA. Indeterminacies in contemporary legislation will therefore continue to be responsible for policy ineffectiveness.

Theory and description of the HRA

In the language of this book, the courts were empowered by the HRA to fix problems in coordinative and communicative discourses. The HRA offers some tools for clarifying the substance and processes of policy, and it came at a time of constitutional reform when the transparency of policymaking and accountability for decisions taken were prominent goals. Besides the HRA, the turn of the millennium saw other major statutes tidy up some of the constitution's 'hidden wiring' (Hennessy 1998). Also around this time came the enactment of the *Freedom of Information Act 2000*, the modernisation of the House of Commons, the devolution of powers to regional and national assemblies, and the reform of House of Lords membership. Later came the *Equality Acts* discussed in Chapter Six, as well as further reforms to parliamentary committees and statutory codes to govern the civil service and the National Health Service. More subtly, the New Labour governments (1997–2010) increased the publication of explanatory notes for legislation, provided more reader-friendly page layouts and increased the use of pre-legislative scrutiny.

The HRA came at a time of constitutional amendment. However, it was not, itself, a major departure from principles of British statecraft. It could not, therefore, be expected to have comprehensively changed the construction of statutory language by judges. Convention rights had been accessible to British litigants in Strasbourg since 1966, and the contents of the ECHR were drafted post-war with extensive input from British lawyers – notably, Sir David Maxwell-Fyfe – applying well-known common law principles. These principles may predominantly be described as 'negative liberties', being freedoms *from* interference, rather than rights *to* outcomes. Remedies for breaches of rights are also limited at the ECtHR and under the HRA. So, the supposed novelty of the HRA needs to be scrutinised carefully.

Core common law principles aspire, broadly speaking, to equality of treatment and procedural fairness. Law is assumed to apply equally and fairly, unless Parliament explicitly states otherwise (Jowell 1994). Sir Edward Coke, in his famous 1610 ruling for *Dr Bonham's Case*, was wrong in one critical respect, therefore:

> in many cases, the common law will control Acts of Parliament, and sometimes adjudge them to be utterly void; for when an Act of Parliament is against common right and reason, or repugnant, or impossible to be performed, the common law will control it, and adjudge such an Act to be void.

The Glorious Revolution of 1688 and the subsequent *Bill of Rights 1688* made clear that common law could not be used to adjudge any Act of Parliament as 'void'. However, Coke's dictum still applies in so far as Parliament is expected to make laws that conform to the underlying principles of equality and fairness. As such, where there is doubt, the courts will interpret legislation by effectively reading in or reading out words that have no clear meaning. A period of enhanced interpretative creativity from the bench came in the post-war period, not just after the HRA came into force. This use of common law to scrutinise government actions accelerated after the 1960s, just as the law was becoming increasingly indeterminate. As Lord Mustill described, *obiter dictum*, in the *FBU*[85] case:

> [567] To avoid a vacuum in which the citizen would be left without protection against a misuse of executive powers the courts have had no option but to occupy the dead ground in a manner, and in areas of public life, which could not have been foreseen 30 years ago.

[85] *R v Secretary of State for the Home Department ex parte Fire Brigades Union* [1995] 2 AC 513.

This dictum pre-dates the HRA, and the case was one of several other pre-HRA assertions by judges of the rule of law against executive overreach (Feldman 2004; Loveland 2006). Perhaps most notable was the case of *Simms*.[86] The House of Lords stated explicitly that human rights existed in the common law and the HRA would merely enhance judges' abilities to declare these rights. As Lord Hoffmann put it:

> [412] The *Human Rights Act 1998* will make ... changes to this scheme of things. First, the principles of fundamental human rights which exist at common law will be supplemented by a specific text, namely the *European Convention*. But much of the Convention reflects the common law.... That is why the United Kingdom government felt able in 1950 to accede to the Convention without domestic legislative change. So the adoption of the text as part of domestic law is unlikely to involve radical change in our notions of fundamental human rights.

Somewhat contrary to this analysis is Keith Ewing's claim that the HRA effected an unprecedented restructuring of the political constitution. Also, Vernon Bogdanor powerfully argued that the HRA (along with devolution and membership of the European Union [EU]) marked the creation of a 'New British Constitution'. This new constitution is based on fundamental laws that limit Parliament's sovereignty (Bogdanor 2009). I agree that the HRA introduced important new tools of statutory construction, but it must be stressed that the HRA is not higher law, and the judiciary are not able to 'strike down' parliamentary legislation with it. Parliament may either assert that a Bill is considered to be compatible with the Convention (using section 19 HRA), or they may choose not to make such an assertion but mandate that the courts implement the law anyway. For instance, the *Communications Act 2003* did not include a 'declaration of compatibility' (Fenwick 2011). Similarly, the *Prevention of Terrorism Act 2005* allowed the creation of 'derogating control orders' that consciously breached Convention rights. Although no derogating control orders were ever issued, it is clear that Parliament may still legislate against the Convention if it wishes to. On top of which, Parliament may ignore the rulings of the British and Strasbourg courts because there are only limited enforcement mechanisms available

[86] *R v Secretary of State for the Home Department ex parte Simms* [1999] UKHL 33, [2000] 2 AC 115, [1999] 3 All ER 400.

to judges. Famously, a Strasbourg ruling against the blanket ban on prisoners' voting did not lead to any remedial action by domestic courts or Parliament.[87]

By international comparison, the HRA's approach to balancing the sovereignty of Parliament against human rights charts a third way between the maximalist approach of Canada's *Charter of Rights and Freedoms* and the minimalist approach pursued under New Zealand's *Bill of Rights Act*. Canada's model allows courts to nullify primary legislation, whereas New Zealand's model tightly constrains judicial autonomy (Feldman 2004: 397). Ultimately, Parliament remains the heart of the British constitution, and it continues to rely on the strong enforcement of the rule of law.

However, it would be misleading to describe the HRA as quotidian. It has been described in court rulings as a 'constitutional statute' of significant importance. A constitutional statute is one that offers guidance on the forms and functions of government, and it is so important that Parliament is assumed not to want to change it implicitly, but only explicitly. According to orthodox accounts of parliamentary sovereignty, statutes are the highest form of law. Therefore, it is not possible for one Parliament to bind its successors, such that more recent enactments were assumed to repeal by implication any previous enactments that were incompatible. However, in the landmark *Factortame* case,[88] it seemed impossible to the House of Lords that the *Merchant Shipping Act 1988* should have repealed by mere implication the *European Communities Act 1972* (ECA). Orthodox constitutionalism might have led to such a conclusion, but that would have meant Britain leaving the EU, unintentionally. The impact that this would have had encouraged judges to suggest a hierarchy of statute laws. Without the ECA, many other Acts of Parliament would cease to operate. Only explicit repeal of this, and other constitution statutes, was to be acknowledged by the courts. It would not be democratic for Parliament to accidentally imply radical policy change that they were unable to exclaim clearly.

This reasoning was developed in the 2002 case of *Thoburn v Sunderland City Council*.[89] Lord Justice Laws ruled that there are constitutional statutes that cannot be repealed by implication. He

[87] *Hirst v the United Kingdom (No 2)* [2005] ECHR 681. Modest steps were taken in 2017 to address the ECtHR ruling on prisoners' voting but these were not mandated by the court.

[88] *R (Factortame Ltd) v Secretary of State for Transport* [1990] UKHL 7.

[89] [2002] EWHC 195 (Admin).

rejected the submission made by the 'metric martyrs' of Sunderland market that they were not bound to sell their produce in kilograms and grams. Their submission was that the ECA had been partly repealed by the *Weights and Measures Act 1985*, which allowed them to sell in pounds and ounces. Laws LJ countered that Acts central to our understanding of the rule of law, such as the ECA and the devolution Acts, must be considered as superior in importance. Crucially, he included the HRA in this roster of superior statutes. These 'constitutional statutes' do not take their superiority from anything said by Parliament. They are superior to 'ordinary' statutes because so many other laws derive validity and meaning from them. The HRA's importance as a constitutional statute was reconfirmed in 2014 by the Supreme Court's *HS2* ruling.[90]

Despite the HRA's importance, there have been significant 'problems with incorporation' (Clayton and Tomlinson 2003). Some cases have been heavily criticised, leading to accusations that judges are applying the HRA without any clear guiding principles (Edwards 2002). Most notably, there has been dispute concerning the point at which the duty set out in the 'compatible construction rule' in section 3 must give way to the power to issue a declaration of incompatibility under section 4 (Bennion 2009). These teething problems will be discussed in greater detail later. However, the cause of the problems with incorporation can be described here. It is due to the fact that the HRA is itself highly indeterminate. It delegates significant powers to both judges and the government to ensure that the British state conforms to the ECHR. More specifically, there has been a need to resolve four intersecting disputes. First, as regards policy feasibility, questions have arisen as to the autonomous power of the judiciary and, second, the accountability of domestic courts. Debates have concentrated on the extent to which a 'margin of appreciation' should be granted to government decisions, and the extent to which domestic courts should follow ECtHR jurisprudence. Third, as regards desirability, debates have focused on the content of rights and, fourth, their application to private disputes. Particularly problematic to resolve have been clashes of opposing rights, and the incompatibility of individual rights and

[90] As per Lords Neuberger and Mance: '207. The United Kingdom has no written constitution, but we have a number of constitutional instruments. They include Magna Carta, the Petition of Right 1628, the Bill of Rights and (in Scotland) the Claim of Rights Act 1689, the Act of Settlement 1701 and the Act of Union 1707. The European Communities Act 1972, the Human Rights Act 1998 and the Constitutional Reform Act 2005 may now be added to this list'. *R (on the application of HS2 Action Alliance Limited) v Secretary of State for Transport and another* [2014] UKSC 3.

corporate policies. Also notable has been the debate as to whether the HRA has horizontal effect in litigation between private individuals, or just vertical effect between the state and citizens.

These four themes constitute the analytic skeleton of this chapter. They will be considered in turn in the following section on the HRA's impact. Before analysing these themes, it is first necessary to analyse the powers and duties created by the HRA, as well as the language used to frame these. The most notable of the new rules of statutory interpretation are contained in sections 2–4 of the Act. Section 2 states that the judiciary 'must take into account' the jurisprudence of the ECtHR and the ancillary human rights institutions of the Council of Europe. While the use of the modal verb 'must' is plain, the duty to 'take into account' is indeterminate. It is a rule of construction that can be satisfied by judges merely acknowledging the existence of ECtHR jurisprudence. There is no compulsion to act in accordance with this jurisprudence. Judges must, specifically, 'take into account' the rulings of their Strasbourg colleagues when using sections 3 and 4. Section 3 is arguably the most significant change in the rules of statutory interpretation, as Lord Hope argued earlier. The section reads as follows: 'So far as it is possible to do so, primary legislation and subordinate legislation must be read and given effect in a way which is compatible with the Convention rights'. This has been taken to mean that the courts must 'read down' or 'read in' language to resolve a breach of Convention rights in any existing legislation. The language of section 3 is plain in so far as it contains no indeterminate adjectives, has few conjunctions and uses the modal verb 'must'. However, as will be discussed later, its interpretation is confused by its relationship with section 4, which is indeterminately framed. Section 4 sets out the means of resolving an incompatibility between legislation and Convention rights: 'If the court is satisfied that the provision is incompatible with a Convention right, it may make a declaration of that incompatibility'. 'Satisfied' is a psychological state that cannot be identified objectively. Once it has been decided that the court is so satisfied, they 'may' then make a declaration of incompatibility. These declarations do not affect the validity of law. As per section 4(6):

> A declaration under this section ('a declaration of incompatibility') – (a) does not affect the validity, continuing operation or enforcement of the provision in respect of which it is given; and (b) is not binding on the parties to the proceedings in which it is made.

Rather than nullifying legislation, a declaration under section 4 initiates a mechanism under section 10, whereby the government 'may' amend the incompatibility: '(2) If a Minister of the Crown considers that there are compelling reasons for proceeding under this section, he may by order make such amendments to the legislation as he considers necessary to remove the incompatibility'. Any amendments considered 'necessary' on account of 'compelling reasons' must be laid before Parliament for 60 days, and then approved by resolution of both Houses. It is a method of legislative reform that has only ever been used to make minor adjustments to legislation, such as in response to a declaration of incompatibility in *R (Baiai and others) v Secretary of State for the Home Department.*[91] In that case, statutory measures to curtail 'sham' marriages were ruled to be disproportionate and discriminatory by the courts. The government used a section 10 remedial order to remove offending sections. More commonly, declarations of incompatibility have been resolved with wholly new primary legislation, enacted in the usual manner. Declarations of incompatibility are nonetheless rare, and declining in use. There were 29 declarations made between October 2000 and June 2015. Of these, nine were overturned. Only three declarations were made in the 2010–15 Parliament (JCHR 2015).

Nonetheless, the powers and duties established by the HRA are framed in indeterminate language. Not all of the indeterminacies take the forms picked up by my machine-reading program. For instance, judges being 'satisfied' under section 4 hinges on a verb, rather than an adjective. Nonetheless, the HRA contains many indeterminate parts of speech that were picked up in the machine reading. Figure 8.1 displays these indeterminacies in each section of the HRA.

On standing and merit, Section 7 stands out as having the most indeterminate parts of speech. It is a long section that is worth quoting at length:

> (1) A person who claims that a public authority has acted (or proposes to act) in a way which is made unlawful by section 6(1) may – (a) bring proceedings against the authority under this Act in the appropriate court or tribunal.... (2) In subsection (1) (a) 'appropriate court or tribunal' means such court or tribunal as may be determined in accordance with rules.... (3) If the proceedings are brought on an application for judicial review, the applicant

[91] [2006] EWHC 823 and 1454.

Figure 8.1: Indeterminate parts of speech in each section of the HRA

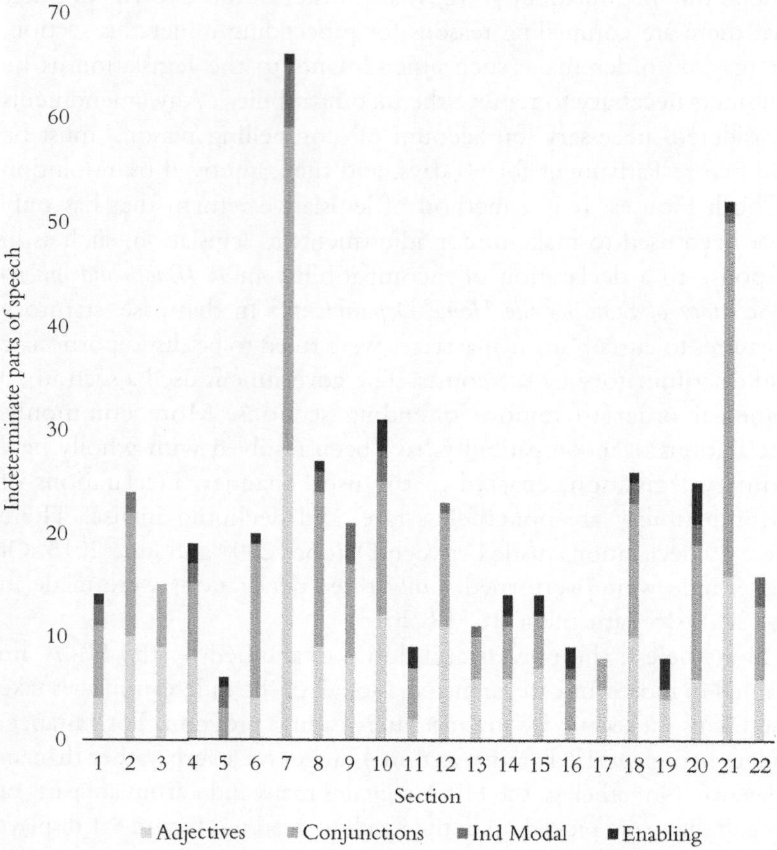

is to be taken to have a sufficient interest in relation to the unlawful act only if he is, or would be, a victim of that act.

(11) The Minister who has power to make rules in relation to a particular tribunal may, to the extent he considers it necessary to ensure that the tribunal can provide an appropriate remedy in relation to an act (or proposed act) of a public authority which is (or would be) unlawful as a result of section 6(1), by order add to – (a) the relief or remedies which the tribunal may grant; or (b) the grounds on which it may grant any of them.

> (12) An order made under subsection (11) may contain such incidental, supplemental, consequential or transitional provision as the Minister making it considers appropriate.

Section 7 relies on several adjectives, conditional conjunctions, indeterminate modal verbs and enabling verbs. It is meant to determine who may bring claims under the HRA. However, constructing this language and ascertaining who 'is, or would be, a victim' is difficult. Having determined victimhood, the potential strength of the HRA is curtailed by its indeterminate stance on remedies in section 8: '8 (3) No award of damages is to be made unless … the court is satisfied that the award is necessary to afford just satisfaction to the person in whose favour it is made'. Added to which, Article 13 of the ECHR (the right to an effective remedy) was not among the rights patriated by the HRA, which segues to considering the language used to frame those rights that were included. Figure 8.2 describes each right and its reliance on indeterminate parts of speech.

Figure 8.2 does not record enabling verbs as the ECHR treaty does not delegate power to agents. It nonetheless contains important sources of indeterminacy. The greatest number of indeterminate parts of speech are contained in Article 6, concerning the right to a fair trial:

> 1 In the determination of his civil rights and obligations or of any criminal charge against him, everyone is entitled to a fair and public hearing within a reasonable time by an independent and impartial tribunal established by law. Judgment shall be pronounced publicly but the press and public may be excluded from all or part of the trial in the interest of morals, public order or national security in a democratic society.

Of course, the overall number of indeterminacies is not the sole consideration. Even very short sentences can introduce significant problems for interpretation. The most notable example of this is Article 3: 'No one shall be subjected to torture or to inhuman or degrading treatment or punishment'. In just 15 words, there are three conjunctions and two adjectives. These are in addition to the conceptual indeterminacy of the noun 'torture'. The point is that both the ECHR and its conduit, the HRA, rely on indeterminate parts of speech that have limited their potential effectiveness in resolving indeterminacies in other laws.

Figure 8.2: Indeterminate parts of speech in each Article of the ECHR included in the HRA

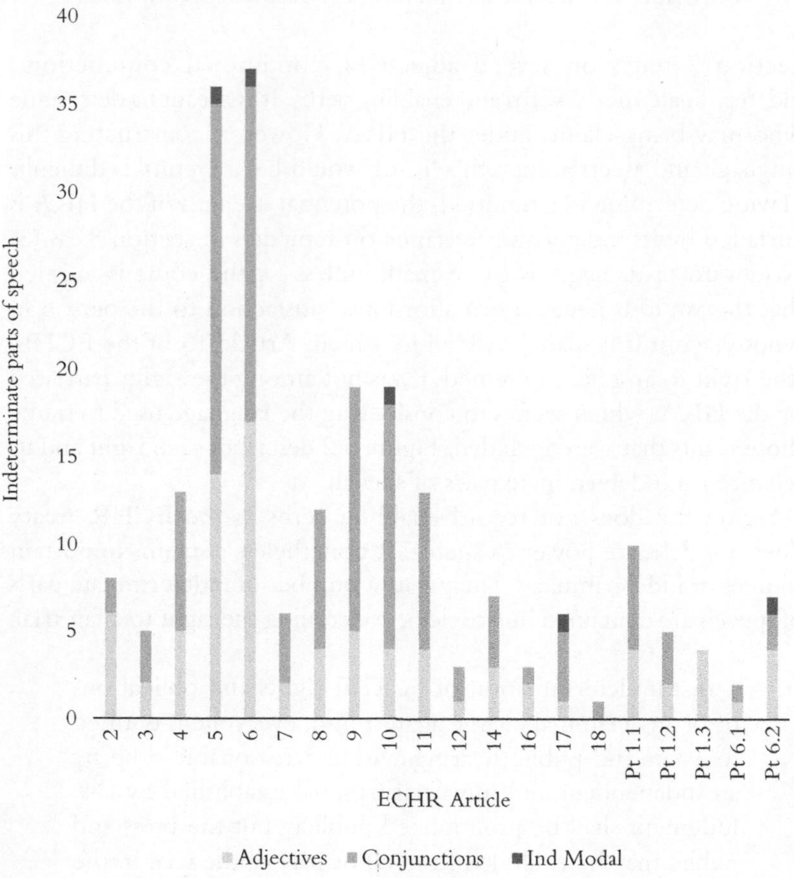

The impact of the HRA

On feasibility

Marking the line between the duty to interpret under section 3 and the power to declare under section 4 has created significant dispute among judges. This debate is relevant here because it concerns when and to what extent courts should defer to democratically accountable agents. The debate therefore considers how state institutions coordinate in applying the law. At the ECtHR, deference to accountable politicians is described as a 'margin of appreciation'. There are circumstances when Convention rights can be breached by politicians, so long as it is in pursuit of a 'legitimate aim'. This is an especially complex problem of coordinative discourse. It affects how powers and duties are distributed between state institutions, and it can implicate the effectiveness of policies. Most notable in this regard have been national security policies. So, has the HRA altered the effectiveness of these policies?

National security is a core competence of executive government. Defending a state's territorial and coastal security, as well as any overseas interests, is a policy space that relies, in part, on secrecy and tactical flexibility. Hence, transparency in national security law is not always conducive to good policy. However, as with any other policy, national security cannot breach the rule of law. This principle is certainly not new to UK law since the HRA. As Lord Atkin stated in his dissentient wartime dictum in *Liversidge v Anderson*[92]:

> [244] In this country, amidst the clash of arms, the laws are not silent. They may be changed, but they speak the same language in war as in peace. It has always been one of the pillars of freedom, one of the principles of liberty for which on recent authority we are now fighting, that the judges are no respecters of persons and stand between the subject and any attempted encroachments on his liberty by the executive, alert to see that any coercive action is justified in law.

Despite this being a minority opinion, it is now recognised as correctly describing the rules of law in wartime (Loveland 2006: 76–9). A more recent test for judges came after the attacks of 11 September 2001, and the subsequent 'War on Terror'. Parliament enacted the *Anti-terrorism, Crime and Security Act 2001* in response. This Act delegated significant discretion to the government to extend counterterrorism measures. However, powers under section 23 of that Act to detain foreign terrorist suspects without charge or trial, pending their deportation, were declared by judges to be incompatible with the Convention:

> (1) A suspected international terrorist may be detained under a provision specified in subsection (2) despite the fact that his removal or departure from the United Kingdom is prevented (whether temporarily or indefinitely) by – (a) a point of law which wholly or partly relates to an international agreement, or (b) a practical consideration.

[92] [1942] AC 206.

This section introduces significant indeterminacy into national security policy by its use of adjectives and adverbs (temporarily, partly, practical), conjunctions (or, or, or, or) and an indeterminate modal verb ('may be detained'). While, in the '*Belmarsh case*' at the House of Lords that considered this section, these indeterminacies were not at issue, a declaration of incompatibility was issued because the power to detain discriminated against foreign terrorist suspects, whereas home-grown terrorists were, in fact, the greater threat.[93] It was ruled that ministers could derogate from the Convention when facing a 'threat to the life of the nation'. However, it was also declared that the government could not respond to such a threat with a policy that fails to achieve its intended purpose and relies on an irrational distinction between foreign and domestic terrorist suspects. The incompatibility was said by judges to be with Article 14 ECHR that guards against unjustifiable discrimination.

Counsel for the government argued that the courts lacked sufficient knowledge to understand the threat posed by foreign terrorist suspects, and some of the judges dissented, claiming that discrimination was not an appropriate basis for declaring against the legislation. Notably, in his dissent, Lord Hoffmann argued that Article 14 was not the point of incompatibility, but Articles 5 and 6 (on restriction of liberty and right to a fair trial) were. Liberty and fair trial procedures can be restricted when pursuing a legitimate aim of defending national security. However, discrimination could not be justified in this instance because it made no sense to use foreign-born terror suspects as scapegoats, giving the appearance of government action when, in fact, a greater home-grown menace was not being managed. The court had accepted by a majority of eight to one that there was a threat, and that it was not in their power to question this. Having accepted that the government was free to conclude that there was a threat, it was then incumbent on the courts to ensure that policy accorded with principles of law. The government had legal cover to detain terrorist suspects without trial, but if that was patently not going to achieve the professed aim, it was not a rational policy.

The conclusions from *Belmarsh* are, first, that the HRA did not clarify indeterminacies in national security policy. Rather, the HRA added further indeterminacies where judges had to reconcile loosely worded rights with ambitious counterterrorism policies. Determination of the law fell back on common law principles: that Parliament is expected to treat all those living under its laws equally,

[93] *A and others v Secretary of State for the Home Department* [2004] UKHL 56.

albeit that the HRA and common law differ in the power available to issue declarations of incompatibility. However, the declarations provided only a partial resolution to policy ineffectiveness in this case. As courts cannot strike down law, the declaration of incompatibility provided time for an alternative policy to be put together. All the while, those who had litigated against the government remained under guard in Belmarsh. To replace section 23, a system of control orders for all terrorist suspects (foreign and domestic) was established under the *Prevention of Terrorism Act 2005* (PTA). These control orders also faced challenge under the HRA, and the courts were again forced to balance a 'margin of appreciation' against the need for legal clarity. In *Secretary of State for the Home Department v. JJ and others*, judges confirmed that six control orders were a nullity because the government did not have sufficient power to make them.[94] It was ruled that undue restrictions on liberty could constitute a breach of Article 5 ECHR. It was concluded that 18 hours of house arrest was a deprivation of liberty, but something less than this could be compatible with the Convention. Lords Hoffmann and Carswell dissented by denying that a court could compare 18 hours of daily house arrest to being in an open prison, as the court's majority had conceived it. They also rejected the analogy of being detained on a remote Italian island, which formed the basis of a similar ECtHR decision.[95] However, the rulings of the High Court, Court of Appeal and House of Lords had to balance executive competence against determinate means of evaluating a deprivation of liberty. These determinate evaluations of deprivation were decided, by judges, to be its 'nature, duration, effects and manner of execution or implementation of the penalty or measure in question'. Again, indeterminate and unworkable national security policy was not much improved by indeterminacies in the HRA, and judges were encouraged to pursue a cautious approach, relying on domestic and foreign precedents.

Similarly, in *Secretary of State for the Home Department v AF and another*, the House of Lords ruled that those suspected of terrorist activities had to be given sufficient information to enable a special advocate to defend them in closed trial.[96] In this case, judges used section 3 of the HRA to read down restrictions in the PTA. By doing so, the court allowed control orders to stay in force but ensured that some basic legal protections were enforced. This balancing act can be construed as

[94] [2007] UKHL 45.

[95] *Guzzardi v Italy* (1980) 3 EHRR 333.

[96] [2009] UKHL 28.

judges taking advantage of legal indeterminacy to manipulate national security policy in accordance with their personal preferences. However, according to Lord Falconer (2006), the former Lord Chancellor, in a government review of the HRA: 'The *Human Rights Act* has had an impact upon the Government's counter-terrorism legislation … [but] The Act has not significantly altered the constitutional balance between Parliament, the Executive and the Judiciary'.

So, as regards the HRA's utility in clarifying inter-institutional discourse, evidence from national security policy suggests that judges had to use the HRA alongside existing legal principles. A further point of analysis as regards inter-institutional coordination is coordination between domestic and international courts. Such coordination is, as mentioned, compelled by the HRA. Section 2 of the HRA calls on judges to 'take into account' judgments or advice handed down by the ECtHR, the Commission (ECmHR) or the Committee of Ministers. Strasbourg jurisprudence is not binding on domestic judges, unlike rulings from the European Court of Justice (CJEU). Nevertheless, Strasbourg case law 'must' be taken into account. This indeterminate section of the HRA alarms critics, who suggest that judges have been handed an open invitation to pick and choose ECtHR jurisprudence to whatever extent they feel best supports their personal objectives.

The most controversial import from Strasbourg and the CJEU is the principle of proportionality. This is a balancing act where a law or executive decision that infringes a right is evaluated in terms of being a 'legitimate aim' that is 'in accordance with law', 'necessary in a democratic society' and therefore 'proportionate'. These concepts are indeterminate, although, as discussed earlier, the balancing of rights and powers is an ancient feature of common law adjudication. However, proportionality review on the continental model was alien to the common law, which instead allowed evaluation of executive decisions according to a narrower test of reasonableness. Since the post-war *Wednesbury* case,[97] it has been recognised that executive action can be technically legal but nullified on account of being 'so outrageous in its defiance of logic or accepted moral standards that no sensible person who had applied his mind to the question to be decided could have arrived at it'.[98]

It had been recognised in 1947 that law can be broken when implemented in an irrational or unjustifiable manner, albeit that this

[97] *Associated Provincial Picture Houses Ltd v Wednesbury Corporation* [1947] 1 KB 223.

[98] Lord Diplock in *Council of Civil Service Unions v Minister for the Civil Service [1983] UKHL 6* at 410.

test was not actually used to settle the *Wednesbury* dispute. Case law from the CJEU and ECtHR applies a more rigorous assessment of proportionality than the narrow *Wednesbury* formula, or even the augmented 'heightened *Wednesbury*' test set out in *R v Ministry of Defence ex parte Smith*.[99] Where, in pre-HRA public law, judicial review of a government decision would look to its reasonableness, at the CJEU and ECtHR, analysis turns on the legitimacy of policy and whether an infringement of rights could be justified. Such a balancing of policy against rights would be difficult to incorporate into the British tradition, where no law supersedes parliamentary statute.[100] Therefore, the most appropriate judicial response was not to adopt proportionality on the same lines as the ECtHR, but to 'take it into account' and assimilate it as an extension of *Wednesbury*. Specifically, judges added rights to the calculus of reasonableness. As Lord Steyn put it in *R v Secretary of State for the Home Department, ex parte Daly*[101]:

> [26–27] There is a material difference between the *Wednesbury* and *Smith* grounds of review and the approach of proportionality applicable in respect of review where convention rights are at stake.... The starting point is that there is an overlap between the traditional grounds of review and the approach of proportionality. Most cases would be decided in the same way whichever approach is adopted. But the intensity of review is somewhat greater under the proportionality approach ... the doctrine of proportionality may require the reviewing court to assess the balance which the decision maker has struck, not merely whether it is within the range of rational or reasonable decisions.

Judges therefore assimilated proportionality review cautiously for lack of clear instructions as to how far they were to take this methodology into account (Loveland 2006: 759–61). Therefore, in clearing up coordinative discourse between institutions, old common law principles were repurposed, and indeterminacies in the HRA stunted its discourse-repairing potential.

---

[99] [1996] QB 517.

[100] See Lords Roskill and Ackner in *R v Secretary of State for the Home Department, ex parte Brind* [1991] UKHL 4.

[101] [2001] UKHL 26.

On desirability

Similarly, as regards communicative discourse, the HRA has introduced some incoherencies and illegitimacy to law. This has further diminished its potential as a tool for repairing indeterminacies in other laws. Only through assimilation with well-worn common law principles have judges been able to make substantial use of the HRA. The HRA's most significant sources of incoherence and illegitimacy have taken four forms. The first is the unclear point at which judges switch from a duty to protect rights, to a power to make a difference. The second is the question as to whether only vertical protection (between state and citizen) or also horizontal protection (between two or more citizens) is provided. The third, and relatedly, is the balancing of individual rights against corporate policies. The fourth is the clashing of mutually exclusive rights between individuals. The first and second factors look more to the HRA's internal coherence, to which the third and fourth factors add consideration of its legitimate operation. Where coherence looks to whether the HRA is comprehensible, legitimacy looks to whether its applications were demanded.

Demarcating the courts' duties and powers has already been analysed with regard to coordinating state action on rights. From here, analysis broadens to consider how the courts' distinction of their duties and powers has affected the public's enjoyment of those rights. Section 3 imposes a duty on judges by stating that they 'must', 'so far as it is possible to do so … read and given effect' to Convention rights when interpreting primary and secondary legislation. Section 4 states that 'If the court is satisfied that [a] provision is incompatible with a Convention right, it may make a declaration of incompatibility'. The point at which the duty under section 3 disappears and is replaced by the power under section 4 is not stated. This indeterminacy as to when it is no longer possible to read and give effect to Convention rights forced judges to determine this for themselves by relying on established principles of justice.

Two of the earliest cases to tackle the duty-to-power problem were *R v A (No 2)*[102] and *R v Lambert*,[103] which were handed down by the House of Lords within two months of each other in 2001. Both were cases in criminal law. *R v A* concerned the admissibility of evidence of past consensual sex in a rape trial. *R v Lambert* interrogated the burden of proof to be placed on an individual caught in possession of

[102] [2001] UKHL 25.

[103] [2001] UKHL 37.

drugs. In *R v A* the court ruled that section 41(3) of the *Youth Justice and Criminal Evidence Act 1999*, if construed according to traditional methods of statutory interpretation, challenged a defendant's right to a fair trial under Article 6 ECHR. However, the case was dismissed pending a reconsideration of the facts by a lower court. There was nonetheless a difficult obiter debate among the judges concerning the line between sections 3 and 4. Principal disputants were Lords Steyn and Hope. The former proposed that section 3 should be used not only to 'read down' language to ensure compatibility, but also to potentially 'read in' words:

> [44] In accordance with the will of Parliament as reflected in s 3 it will sometimes be necessary to adopt an interpretation which linguistically may appear strained. The techniques to be used will not only involve the reading down of express language in a statute but also the implication of provisions. A declaration of incompatibility [under section 4] is a measure of last resort. It must be avoided unless it is plainly impossible to do so. If a clear limitation on convention rights is stated in terms, such an impossibility will arise.

This argument was rejected by Lord Hope, who instead suggested that Parliament be allowed to resolve the incompatibility:

> [58] As I said in *R v DPP, ex p Kebeline*, it is appropriate in some circumstances for the judiciary to defer, on democratic grounds, to the considered opinion of the elected body as to where the balance is to be struck between the rights of the individual and the needs of society.

Lord Hope opposed the idea of 'reading in' language as he argued that it tipped over from interpretation to legislation. However, when it came to *R v Lambert*, his position was that 'reading in' was possible but needed careful handling:

> [80] So far as possible judges should seek to achieve the same attention to detail in their use of language to express the effect of applying section 3(1) as the parliamentary draftsman would have done if he had been amending the statute. It ought to be possible for any words that need to be substituted to be fitted in to the statute as if they had been inserted there by amendment. If this cannot be done

> without doing such violence to the statute as to make it unintelligible or unworkable, the use of this technique will not be possible. It will then be necessary to leave it to Parliament to amend the statute and to resort instead to the making of a declaration of incompatibility.

One can see that the conceptual distinction between interpretation and amendment was blurred. However, it was not an unknown problem before 2000, and earlier precedents were used to resolve indeterminacies in the HRA. A notable precedent was *Fitzpatrick v Sterling Housing Association Ltd*, decided just before the HRA came into force.[104] The House of Lords ruled by a majority that Schedules to the *Rent Act 1977* should be read as if 'living with the original tenant as his or her wife or husband' in paragraph 2(2) included homosexual couples. In a strikingly similar case under the HRA, the same reading in of words was achieved under the guidance of section 3. This case – *Ghaidan v Godin-Mendoza* – became a central precedent in the use of section 3.[105] However, reading 'as if … wife or husband' to include non-heterosexual relationships was an interpretative step taken before the HRA came into force.

Besides *Ghaidan*, other test cases determined when section 4 should be engaged, and when no rights protection could be offered. Notable were the cases of *Bellinger*[106] and *Wilkinson*.[107] In *Bellinger*, a transsexual woman sought to have her marriage recognised under section 11(c) of the *Matrimonial Causes Act 1973*. In this case, the House of Lords issued a declaration of incompatibility, claiming that they could not use the 'compatible construction rule' in section 3. Specifically, it was considered impossible to 'read in' or 'read down' words from the gender recognition test performed at birth that was used in those days to recognise marriages between a 'male' and a 'female'. In *Wilkinson*, a bereaved husband was unable to have the term 'widower' read into section 262 of the *Income and Corporation Taxes Act 1988*, which provided tax relief to widows. Use of section 3 to resolve *Ghaidan*, section 4 to resolve *Bellinger* and neither to resolve *Wilkinson* is evidence of judges applying well-worn techniques of statutory construction under the HRA. First, in *Ghaidan*, the use

---

104 [1999] All ER (D) 1171.

105 [2004] 2 AC 557.

106 *Bellinger v Bellinger* [2003] UKHL 21.

107 *R (on the application of Wilkinson) v Inland Revenue Commissioners* – [2005] All ER (D) 68 (May) [2005] UKHL 30.

of section 3 was 'possible' because a very similar interpretation had been used in *Fitzpatrick*, and the disputed legislation was sufficiently indeterminate by catering to any couples living 'as his or her wife or husband'. To live 'as' a wife or husband implies fulfilling a role associated with those labels, without necessarily being a literal wife or husband.[108] Parliament could have adopted a more determinable construction, such as 'being his or her wife or husband', to prevent the courts from reading in language. However, in *Bellinger*, the language to be interpreted was: 'A marriage celebrated ... shall be void on the following grounds ... that the parties are not respectively male and female'. There is no indeterminacy here because Parliament provided specific (albeit contestable) definitions for male and female as being determined at birth. *Wilkinson* concerned the 'Widows' bereavement allowance', and if the courts had read in 'widower', it would have had dramatic repercussions for the tax code and other social policies where discrimination was pursued to address specific gendered inequalities. The reason for denying a declaration of incompatibility was justified by the court on the grounds that the infringement of a right to enjoy property (under Article 1 of the First Protocol ECHR) was justified in this case in pursuit of legitimate and democratic aims.

Therefore, despite early problems in resolving the demarcation issues in *R v A*, *R v Lambert*, *Ghaidan*, *Bellinger* and *Wilkinson*, there are now clear principles of statutory interpretation that accord with the traditional constitutional role of the judiciary – of maximising certainty in the rule of law through interpretation rather than legislation. As Aileen Kavanagh (2009: 280) has argued:

> the power given to the courts under sections 3 and 4 is a constitutional power, because it enables the courts to shape the content of the human rights guarantees. Not only is it a power to enforce those rights and comply with them in common law adjudication, it is also a power to enforce those rights against the elected branches of government if required. The performance of this constitutional role is one which has traditionally been exercised by the courts, but has been enhanced by the HRA in various subtle ways, most notably in giving the courts a greater sense of legitimacy in opposing and limiting the law-making powers of Parliament. So the courts did not acquire a novel kind

---

108 See Lord Hoffmann in *Wilkinson* at 16–18.

> of power by the enactment of the HRA – rather, their existing constitutional role was strengthened and enhanced.

Lord Nicholls made a similar argument as to the reconciliation of common law and HRA interpretation techniques in *Re S*[109]:

> [40] The area of real difficulty lies in identifying the limits of interpretation in a particular case. This is not a novel problem. If anything, the problem is more acute today than in past times. Nowadays courts are more 'liberal' in the interpretation of all manner of documents. The greater the latitude with which courts construe documents, the less readily defined is the boundary. What one person regards as sensible, if robust, interpretation, another regards as impermissibly creative. For present purposes it is sufficient to say that a meaning which departs substantially from a fundamental feature of an Act of Parliament is likely to have crossed the boundary between interpretation and amendment.

Lord Nicholls' claim that statutory interpretation has become more 'liberal' chimes with this book's thesis. Judges need to be more creative because identifying the 'fundamental feature' of increasingly indeterminate legislation is difficult. Besides these difficulties in finding coherence between sections 3 and 4, there has been difficulty in interpreting section 6. This has relevance for whether Convention rights under the HRA can only apply vertically (between state and citizen) or whether there can be horizontal application (between private citizens). Section 6 describes the Act's reach:

> (1) It is unlawful for a public authority to act in a way which is incompatible with a Convention right.... (3) In this section 'public authority' includes – (a) a court or tribunal, and (b) any person certain of whose functions are functions of a public nature.

Parliament was explicitly excluded from the definition of a public authority. This was to ensure that no cases could be brought against the sovereign in court, thereby breaching its privileges under Article 9

[109] *Re W (children: care plan) Re S (children: care plan)* [2002] UKHL 10 All ER (D) 212 (Mar).

of the *Bill of Rights 1688*. Nevertheless, Parliament gave scant guidance as to what 'functions of a public nature' are. This has forced judges to remove the indeterminacy by relying on past precedent.

In pre-HRA cases, the extent to which private interactions could be subject to public law had developed a relatively stable jurisprudence. Cases such as *R v Panel on Take-overs and mergers ex parte Datafin*[110] established a principle that where a private body takes on a role that would have to be performed by the government in its absence, that role can be considered essentially a public function. Also, the courts have long recognised that, for consistency's sake, they cannot totally compartmentalise public and private law rights as it creates an arbitrary division in the rule of law that is not in the tradition of the common law (Woolf 1995). This is fundamentally different to civil law systems, such as in continental Europe, where public and private law are often administered by different courts, let alone different laws. Therefore, the HRA does not mark a critical turning point in the development of English public law. It made explicit what had been implicit: that private relations can be subject to public rights. Indeed, indeterminacy in the HRA forced judges into creating new ligatures to link Convention rights to pre-existing rules of law. As Gavin Phillipson (2011) has argued:

> given the paradox set up by section 6(1) and (3)'s inclusion of judges within those public authorities bound to act compatibly with the Convention rights taken together with the Act's presumably deliberate silence on private law and common law, we must turn to existing constitutional principles governing the role of the judiciary, which provide the 'constitutional constraint' of incrementalism; this supplies the necessary definition of and limitation upon the judicial role in developing common law compatibly with the Convention rights.

These incoherencies on the law's face have had implications for its operation, and these operational difficulties have had especial impact on the HRA's legitimacy. First, there has been difficulty in balancing Convention rights against corporate policies. In the case of *Sakira*, a young woman practising Sikhism was supported by the courts in her

110 [1987] QB 815.

fight to wear a religiously significant bracelet to school (the Kara).[111] However, in the case of *Denbigh*,[112] a young woman practising Islam could not use the HRA to defend her choice to wear a long loose-fitting coat to school (the Jilbab). Also in *Eweida*,[113] a woman working for British Airways lost her case to be allowed to wear a crucifix at work. These decisions, when taken together, appear arbitrary and inconsistent. In reality, each case was decided differently because of difficulties in applying the HRA. The ruling in *Sakira* relied predominantly on anti-discrimination law in the *Race Relations Act 1976* (as amended), rather than utilising the HRA. Counsel for Sakira avoided heavy reliance on Convention rights because of a string of failed attempts to use the HRA to defend individual clothing choices against corporate clothing policies.[114] The Act simply did not work consistently and was eclipsed by other pre-existing laws.

However, of course, not all uncertainty in law encourages restraint from judges. Incorporating Convention rights did lead to some legal innovations, but these were not expected and therefore not fully legitimised. The most prominent innovations came in privacy law, under the auspices of section 6, described earlier. Developments came as a result of some determinate language in the HRA that created unexpected consequences as a result of indeterminacy in the ECHR. Section 6 makes plain that: 'It is unlawful for a public authority to act in a way which is incompatible with a Convention right … [and] "public authority" includes – (a) a court or tribunal'. The courts, as a public authority, are compelled to apply Convention rights to all cases, including those with only private disputants. However, this compulsion to act is complicated by the clash between Article 8 ECHR, which sets out a right to a 'private and family life', and Article 10, which establishes 'freedom of expression':

> 8 (1) Everyone has the right to respect for his private and family life, his home and his correspondence. (2) There shall be no interference by a public authority with the exercise of this right except such as is in accordance with the law and is necessary in a democratic society.

---

111 *R(Sarika Watkins-Singh) v Aberdare Girls High School Governors and Rhondda Cynon Taf Unitary Authority* [2008] EWHC 1865 (Admin).

112 *R(SD) v The Governors of Denbigh High School* [2007] 1 AC 100.

113 *Eweida v British Airways* [2010] EWCA Civ 80.

114 See also *R (on the application of Playfoot) v Governing Body of Millais School* [2007] ELR 484; and *R (on the application of X v Head Teacher and Governors of Y School* [2008] 2 All ER 249.

> 10 (1) Everyone has the right to freedom of expression. This right shall include freedom to hold opinions and to receive and impart information and ideas without interference by public authority.... (2) The exercise of these freedoms ... may be subject to such formalities, conditions, restrictions or penalties as are prescribed by law and are necessary in a democratic society.

In a number of cases, privacy law developed rapidly by judges seeking to resolve this clash of rights. For instance, in *Mosley v News Group Newspapers*,[115] Mr Justice Eady used the HRA to award damages to Max Mosley, the former head of Formula One's governing body, after he was alleged to have committed acts of sadomasochism with prostitutes by the *News of the World* newspaper. The response from Paul Dacre, editor of *The Daily Mail*, was to accuse Eady J of fundamentally altering law 'with a stroke of his pen' (Holmwood and Fitzsimmons 2008). This argument mistakenly assumes that there was determinable law for Eady J to apply.

Even more controversial was the development of 'super-injunctions' in privacy law. These were injunctions against reporting a story where even the existence of any injunctions could not be reported. It was a meta-injunction: an injunction against disclosing an injunction. This could have resulted, hypothetically, in an individual being held in contempt of court for revealing the existence of an injunction but not being allowed to know the reasons for their incarceration because of the injunction. It could therefore have led to secret trials. Some pre-HRA case law prefigured the development of super-injunctions.[116] However, the HRA significantly extended their development due to the indeterminate mix of Articles 8 and 10, taken together with section 6 and, the hitherto unmentioned, section 12 on freedom of expression:

> (1) This section applies if a court is considering whether to grant any relief which, if granted, might affect the exercise of the Convention right to freedom of expression.... (3) No such relief is to be granted so as to restrain publication before trial unless the court is satisfied that the applicant is likely to establish that publication should not be allowed.

115 [2008] EWHC 1777.

116 *American Cyanamid Co. v Ethicon Ltd* [1975] 2 WLR 316, [1975] AC 396, [1975] UKHL 1.

This language utilises several indeterminacies that force statistical, rather than logical, reasoning. This is especially in so far as no relief will be granted unless judges are 'satisfied that the applicant is likely to establish that publication should not be allowed'. To cut through these indeterminacies, judges provided evidence of trying to reconcile the HRA with existing rules of law. As can be seen from Eady J in a case concerning a celebrity chef[117]:

> [5] … it is clear that an applicant who seeks to restrain publication of personal information will need to approach the matter in two stages. First, it is necessary to demonstrate that he has a reasonable expectation of privacy in respect of the subject-matter in question, having regard to Article 8 of the *European Convention on Human Rights*. If that hurdle is overcome, it next has to be shown that there is no countervailing public interest sufficient to outweigh his right to protect that information. At the second stage, the court will apply what has been termed 'an intense focus' to the particular circumstances of the case, in order to arrive at a determination of where the balance lies between the competing rights concerned.

In this particular case, Gordon Ramsay did not establish a strong enough case on Convention grounds, and his request for a super-injunction was declined. Assessing where public interest and private lives should be balanced is a standard common law solution to such matters. It was engaged in this case when the Article 8 hurdle was not overcome. Balancing rights in this manner is complex and can be controversial, but it is the essence of adjudication. This has only been made more complex and controversial as a result of indeterminate legislation. These consequences of indeterminate language in the HRA were not desired, in that they were not fully anticipated. Coordinative and communicative language in the HRA was not capable of establishing meaning without heavy reliance by judges on well-worn principles of law.

---

[117] *KGM v News Group Newspapers Ltd and others* [2010] EWHC 3145 (QB).

Conclusion

The principal question posed for this chapter was: has the HRA provided means for agents of Parliament (most notably, judges) to construct a logic of communication? A subsidiary question was whether new rules of statutory construction provided a legal base onto which Britain's 'political constitution' has been tethered. My argument was that due to indeterminacies in the HRA and ECHR, these new tools of construction have themselves needed to be carefully constructed by judges. They have not, therefore, imposed wholly new rules of law onto indeterminate policies. Indeed, a claim that prior to the HRA, there was subordination of law to politics is flawed. Parliamentary sovereignty cannot exist independently of the rule of law. For Parliament's laws to have their intended effects and be seen as legitimate depends on their comprehensibility and consistent application. In Britain, where there is a single source of public law and no codified constitution or civil code, the precise meaning of the sovereign's utterances must be clearly understood or else its intentions will be mistaken or ignored. Therefore, the idea that there can be a political constitution that does not depend on clarity in the law is arguably mistaken. The rule of law and parliamentary sovereignty are mutually supporting (Phillipson 2011).

The common law judge must integrate relevant law with principles of justice so as to resolve the case at hand. This is the crux of what Neil MacCormick (2005) described as 'post-positivism', where gaps and incoherencies in 'positive' law are corrected by judges applying theory and rhetoric. In a similar vein, David Robertson (2010) argued that judges increasingly need to act as political theorists for want of clear guidance from politicians. The 'compatible construction rule' and declarations of incompatibility fit with these descriptions of modern law. Judges read law so 'far as it is possible to do so' in accordance with Convention rights. When it is impossible to declare what the law says, judges declare that it says nothing coherent at all and issue a declaration of incompatibility. So, as Ronald Dworkin (1986: 8–9) has argued, the task of the judiciary is to establish what the law ought to mean in situations where the sovereign power has left doubt:

> the law may be silent because the pertinent institutional decision stipulated only vague guidelines by declaring, for example, that a landlord must give a widow a 'reasonable' time to pay her rent.... Then the judge has no option but to exercise a discretion to make new law by filling gaps

> where the law is silent and making it more precise where it is vague.

Judges do, clearly, have an important role in repairing logics of communication. They improve the feasibility, the desirability and, thereby, the effectiveness of public policies. This enhanced role for judges is a result not only of complex policies leading to clashing outcomes, but also of a degree of ambivalence with regard to human rights. To a certain extent, the HRA was part of a modernisation agenda that saw keeping up with the world on such matters as an end in itself. Besides the modernisation of domestic law, there was also a cosmopolitan spur (Posner 2003). In other words, there was the desire to connect British human rights practices to, in particular, European norms. However, modernising and 'keeping up with the Joneses' do not in themselves lead to clear, coherent human rights protection. These motives have instead compounded the confusion felt by judges and citizens, who see rights both lauded and castigated by policymakers. Lord Sumption SCJ made much this point just prior to his elevation to the Supreme Court bench:

> The tendency of the courts to intervene in the making of 'macro-policy' has become more pronounced.... The Strasbourg court has treated the Convention not just as a safeguard against arbitrary and despotic exercises of state power, but as a template for most aspects of human life. These include many matters which are governed by no compelling moral considerations one way or the other.[118]

While the judiciary faced difficulties in interpreting Convention rights, it would be wrong to say that their decisions were tantamount to legislation, rather than interpretation. Indeterminacy in law does not release judges to rule as they please. Constraints on judges encourage caution. Judges try to avoid being overruled at a higher court for some flight of fancy; far better to play it safe and tether a ruling to clearly recognised principles of law. The mere fact that different rights claims clash is also not enough to contend that judges can make law according to their personal interests. Common law is founded on the adversarial principle. It is a principle that would quickly be delegitimised if judges were not seen to be applying the law equally and fairly. Therefore, the HRA has not initiated a new constitutional

[118] F.A. Mann lecture in Lincoln's Inn, November 2011.

paradigm, but rather reinvigorated clashes that have been common law mainstays for centuries. Research showed a substantial increase in human rights litigation under the HRA in its early years of operation: as many as 37.5% of cases brought to the House of Lords between 2002 and 2008 were related to the HRA (Blom-Cooper et al 2009: 546). Many of the early litigations brought under the HRA were speculative attempts by counsel to test the new legislation, and we cannot accurately measure what the comparative figure was before October 2000. While there was no HRA, it would be wrong to say that there were no human rights-related cases (Clayton and Tomlinson 2003). Indeed, where Parliament has issued indeterminate commands, it has always been up to the courts to cobble together a workable rule of law. This construction of a logic of communication is as old as the common law itself and was not changed by one of the more indeterminate Acts of the new millennium.

NINE

Conclusions

> (1) The Chimney Sweepers and Chimneys Regulation Acts, 1840 and 1864, the Chimney Sweepers Act, 1875, and the Chimney Sweepers Act, 1894, are hereby repealed.
> (2) This Act may be cited as the Chimney Sweepers Acts (Repeal) Act, 1938, and shall not apply to Scotland or to Northern Ireland.
>
> *Chimney Sweepers Acts (Repeal) Act 1938*

> (1) The Treasury or the Secretary of State may make provision by regulations requiring institutions to which this section applies to provide information about the exercise of voting rights attached to shares to which this section applies.... (5) Regulations under this section may make different provision for different descriptions of institution, different descriptions of shares and for other different circumstances.
>
> *Section 1,277 of the Companies Act 2006*

Sovereignty is as sovereignty does

An apocryphal story is told of Stalin's choice of design for the Hotel Moskva. In the midst of interwar purges, a nervy architect presented two visions to the Chairman. Instead of choosing, Stalin grunted, registering no preference. Not wanting to displease his mercurial leader, the architect built a hotel according to both styles. It was one building constructed in two totally different halves. This absurd result came about because the leader's will was incomprehensible. To be sovereign, it is necessary to act like a sovereign. More specifically, absolute power must be at least partly comprehensible if it is to be usable. Stalin could not have ruled effectively through grunts alone.

This is also true for the Queen-in-Parliament. The sovereign increasingly fails to communicate its will in clear terms. To remedy this, agents of Parliament try to infer intent, rather than make messes like the hapless architect. Sovereignty will diminish or deform without comprehensible language. Comprehensibility depends on rules of recognition, which are not fixed, but change with shifts in context and communal norms (Hart 1961). This means that the government, administrators and judges are constantly groping to interpret public reason, and this task is made all the more difficult by Parliament's increasing resort to indeterminate language.

Quoted at the opening of this chapter are, respectively, the shortest and longest statutes found from the 6,635 Acts surveyed in these pages. The *Chimney Sweepers Acts (Repeal) Act 1938* is just a single section long. This is exceptionally rare. Only six other statutes in 115 years were similarly diminutive. By sharp contrast, the *Companies Act 2006* rolls out its instructions through 1,300 sections. On its own, the *Companies Act* contains more sections than were enacted in 1900, 1901 and 1902 combined; that was across 134 separate pieces of legislation. As noted, the changes in legislative language have been not just in terms of volume, but also in style and comprehensibility. Section 1,277 of the *Companies Act*, quoted earlier, demonstrates the degree of indeterminacy that Parliament is capable of, even from an exceptionally detailed law. By regulations, the government may 'make different provision for different descriptions of institution, different descriptions of shares and for other different circumstances'. This is not a rule of law that would be recognisable to previous generations of lawmakers (Thring 1902). There is nothing typically 'rule-like' in its language. Notably, it does not outline concept, action and consequence in a logical succession of points. Rather, it allows the government to determine rules according to 'different circumstances'. It is not law that establishes a standard, but law that enables policy executives to work out standards as they go. It is, therefore, an analogic form of communication, rather than language based on logic.

The consequences of this diminished 'logic of communication' on policy have been significant (Schmidt 2008). We have seen a 14-fold increase in the likelihood of government defeat in immigration appeals caused by conditional conjunctions. We have seen evidence that as many as 50,000 individuals were deemed not to be in 'priority need' of housing after the introduction of adjectives to homelessness law. With regard to anti-discrimination and equality law, we have seen over 800 regulations in secondary legislation introduce 400 substantive amendments to primary law, as well as 116 new offences and umpteen new indeterminacies. We have even seen evidence of a correlation between the number of adjectives in constitutional law and sluggish economic performance and increased corruption around the world. Any supposed benefits of indeterminate law – most notably, in policy flexibility – must be considered against the effects wrought on delegation, accountability, coherence and legitimacy. In other words, the feasibility and desirability of policies are directly implicated by the language used to frame them (Pollitt and Bouckaert 2004).

This concluding chapter begins with a brief restatement of the book's central argument, and discussion of its implications. After which, some broader historical lessons are drawn, with particular interrogation of the Westminster model. Finally, moral implications are considered, along with some possible solutions to a failing logic of communication.

The argument and its implications

Four principal questions were asked in the introductory chapter. First, how has Parliament's use of language changed? Second, why has Parliament's use of language changed? Third, what impact have the changes had on policy? Fourth, what can and has been done to address indeterminate legislation in the UK and overseas?

With regards to how Parliament's language has changed, the principal contribution of this book has been its description, in unusual detail, of the increasing use of indeterminate parts of speech in legislation. Previous works on political history have produced rich narratives of events, with focuses on individual actors and policy environments. These histories have been unimpeachably useful, but somewhat overlooked has been the medium through which actors have propelled policy change. The quantitative history offered in Chapters Two and Three of this book demonstrated significant changes in Parliament's use of language. These changes are summarised in Figure 9.1, which displays the sum of all four indeterminate parts of speech measured: adjectives and adverbs; conditional conjunctions; indeterminate modal verbs; and enabling verbs.

Figure 9.1 displays results from machine reading 41.5 million words of legislation, and these results describe increases in both the volume of legislation enacted and the reliance on indeterminate parts of speech. These changes came slowly and subtly, such that they were barely perceptible. It is through a wide-angle lens, capable of

Figure 9.1: Changes in the number of sections, and indeterminacies per section enacted by Parliament, 1900–2015

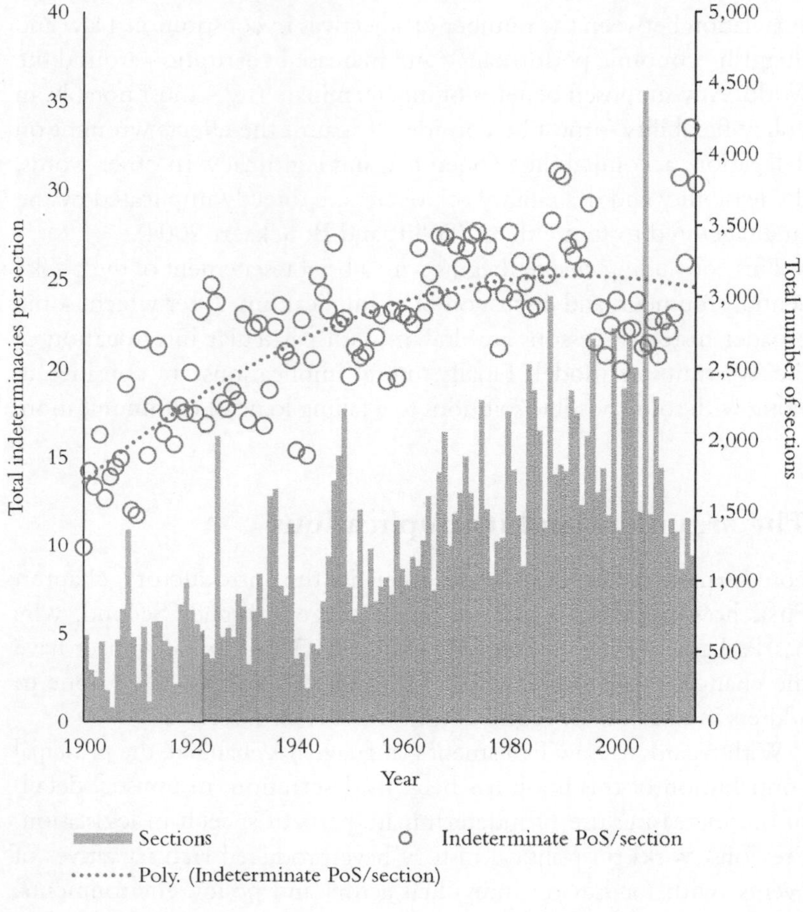

viewing all legislation across over a century, that the scale of change can be appreciated. As hypothesised, because of its indeterminacy, legislation does not mark the end of the political fight. Parliament's use of language does not typify a neat process where politics morphs into law. The texts of law remain intensely political. This is not just the case for so-called 'Henry VIIIth clauses', where power to amend primary legislation has been delegated by Parliament to the government. See, for example, section 5(3) of the *Extradition Act 1989*:

> (3) Her Majesty may by Order in Council direct that this Act shall have effect in relation to the return of persons to, or in relation to persons returned from, any designated

> Commonwealth country or any colony subject to such exceptions, adaptations or modifications as may be specified in the Order.

This section allows primary law to be changed by Order in Council. Furthermore, it is not just the power to change law that affects policy outcomes; also important are more subtle uses of adjectives, conjunctions and verbs. This includes the use of conjunctions in immigration law or framing a duty to house with the adjective 'vulnerable'.

Driving these changes have been increases in the size and responsibilities of the British state. Size is an objective measure, while responsibility is subjective. They therefore represent the 'is' and 'ought' of modern British politics. Size can roughly be measured as the share of gross domestic product (GDP) that is spent by the state, which has increased significantly in post-war Britain (Foster and Plowden 1996: 3–4). The responsibility of the state concerns expectations of what it ought to be achieving. This has also expanded, with voters increasingly looking to government as the primary solution to economic and social problems. However, what the state is capable of has not kept pace with expectations of what it ought to be doing. The consequences are policy instability as governments try to manage voter demands as far as possible and rival parties trade in unrealistic expectations. Large quantities of indeterminate legislation offer both intrinsic and functional utilities to struggling governments. Working to produce large volumes of indeterminate law is intrinsically useful in so far as it gives an appearance of activity while not committing the government to many specific policy constraints. Also, there is functional utility here because when actual policy change is needed, indeterminate law facilitates quick and cheap adaptations. Indeterminate law can therefore suit both structural and ideological needs, with structural needs being the gap between what is demanded and what can be delivered, and ideological needs being any desires to 'roll back the state' and enable individual ministers to decide how best to respond to changing circumstances.

This is not to say that post-war state expansion has been inexorable and will continue. Indeed, the data in Figure 9.1 suggest that the volume and indeterminacy of legislation declined at the turn of the millennium. This is likely to have been the result of New Public Management reforms and the devolution of powers pushed during the 1990s. Nonetheless, it is clear that the state expanded relative to pre-war levels, and despite peaks and troughs, there has been an upward trend. Separately, it would also be implausible to conclude that governments have always been incapable of satisfying voter demands. Mine is not a deterministic argument, but a probabilistic one. Given that there has been a widening gap between voter demand and state capacity to supply policy, the use of indeterminate language to frame state powers is a likely and common consequence, but not the only consequence.

Figure 9.2 demonstrates relative changes in the use of language. Displayed in Figure 9.2 are z-scores. These z-scores describe distances from the mean at various points in time. What the graph shows is that the mean level of indeterminacy (z-score = 0) came in the late 1950s. This tipping point in language use fits the theory: that post-war changes in policy were consummated with increasingly indeterminate instructions from Parliament. The graph also shows, as theorised, that

Figure 9.2: Relative changes in indeterminate parts of speech (PoS) per section, 1900–2015

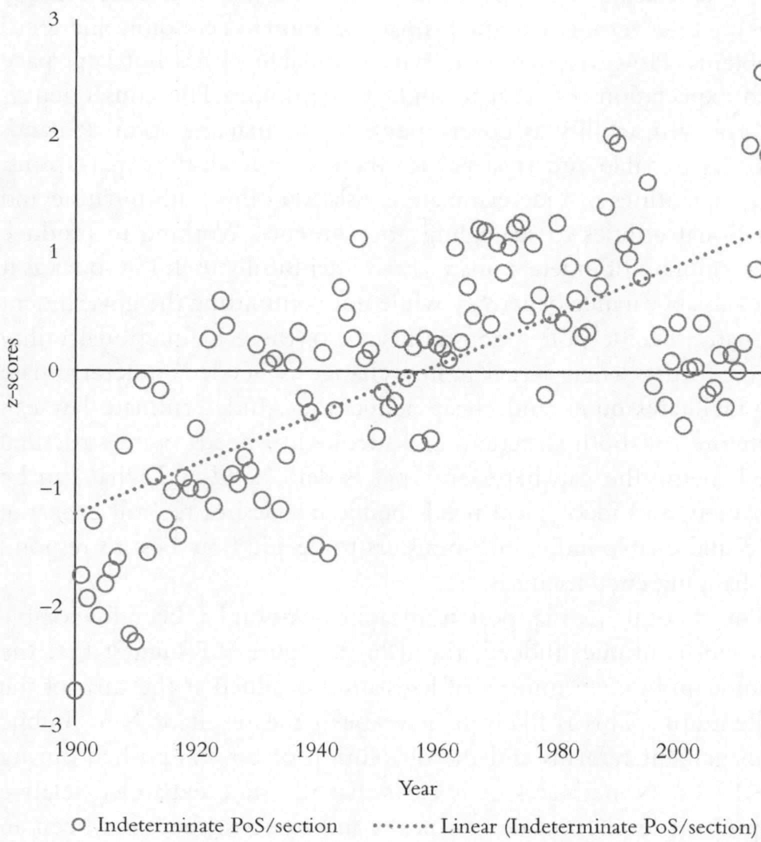

periods of change in policy 'consensus' saw peaks in indeterminacy (above 0), and institutional reforms at the turn of the millennium were coincident with a trough in indeterminacy (at or below 0).

While absolute policy stability, or stasis, can threaten a regime's legitimacy (Tsebelis 2002), the alternative of high instability and unpredictability can undermine the effectiveness of government. High levels of policy instability in post-war Britain can be observed from increasing 'government overload' (King 1975), a lack of coherent policy strategy (Flinders 2008), a fragmentation of policymaking and delivery in a hollowed-out state (Rhodes 1996), a hostile media reaction to policy ineffectiveness (Dean 2012), and, ultimately, the breakdown of effective relations between politicians, on the one hand, and interest groups, policy networks and civil servants, on the other (Rhodes 1997; Foster 2005). Hence, as Sir Christopher Foster argued, a 'crisis' developed in British government, with symptom and cause being the increased volume and indeterminacy of legislation. Resolving this will not be easy, but will require careful and comprehensive policymaking, relying on detailed consultation on how best to proceed (Foster 2005: 288). It is, of course, not true to say that this never happens in modern British politics, but the argument of Foster is that such policymaking is increasingly the exception rather than the norm.

A prominent example of expanding state responsibilities, and the extensive use of indeterminate law, comes from criminal justice policy. Governments have sought greater flexibility in law so as to manage public expectations. A result was that, during the New Labour years, 3,605 new offences were created through a vast amount of primary legislation (1,238 offences) and secondary legislation (2,367 offences) (Morris 2008). Nearly two thirds of the new criminal offences were created in secondary legislation under the authority of decentralised powers in primary legislation. When considering the sum total of modern criminal law, there have been significant increases in volume and indeterminacy, leaving judges and administrators to work out how a rule of law is to be inferred from this new statutory material (Calabresi 1982).

At root, this was a book about institutions. Indeterminate legislation is evidence of deinstitutionalisation, in that indeterminacy signifies a breakdown of rule-bound behaviour, seen through the dilapidation of the medium through which rules are communicated. Since the 1980s, there has been renewed interest from political scientists in institutions and their operation. This 'new institutionalism' saw political scientists 'bringing the state back in', rather than ignoring the rules of government as ephemeral (Evans et al 1985). This book has identified how institutions, sitting at the midpoint between broader social forces and specific actions, depend for their efficacy on clear discourse. This was a claim made most forcefully by Vivien Schmidt (2008, 2010). In this book, I offered detailed empirical evidence of the importance of a 'logic of communication' for policy effectiveness. In particular, dilapidations in coordinative and communicative discourses have, through specific parts of speech, been shown to have had marked effects on policy. The research designs used have allowed observation of the counterfactual, meaning that we have seen what effects more or less determinable language has had. The findings cast doubt on arguments that flexible governance is automatically preferable on the grounds of pragmatism. For the most part, more consensual governance with clearer accountability, and founded on clear public reasoning, will lead to more effective governance (Lijphart 2012).

More specific implications of the theory include, first, that law with indeterminate meaning is an abnegation of sovereign authority. Indeterminacy increases the likelihood that powers will be exaggerated, that duties will be shirked and that any new rights will be only partially enforced. The social implications are that more powerful individuals, with extensive resources, with social capital and embedded in elite networks, are better placed to determine the meaning of Parliament's legislation. Without Parliament being clear as to what it wants, the interpretation of statute becomes reliant on ministers, lawyers, judges and bureaucrats. This undermines democracy by creating an expensive market in authoritative discourse. Even laws intended to benefit the weak (including immigrants, the homeless and victims of discrimination) will favour the well resourced.

As Dani Rodrik (2000) argued, there is a trilemma in modern politics between global economic integration, national sovereignty and democratic politics. Democracy has lost this three-way battle and been 'diminished'. The observable implication of this is institutions that do not produce clear and authoritative language. This links to other debates, such as whether modern politics is able to secure losers' consent (Anderson et al 2005). In other words, can those who lose battles over policy and resources accept their losses as legitimate? When the outcome of these battles over policy is an indeterminate communiqué that can be twisted by a small elite, it is intuitive that losers' consent will also diminish. This speaks to the recent growth in populist politics worldwide.

Populism was, in part, fuelled by technocracy. Cold, rationalist policymaking that is incomprehensible to voters has been rebuffed in major electoral surprises, from Brexit to the Trump presidency. From the 1950s, technocracy was facilitated by a form of political cybernetics that moved away from a clear command language based on a logic of communication. Now, the form of cybernetics used in legislation is closer to an artificial neural network, also known as a learning algorithm. The programming language of legislation is not fixed, but adapts new policy outputs in response to previous outputs and new inputs. It is language that learns from context, and that changes by user discretion, rather than being rooted to pre-set commands. This language has many advantages in managing complexity. However, it is dehumanising by its reliance on contextual factors and individual whim. The language has also been shown to be ineffective in many cases. The point is made most clearly by Lord Atkin's withering dissent in the wartime case of *Liversidge v Anderson*.[119] He quoted Lewis Carroll to underscore the absurd potential of indeterminate language:

> 'When I use a word,' Humpty Dumpty said, in rather a scornful tone, 'it means just what I choose it to mean – neither more nor less.'
>
> 'The question is,' said Alice, 'whether you can make words mean so many different things.'
>
> 'The question is,' said Humpty Dumpty, 'which is to be master – that's all.'

Of course, it is important not to overstate conclusions and implications. This book covered a relatively modest empirical range by focusing predominantly on the UK. It could be argued that the book's wide historical sweep and policy-focused analyses do not support inferences for social sciences more broadly. Put technically, the number of observable implications of the theory are relatively limited and UK-centric (King et al 1994). However, social sciences are trending towards more detailed, but contextually contingent, theories. This has been in response to past attempts at general theories of politics that tended to shift like sandcastles with every new empirical development (Geddes 2003). Precision in both theory and evidence has been promoted as part of a 'historical turn' in political science (Capoccia and Ziblatt 2010). This book charted a path between huge quantities of data and grounding in specific and important policy problems. Needless to say, much more research is needed to flesh out the causes and implications of legislative indeterminacy.

---

119 [1942] AC 206, [1941] UKHL 1.

Broader historical implications

Considering the UK, what implications does legislative language have for the Westminster model of government? More precisely, how important is a logic of communication to British constitutionalism? This section will consider, in turn, how the British legislature, executive and judiciary are affected, and have been affected, by indeterminate institutional communication. Starting with the legislature, Parliament's predominance is the essential maxim of Britain's constitution and the Westminster model. The doctrine of parliamentary sovereignty is, on its face, uncluttered by detail. The doctrine is so simple, indeed, that were the British constitution to be written up comprehensively it could be done in just eight words – 'what the Queen in Parliament enacts is law' (Bogdanor 2009). Anything else would be needless embellishment.

Britain's is therefore an empirical constitution. It is set up to deal with the world as it is, rather than how it could be. The constitution is intended to be flexible and adaptive to shifting power constellations. However, underscoring this simple design is the legitimacy of Parliament. This legitimacy derives from form and function, in that Parliament is a mechanism for enabling peaceful decision-making. It is a bundle of processes which ensures that a plurality of views can be reconciled to solve shared problems. While the processes are flexible, the outputs need to be clearly stated if they are to hold. Indeterminate legislation is indicative of the parliamentary process failing to establish a reconciliation of competing views. Limited delegations of power will occasionally be required to manage changeable problems, but persistent indeterminacy devalues law as a guide to action. Also, indeterminacy favours the executive, which is especially problematic in a delicate balance of forces that enjoys no constitutional backstop. Of course, as will be acknowledged in the following, the Westminster model relies on a powerful executive and law-making judges. However, after a certain point, indeterminacy in law undermines the concept of law as a guide to action. The parameters of what is and is not acceptable become so blurred that almost any policy decision could be retroactively justified as being 'within the four corners of law'. To my mind, this point has never been better made than by Ian Loveland (2006: 504):

> the content of legislation, in so far as it can be presented as having a geometrical shape, may look less like a neat

> rectangle and more like a blob of custard dropped from a great height onto a hot plate.

Parliament's sovereignty was, for the most part, won in battle. The English Civil War was a battle over what kind of power did, and should, govern the land. This, the bloodiest war that ever occupied the islands, reached a somewhat trite conclusion: might was right. The 'ultimate political fact' of the English, and later British, constitution was that the people were in charge via their agents in Parliament (Wade 1955: 188). The divine and transcendental powers claimed by the crown were to be subject to the humanist and terrestrial powers of Parliament. This conclusion was consummated in the Glorious Revolution of 1688–89. The king, James II, was encouraged to leave crown and country behind. James was replaced by the more pliable (and more protestant) William and Mary. They dutifully signed the *Bill of Rights* and, in so doing, consigned their successors to a permanently diminished role as constitutional monarchs. Divinity remains, in theory, as the source of royal and parliamentary authority, but, for now, the UK is under the stewardship of Parliament. Also, the *Bill of Rights* uses a didactic rather than volitional register, in that it does not create or aspire to new rights, butt states what in the opinion of its authors had always been true:

> And thereupon the said Lords Spirituall and Temporall and Commons pursuant to their respective Letters and Elections being now assembled in a full and free Representative of this Nation takeing into their most serious Consideration the best meanes for attaining the Ends aforesaid Doe in the first place (as their Auncestors in like Case have usually done) for the Vindicating and Asserting their auntient Rights and Liberties, Declare — That the pretended Power of Suspending of Laws or the Execution of Laws by Regall Authority without Consent of Parlyament is illegall.

The rights enumerated were considered so ancient as to be beyond doubt, or 'self-evident' as Thomas Jefferson (1774) would put it a hundred years later. Here, he is quoted from Willamsburg, Virginia, in 1774. It is a city named after William of Orange, no less. Jefferson was hammering home the point that laws, freely made in Parliament, were intended by the *Bill of Rights* to dominate executive discretion:

> Since the establishment, however, of the British constitution, at the glorious revolution, on its free and antient principles, neither his majesty, nor his ancestors, have exercised such a power of dissolution in the island of Great Britain; and when his majesty was petitioned, by the united voice of his people there, to dissolve the present parliament, who had become obnoxious to them, his ministers were heard to declare, in open parliament, that his majesty possessed no such power by the constitution.

However, these free and ancient principles are not enshrined in any codified constitution. As a consequence, the distribution of powers and rights in Britain depends on the messy vicissitudes of politics, rather than depending upon any agreed principles of justice. Put simply, whichever faction controls Parliament controls sovereign power. However, there is, by logical necessity, a constraining force on Parliament's power, that is, the rule of law. Logic dictates that for a sovereign to sustain its sovereignty, its commands have to be comprehensible. This is a point raised most famously by two giants of 19th-century constitutional theory, A.V. Dicey and Thomas Erskine May:

> Parliamentary sovereignty has favoured the rule of law, and that the supremacy of the law of the land both calls forth the exertion of Parliamentary sovereignty, and leads to its being exercised in a spirit of legality.
> *Dicey 1915: 273*

> The legislative authority of Parliament extends over the United Kingdom, and all its colonies and foreign possessions; and there are no other limits to its power of making laws for the whole empire than those which are incident to all sovereign authority – the willingness of the people to obey, or their power to resist.
> *Webster 1917: 44*

Dicey described a complex back and forth. The rule of law, he explained, 'calls forth the exertion of Parliamentary sovereignty, and leads to its being exercised in a spirit of legality'. The rule of law both creates and is created by Parliament. The formulation is elegant, but it does not help us understand how this positive feedback emerges and is sustained. Dicey's formulation is functionalist. The rule of law and the sovereignty of Parliament are mutually reinforcing concepts that grow as they are used. The problem with this theory is that it bleaches out the role of individual citizens.

Sir Thomas Lonsdale Webster (writing in an update of Sir Thomas Erskine May's book) adds the missing ingredient of politics. For him, it is clear that parliamentary sovereignty is not an irresistible force, but vulnerable, and must be tended. It depends most crucially 'on the willingness of the people to obey, or their power to resist'. This idea is described by the Latin phrase *salus populi est suprema lex* – the welfare of the people is the highest law. In other words, Parliament is not omnipotent; it relies on resources that are beyond the simple command of its statutes. Foremost of these resources is the consent of the governed. Dicey, it should be noted, had a different agenda. In the eight editions of his *Law and the Constitution* published between 1885 and 1915, he persistently tried to prevent Home Rule being granted from Westminster to Ireland. He needed to make a case that dispelled even the possibility. By describing Parliament's sovereignty as indivisible, he hoped to check any centrifugal forces. His work should not by any means be disdained as a result. It stands up as a classic statement of English revolutionary essentials. However, like similar celebrations of revolutionary principles, Dicey's account is fundamentally conservative and is therefore undermined by his biases.

Dicey's particular concern for Ireland provides a prime example of the limits to statute. In response to the third attempt at a *Home Rule Bill* in 1912, the north of Ireland came close to civil war. Many were planning to disobey Westminster if it was to grant law-making power to Dublin. Over half a million signed the Ulster Covenant, and many thousands prepared for armed insurrection. Supporting this was the Leader of His Majesty's Loyal Opposition – Andrew Bonar Law. In the end, the onset of world war encouraged the Liberal Prime Minister, Herbert Asquith, to call on Parliament to suspend the *Government of Ireland Act 1914*. Promises were also made to recognise the different demands of the north and south of Ireland in any settlement. This settlement was the *Government of Ireland Act 1920*. If Dicey were correct, the sovereign Parliament could repeal this Act and demand that the Republic of Ireland once again become part of the UK. This argument is legally accurate but politically preposterous. Equally preposterous would be any attempt to govern Australia, New Zealand, Canada, South Africa or, again, Ireland by repeal of section 4 of the *Statute of Westminster 1931*:

> No Act of Parliament of the United Kingdom passed after the commencement of this Act shall extend, or be deemed to extend, to a Dominion as part of the law of that Dominion, unless it is expressly declared in that Act that that Dominion has requested, and consented to, the enactment thereof.

Statute law is a statement of intent. It describes the desirable ends but cannot guarantee the means. The means are political and material. These forces cannot be managed by fine words alone. That said, statute law is a very effective way of guaranteeing minimum levels of coordinated power. This is because statutory pronouncements are, for the most part, considered to be legitimate. Those subject to them will yield, even if the law disadvantages them personally or corporately. Parliament is the best way of organising shared power in the UK. Its status as sovereign comes from social and political history, and its status depends, in part, on the 'manner and form' in which it produces laws (Lee 1992). In other words, laws have to be comprehensible to work. It is the *Parliament Act 1911* (as amended by the *Parliament Act 1949*) that lays down requirements on 'manner':

> 2(1) If any Public Bill (other than a Money Bill or a Bill containing any provision to extend the maximum duration of Parliament beyond five years) is passed by the House of Commons in three [now two] successive sessions (Whether of the same Parliament or not), and, having been sent up to the House of Lords at least one month before the end of the session, is rejected by the House of Lords in each of those sessions, that Bill shall, on its rejection for the third [now second] time by the House of Lords, unless the House of Commons direct to the contrary, be presented to His Majesty and become an Act of Parliament on the Royal Assent being signified thereto.

While this 1911 Act prescribes the manner, an unmentioned, but logically necessary, element of effective legislation is its 'form', specifically, its comprehensibility. In its earliest years of operation, the sovereign Parliament made declarations of how rulings in common law needed to be revised and corrected. It also sanctioned taxation and appropriation. Parliament was, therefore, a master of detail. It responded to specific demands from constituents and the crown, but it had practically no role in leading either. This is because

Parliament has never been well suited to proposing ambitious or ideological programmes. There are, today, nearly 1,500 members of the sovereign corporation. The Queen, Lords Spiritual, Lords Temporal and Commons collectively comprise the largest legislature in the democratic world. Only China's near-3,000-strong National People's Congress is larger. Coming up with tight instructions for indicative planning, behavioural manipulation or market oversight is almost impossible without leadership.

The form of power that Parliament wields is mostly negative therefore. As the *Bill of Rights* states, Parliament has the ability to stop transgressions of ancient privileges, but this translates poorly to power for effecting change. The English constitution is a creature of two major post-conflict settlements: *Magna Carta* and the *Bill of Rights*. These laws are closest in form to treaties. Most countries' institutions similarly emerge from the crucible of conflict, but the Westminster model gave a lot of power to both sides after the truce. It was intended in both 1215 and 1688/89 to retain monarchical power, not only because of its supposedly divine origins, but also because of its efficiency. The monarch and the Cabinet were better placed to identify complex problems and propose effective solutions. Parliament would fund schemes and vote its approval where statute law was required. Parliament's sovereignty was therefore designed to sustain order, rather than enable the creative use of power. Walter Bagehot (1873: 194) set out the importance of parliamentary constraint in his classic work *The English Constitution*:

> Now a competent legislature is very rare. Any permanent legislature at all, any constantly acting mechanism for enacting and repealing laws, is, though it seems to us so natural, quite contrary to the inveterate conceptions of mankind. The great majority of nations conceive of their law, either as something Divinely given, and therefore unalterable, or as a fundamental habit, inherited from the past to be transmitted to the future. The English Parliament, of which the prominent functions are now legislative, was not all so once. It was rather a preservative body. The custom of the realm – the aboriginal transmitted law – the law which was in the breast of the judges, could not be altered without the consent of parliament, and therefore everybody felt sure it would not be altered except in grave, peculiar, and anomalous cases. The valued use of parliament was not half so much to alter the law, as to prevent the laws being

> altered. And such too was its real use. In early societies it matters much more that the law should be fixed than that it should be good.

Parliament's role in the constitution was one of superintendence, rather than creativity. As such, creative power has been delegated by Parliament to agents that are better placed to innovate. The constitution's mixture is comprised of the three estates set out in Aristotle's *Politics* – monarchy, aristocracy and civil government, in Queen, Lords and Commons. This design, much praised in the 18th and 19th centuries, is still the official set-up. All statutes to this day begin with a reaffirmation. Here is the *Cultural Property (Armed Conflicts) Act 2017*:

> An Act to enable the United Kingdom to implement the Hague Convention for the Protection of Cultural Property in the Event of Armed Conflict of 1954 and the Protocols to that Convention of 1954 and 1999. [23rd February 2017]
>
> Be it enacted by the Queen's most Excellent Majesty, by and with the advice and consent of the Lords Spiritual and Temporal, and Commons, in this present Parliament assembled, and by the authority of the same, as follows:–

The problem is that the Westminster model set out in this declaration does not reflect reality. Responsibility for delivering policies is concentrated in Her Majesty's Government, with Commons and Lords playing only a supporting role. Given modern policy priorities, this is unsurprising, and not unique to the UK. The Commons is an institution founded on simple principles: the equality of all members and their ability to represent 650 discrete constituencies. However, the only way to produce coherent social policy from 650 equal members is to create petty tyrannies to mute dissent and build agreement. No insult is meant by the term 'tyranny' here; it is a statement of fact. If all parliamentary business were transacted in plenary, the Commons would descend into a 'legislative state of nature' (Cox 2008). Thus, the government, along with Public Bill Committees and select committees, perform most of the work of drafting, amending and scrutinising law. Parties and their enforcing whips are also necessary if coherent statements of intent are to emerge from the 650-headed hydra.

However, ultimately, it is Her Majesty's Government who leads Parliament towards ambitious and ideological projects. By sustaining the confidence of a majority in the Commons, the crown can ensure that the Queen's Speech is accepted and grants of supply are provided. A loyal majority can also allow the crown to manipulate standing orders and use motions of closure (also called guillotine motions) to speed up the passage of a law and curtail filibusters. While its power depends on the confidence of Parliament, the government controls membership of the Lords, and the Commons has only withdrawn confidence twice in the last hundred years. To all intents and purposes, the enacting of statutes is dominated by the government.

The execution of law is also changing. At the time of writing, there were 25 ministerial departments operating under the Prime Minister's Office.[120] These work with 22 non-ministerial departments, such as the Crown Prosecution Service, the Forestry Commission and Her Majesty's Revenue and Customs. There are 378 other executive agencies and public bodies, including the Bank of England. The government delegates many of the tasks of service delivery to 418 local authorities in England, Wales, Scotland and Northern Ireland. The powers of local government have declined significantly since reforms to their finance in the 1980s. The great exception to this centripetalism is the devolution of powers to Scotland, Wales and Northern Ireland, as well as the devolution of strategic decision-making to Greater London and Greater Manchester. The movement of power down to the nations, up to the European Union (EU) and across to Whitehall has 'hollowed out' Westminster (Rhodes 1996). Parliament remains sovereign but has little influence over policymaking.

The constitutional problem is that while the 'form' of sovereign communication has changed, judges are still working off the original script. They still try to work out what the sovereign intended from the language used. The jurisdiction of the courts draws from the vestigial prerogatives of the crown, as well as from judge-made common law. Parliament's statutes have always been 'the carpet to cover the floor', the floor in the metaphor being the common law. This is not to say that judge-made common law is more important; it simply means that when statutes leave gaps, as they inevitably will, it is up to the judges to reveal that some law is there. Without this, there would be disputes that could not be settled by legal means. This would lead to more citizens extracting themselves from society and settling matters by their own hands. So, judges are increasingly resorting to various principles of justice to settle cases where statutes do not cover the floor.

[120] See: https://www.gov.uk/government/organisations

Figure 9.3[121] displays the number of cases from all courts that contain references to principles of law.

Figure 9.3 shows that judges have used the concepts of fairness and reasonableness to settle cases since at least 1950. These are means of reviewing the process by which law is executed. Their use has increased, but before the 1970s, there were no cases where judges explicitly referred to the concepts of human rights and proportionality when adjudicating. Human rights and proportionality are tools used to analyse the substance of law, which is typically the concern of politicians, rather than judges. Of course, the concepts of human

Figure 9.3: Total number of court cases categorised as relying on non-statutory principles of justice

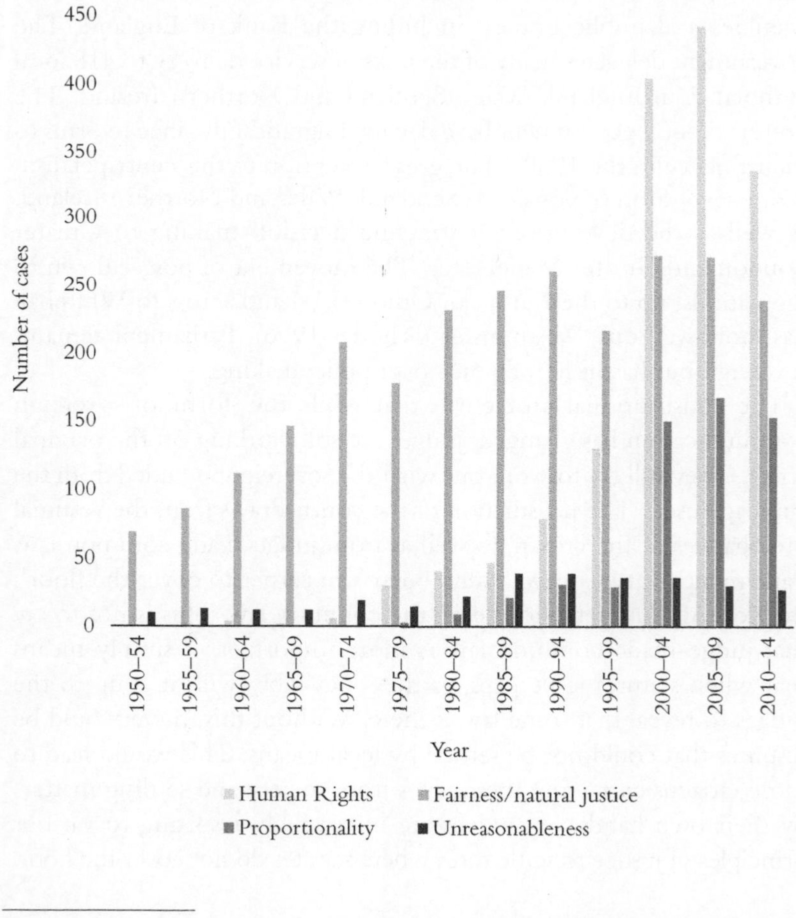

[121] See: https://www.gov.uk/government/organisations/ministry-of-justice/about/statistics

rights and proportionality would have been familiar to British judges before the 1970s, but it was exceptionally unusual for judges to rely on such ideas to settle disputes. Several factors explain these changes. First, there were deliberate grants of power to the courts by Parliament. Notably, the *Crown Proceedings Act 1947* allowed citizens to sue representatives of the crown for civil liability (not including the Sovereign himself). Also, court doors were opened to poorer litigants with the *Legal Aid Act 1949*. This reduced the comparative advantage of wealth in justice, which, in the past, had allowed the richer party to muscle out the poorer by appealing cases and winning by default rather than on merit. Furthermore, the Franks Report of 1957 led to the *Tribunals and Inquiries Act 1958*, which tidied up the tribunal system and ensured supervision by the courts of statutory tribunals. The report was commissioned after the Crichel Down affair, where land requisitioned for war use was not returned to its owners despite a promise to that effect from Churchill himself.

Second, the sovereign bound itself to international and supranational laws. Most notable in this regard were EU, Council of Europe and United Nations (UN) laws. It was via this internationalism that the *Human Rights Act* was domesticated in 2000. Third, public distrust of politics and politicians has encouraged more citizens to rely on adjudication over lobbying and legislation. Judges, as technical experts with no constituents, lobbyists or journalists to please, are often more trustworthy. Fourth, the decline of two-party politics in the UK means that fewer voters are represented by the party in government. These voters without a political constituency will resort to alternative institutions to redress their grievances, including the courts.

This last reason is a product of the political upheavals of the late 20th and early 21st centuries. Figure 9.4 shows a widening democratic deficit. Displayed is the gap between the seat share of the government in the Commons and the vote share they received from all eligible voters (voting age population [VAP]). In 2010, with the formation of the Conservative–Liberal Democrat Coalition, the post-war widening of the democratic deficit reversed. In 2015, the gap returned, with a government securing over half the seats in the Commons with support from little over a fifth of those eligible to vote. In 2017, with two-party politics revived, there was again a modest narrowing of the gap between votes and seats, but the deficit is still just under 20%.

The powers granted to judges, the expectations of the public and international norms are all important factors. However, on their own, these provide an incomplete explanation. Specifically, these factors do not tell us exactly when judges use concepts such as human rights

Figure 9.4: The democratic deficit, 1945–2017

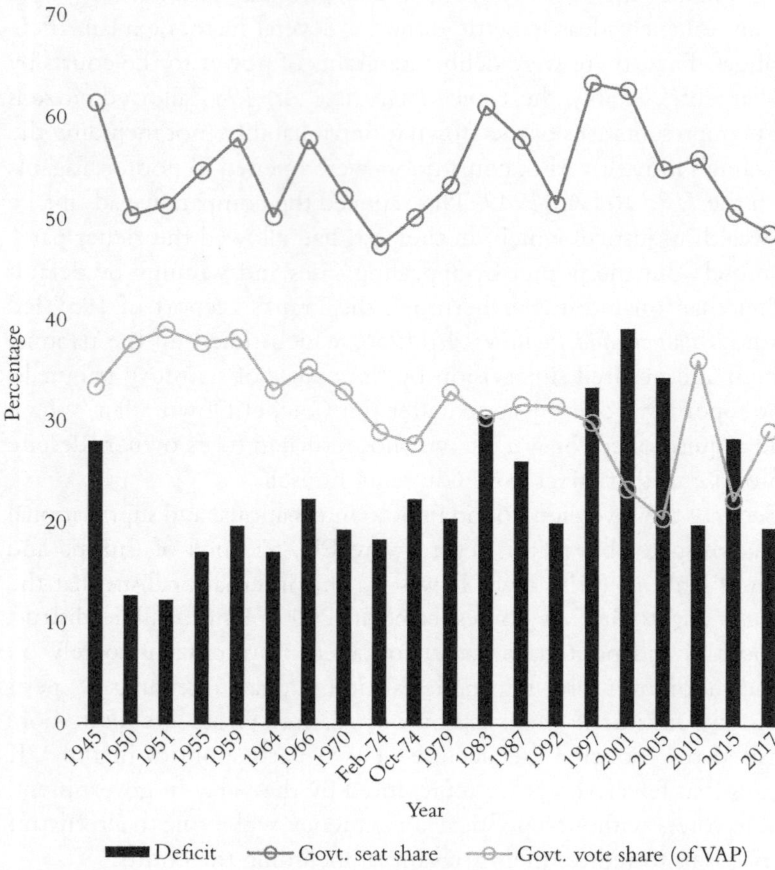

or proportionality to change law. Judges could not legally reject Parliament's will if it was stated without ambiguity. Such a rejection would be unconstitutional and illegitimate. Without good reasons to make the law, judges would be acting for themselves and would be little more than politicians in robes. Judges make law in response to constitutional deformation. The original model of the constitution is deforming in response to demands for Parliament to create more law, without clear guidance on whether the law does, in fact, represent the sovereign will. Law is made in the correct manner, but the form of legislation is increasingly becoming indeterminate.

Moral implications of indeterminacy and some possible solutions

Having considered some theoretical implications of increasing indeterminacy in law, what, if any, are the moral implications? Does it matter, from a moral perspective, how the sovereign Parliament expresses its will? The analysis here focuses on who, by rights, should be empowered and who disempowered in a democracy. The crux is: who wins and who loses from indeterminate legislation? It has been argued, with considerable plausibility, that fuzzy concepts in law and politics are, in fact, more democratic. What has been technically described as 'heteroglossia' (meaning multiple possible interpretations of the same text) enables individuals and communities to take ownership of authoritative language and remake it as it suits them (Crowley 1989). However, in public policy, heteroglossia is not permitted. Legal language may be capable of multiple interpretations but, ultimately, both the executive and judiciary will work towards settled, 'monoglossic', clarity. The consequence is that with rising indeterminacy, what policy has meant depended on which individuals controlled the words. This is because shared meaning has not been effectively established at the ballot box or in legislation. As mentioned previously, Henry Maine (1861) described a move from 'status to contract' in 19th-century law. Charismatic leaders, he argued, were brought to heal by cold, rational contracts. However, as legislation increasingly lacks determinate meaning, the contracts between state and citizen are not fixed, but fluid. As a consequence, status can dominate contract. This executive-dominated phase in modern politics can been described as post-democratic (Crouch 2004). Leadership is not tethered to public reasoning, but acts on the perceived requirements of circumstance and in accordance with individual whim. To get here, Parliament is writing vastly more law, but is saying much less.

What is considered as good legislation ought to consider the language used, and not just its contents. Reforms to parliamentary procedure that have allowed for more pre-legislative and post-legislative scrutiny, as well as the increased use of evidence-gathering Public Bill Committees, are steps in this direction. Civil service 'Bill Teams' and parliamentary counsel are also implicated in this call for clarity. However, it must be stressed that civil servants and government lawyers act on instructions from ministers; they are unable to change the genre of legal language unilaterally.

Some other solutions are already to hand. As was demonstrated in Chapter Two, financial legislation attains a far higher degree of determinacy than does all other legislation. These laws could present a model for plain drafting. Take, for instance, this 'tax lock' from the *Finance (No. 2) Act 2015*:

> 1 Income tax lock (1) For any tax year to which this section applies – (a) the basic rate of income tax shall not exceed 20%, (b) the higher rate of income tax shall not exceed 40%, and (c) the additional rate of income tax shall not exceed 45%.

There are, strictly speaking, adjectives (basic, higher, additional) and conjunctions (and) used in this section. However, the computer program used for this book was able to filter out these more determinate parts of speech from analyses. This section is, therefore, as close to a mathematical formula as is possible to achieve in natural language. So, perhaps more laws framed like this would be preferable. However, the disadvantages for social policy are fairly obvious. There are very few policy spaces capable of being distilled down to such plain prescriptions. Some flexibility and adaptability is needed in most policy spaces. The problem is that modern law has taken flexibility too far.

Solutions could include more codification of laws. If not a fully codified constitution, then at least some more codified policy spaces would improve the comprehensibility of subordinate laws. For instance, a single criminal code, or a unified tax code, could provide indexes of meanings to clarify all related laws. Clearly, this would be a major undertaking. Perhaps a more practical solution would be greater decentralisation of power. If communities and local authorities were able to make laws in a more participatory fashion, they would likely not bear indeterminate language that could empower a narrow elite. More evenly distributed 'stakeholding' – where a wider pool of citizens is responsible for policy – would make clarity in law a higher priority (Dowding et al 2003). An even simpler step would be for politicians to make clear some 'basic norms' of British statecraft, à la Hans Kelsen. This could be achieved with a convention, followed by a proclamation and authorised by an election. Or, the proposed *British Bill of Rights* that is intended to replace the *Human Rights Act* could clarify in a 'constitutional statute' what, exactly, the core values of democracy are. While the *Human Rights Act* goes some way to achieving this, its own indeterminacies have lessened its potential impact.

Alternatively, we could look to society to address the problem. If indeterminacy is, in part, a consequence of policy demands not being realistic, education could help citizens 'settle for less'. The problem here is that the rules of the electoral game disincentivise any such honesty from politicians. Straight-talking politicians, so desired by voters, tend to fail because elections are won by those able to spin the best yarn. As such, the 'superfluity of talking', and 'eloquence', much derided by Bishop Sprat in the book's opening quote is, at present, unavoidable. However, the effects of indeterminate language on policy are such that citizens and politicians ought to consider, much more seriously, the importance of a clear logic of communication.

Appendix

Acts missing from the analysis of legislation in Chapter Two

- *Appropriation Act 1900, Session 2*
- *Dublin Improvement (Bull Alley Area) Act 1903*
- *Fatal Accidents (Damages) Act 1908*
- *Children (Employment Abroad) Act 1913*
- *Army (Annual) Act 1914*
- *Arrest of Suspected Persons (Ireland) Act 1916*
- *House-Letting and Rating Suspensory (Scotland) Act 1920*
- *Irish Free State (Consequential Provisions) Act 1922*
- *Board of Guardians (Default) Act 1926*
- *Patents and Designs (Convention) Act 1928*
- *Amendment Act 1931*
- *Registration of Births, Deaths, and Marriages (Scotland) Act 1938*
- *Local Elections and Register of Electors (Temporary Provisions) Act 1944*
- *British Transport Commission Act 1949*
- *National Insurance Act 1953*
- *Requisitioned Houses and Housing (Amendment) Act 1955*
- *Family Allowances and National Insurance Act 1959*
- *Dog Licences Act 1959*
- *Appropriation Act 1959*
- *Requisitioned Homes Act 1960*
- *Agriculture and Forestry Associations Act 1962*
- *Burgh Police (Amendment) (Scotland) Act 1964*
- *Ministers of the Crown Act 1964*
- *Consolidated Fund (No. 2) Act 1965*
- *Representation of the People (Armed Forces) Act 1976*

Immigration and asylum legislation analysed for Chapter Four

- *Aliens Act 1905*
- *Aliens Restriction Act 1914*
- *British Nationality and Status of Aliens Act 1914*
- *Aliens Restriction (Amt) Act 1919*
- *British Nationality and Status of Aliens Act 1922*
- *Former Enemy Aliens (Disabilities Removal) Act 1925*
- *British Nationality and Status of Aliens Act 1933*
- *British Nationality and Status of Aliens Act 1943*
- *British Nationality Act 1948*
- *Aliens' Employment Act 1955*
- *British Nationality Act 1958*
- *Commonwealth Immigrants Act 1962*
- *British Nationality Act 1964*
- *British Nationality (No 2) Act 1964*
- *British Nationality Act 1965*
- *Commonwealth Immigrants Act 1968*
- *Immigration Appeals Act 1969*
- *Immigration Act 1971*
- *British Nationality Act 1981*
- *British Nationality (Falkland Islands) Act 1983*
- *Immigration (Carriers' Liability) Act 1987*
- *Immigration Act 1988*
- *British Nationality (Hong Kong) Act 1990*
- *Asylum and Immigration Appeals Act 1993*
- *Asylum and Immigration Act 1996*
- *British Nationality (Hong Kong) Act 1997 (Con)*
- *Special Immigration Appeals Commission Act 1997 (Lab)*
- *Immigration and Asylum Act 1999*
- *Nationality, Immigration and Asylum Act 2002*
- *Asylum and Immigration (Treatment of Claimants, etc.) Act 2004*
- *Immigration, Asylum and Nationality Act 2006*
- *UK Borders Act 2007*
- *Criminal Justice and Immigration Act 2008*
- *Borders, Citizenship and Immigration Act 2009*
- *Immigration Act 2014*
- *Immigration Act 2016*

Housing and homelessness legislation analysed for Chapter Five

- *Housing of the Working Classes Act 1903*
- *Housing of the Working Classes (Ireland) Act 1908*
- *Housing Act 1914*
- *Housing (No. 2) Act 1914*
- *Housing (No. 2) (Amendment) Act 1914*
- *Housing (Additional Powers) Act 1919*
- *Housing (Ireland) Act 1919*
- *Housing (Scotland) Act 1920*
- *Housing, &c. Act 1923*
- *Housing (Financial Provisions) Act 1924*
- *Housing Act 1925*
- *Housing (Scotland) Act 1925*
- *Housing Act 1930*
- *Housing (Scotland) Act 1930*
- *Housing (Rural Workers) Amendment Act 1931*
- *Housing (Rural Authorities) Act 1931*
- *Housing (Financial Provisions) Act 1933*
- *Housing (Financial Provisions) (Scotland) Act 1933*
- *Housing Act 1936*
- *Housing (Financial Provisions) Act 1938*
- *Housing (Rural Workers) Amendment Act 1938*
- *Housing (Agricultural Population) (Scotland) Act 1938*
- *Housing (Rural Workers) (Scotland) Act 1942*
- *Housing (Agricultural Population) (Scotland) Act 1943*
- *Housing (Temporary Provisions) Act 1944*
- *Housing (Temporary Accommodation) Act 1944*
- *Housing (Scotland) Act 1944*
- *Housing (Temporary Accommodation) Act 1945*
- *Housing (Financial and Miscellaneous Provisions) Act 1946*
- *Housing (Financial Provisions) (Scotland) Act 1946*
- *Housing (Temporary Accommodation) Act 1947*
- *National Assistance Act 1948*
- *National Assistance (Amendment) Act 1951 c.51*
- *National Assistance (Amendment) Act 1951 c.57*
- *Housing Act 1952*
- *Housing (Scotland) Act 1952*
- *Housing Act 1957*
- *Housing (Financial Provisions) Act 1958*
- *Housing Act 1961*

- *Housing Act 1969*
- *Housing Act 1971*
- *Housing (Amendment) Act 1973*
- *Housing Act 1974*
- *Housing (Homeless Persons) Act 1977*
- *Housing Act 1985*
- *Housing and Planning Act 1986*
- *Housing (Scotland) Act 1987*
- *Housing (Scotland) Act 1988*
- *Housing Act 1988*
- *Housing Act 1996*
- *Homelessness Act 2002*
- *Civil Contingencies Act 2004*
- *Housing and Regeneration Act 2008*
- *Prevention of Social Housing Fraud Act 2013*
- *Homelessness Reduction Act 2017*

Anti-discrimination and equality legislation analysed for Chapter Six

- *Employment of Women Act 1907*
- *Married Women's Property Act 1907*
- *Matrimonial Causes Act 1907*
- *Qualification of Women (County and Borough Councils) Act 1907*
- *Qualification of Women (County and Town Councils) (Scotland) Act 1907*
- *Married Women's Property Act 1908*
- *Parliament (Qualification of Women) Act 1918*
- *Sex Disqualification (Removal) Act 1919*
- *Jurors (Enrolment of Women) (Scotland) Act 1920*
- *Married Women (Maintenance) Act 1920*
- *Married Women's Property (Scotland) Act 1920*
- *Matrimonial Causes Act 1923*
- *Roman Catholic Relief Act 1926*
- *Representation of the People (Equal Franchise) Act 1928*
- *Law Reform (Married Women and Tortfeasors) Act 1935*
- *Disabled Persons (Employment) Act 1944*
- *Married Women (Restraint upon Anticipation) Act 1949*
- *Married Women (Maintenance) Act 1949*
- *Matrimonial Causes Act 1950*
- *Matrimonial Causes (Property and Maintenance) Act 1958*

- *Law Reform (Husband and Wife) Act 1962*
- *Married Women's Property Act 1964*
- *Race Relations Act 1965*
- *Race Relations Act 1968*
- *Equal Pay Act 1970*
- *Sex Discrimination Act 1975*
- *Race Relations Act 1976*
- *Sex Discrimination Act 1986*
- *Race Relations (Remedies) Act 1994*
- *Disability Discrimination Act 1995*
- *Disability Rights Commission Act 1999*
- *Race Relations (Amt) Act 2000*
- *Special Educational Needs and Disability Act 2001*
- *Sex Discrimination (Election Candidates) Act 2002*
- *Disability Discrimination Act 2005*
- *Equality Act 2006*
- *Equality Act 2010*
- *Marriage (Same Sex Couples) Act 2013*
- *Lords Spiritual (Women) Act 2015*

References

Anderson, C.J., Blais, A., Bowler, S., Donovan, T. and Listhaug, O. (2005) *Losers' Consent: Elections and Democratic Legitimacy* (Oxford: Oxford University Press).

Arnarsdóttir, E.S. (2015) 'Icelandic journalist wins freedom of expression case', *Icelandic Review*. Available at: http://icelandreview.com/news/2015/06/02/icelandic-journalist-wins-freedom-expression-case (accessed 19 July 2016).

Bagehot, W. (1873) *The English Constitution* (2nd edn) (London: Kegan Paul, Trench, Trübner & Co).

Bates, D.M. (2010) 'lme4: mixed-effects modeling with R'. Available at: http://lme4.r-forge.r-project.org/book

Bauman, Z. (1991) *Modernity and Ambivalence* (Cambridge: Polity Press).

BBC (British Broadcasting Corporation) (2016) 'Wales "leading way" tackling homeless, expert says'. Available at: http://www.bbc.co.uk/news/uk-wales-35528721 (accessed 1 March 2016).

Bell, M. (2002) *Anti-Discrimination Law and the EU* (Oxford: Oxford University Press).

Bell, M. (2009) *Racism and Equality in the European Union* (Oxford: Oxford University Press).

Bennion, F.A.R. (2008) *On Statutory Interpretation: A Code* (5th edn) (London: LexisNexis).

Bennion, F.A.R. (2009) *Understanding Common Law Legislation: Drafting and Interpretation* (Oxford: Oxford University Press).

Bevan, V. (1986) *The Development of British Immigration Law* (London: Croom Helm).

Bix, B. (1993) *Law, Language, and Legal Determinacy* (Oxford: Clarendon).

Bjørnskov, C. and Voigt, S. (2014) 'Constitutional verbosity and social trust', *Public Choice*, 161:1, 91–112.

Blom-Cooper, L., Dickson, B. and Drewry, G. (2009) *The Judicial House of Lords* (Oxford: Oxford University Press).

Blume, L., Müller, J. and Voigt, S. (2009) 'The economic effects of constitutions: replicating – and extending – Persson and Tabellini', *Public Choice*, 139:1, 197–225.

Bogdanor, V. (2009) *The New British Constitution* (Oxford: Hart).

Bulpitt, J. (1986) 'The discipline of the new democracy: Mrs Thatcher's domestic statecraft', *Political Studies*, 34:1, 19–39.

Butt, P. and Castle, R. (2007) *Modern Legal Drafting: A Guide to Using Clearer Language* (Cambridge: Cambridge University Press).

Calabresi, G. (1982) *A Common Law for the Age of Statutes* (Cambridge, MA: Harvard University Press).

Capoccia, G. and Ziblatt, D. (2010) 'The historical turn in democratization studies: a new research agenda for Europe and beyond', *Comparative Political Studies*, 43:8–9, 931–68.

Card, D. and Krueger, A.B. (1994) 'Minimum wages and employment: a case study of the fast-food industry in New Jersey and Pennsylvania', *American Economic Review*, 84:4, 772–93.

Carrubba, C.J., Gabel, M. and Hankla, C. (2008) 'Judicial behavior under political constraints: evidence from the European Court of Justice', *American Political Science Review*, 102:4, 435–52.

Charrow, R.P. and Charrow, V.R. (1979) 'Making legal language understandable: a psycholinguistic study of jury instructions', *Columbia Law Review*, 79:7, 1306–74.

Christensen, T. (2008) 'Smart policy?', in Moran, M., Rein, M. and Goodin, R.E. (eds) *Oxford Handbook of Public Policy* (Oxford: Oxford University Press), pp 448–68.

Clayton, C. and Gillman, H. (1999) *Supreme Court Decision-Making: New Institutionalist Approaches* (Chicago, IL: Chicago University Press).

Clayton, R. and Tomlinson, H. (2003) *The Law of Human Rights* (Oxford: Oxford University Press).

Cohen, M.D., March, J.G. and Olsen, J.P. (1972) 'A garbage can model of organizational choice', *Administrative Science Quarterly*, 17:1, 1–25.

Collier, R.B. and Collier, D. (2002) *Shaping the Political Arena: Critical Junctures, the Labor Movement, and Regime Dynamics in Latin America* (Princeton, NJ: Princeton University Press).

Connolly, W.E. (1974) *The Terms of Political Discourse* (London: Heath).

Cox, G.W. (2008) 'The organization of democratic legislatures', in Wittman, D.A. and Weingast, B.R. (eds) *The Oxford Handbook of Political Economy* (Oxford: Oxford University Press).

Crenshaw, K.W. (1989) 'Demarginalising the intersection of race and sex: a black feminist critique of anti-discrimination doctrine, feminist theory and anti-racist politics', *University of Chicago Legal Forum*, 1989:1 139–68.

Cross, R., Bell, J. and Engle, G. (1995) *Cross: Statutory Interpretation* (London: LexisNexis Butterworths).

Crouch, C. (2004) *Post-Democracy* (Cambridge: Polity).

Crowley, T. (1989) *The Politics of Discourse: The Standard Language Question in British Cultural Debates* (Basingstoke: Macmillan Education).

Crystal, D. and Davy, D. (1969) *Investigating English Style* (Harlow: Longmans).

Dahl, R.A. (1957) 'Decision-making in a democracy: the Supreme Court as a national policy-maker', *Journal of Public Law*, 6, 279–95.

Dahl, R.A. (1989) *Democracy and its Critics* (New Haven, CT: Yale University Press).

Danet, B. (1980) 'Language in the legal process', *Law and Society Review*, 14:3, 445–564.

Danet, B. (1985) 'Legal Discourse', in Van Dijk, T.A. (ed) *Handbook of Discourse Analysis: Volume One* (London: Academic), pp 273–91.

Dean, M. (2012) *Democracy Under Attack: How the Media Distort Policy and Politics* (Bristol: The Policy Press).

Desjardins, J. (2017) 'How many millions of lines of code does it take?'. Available at: http://www.visualcapitalist.com/millions-lines-of-code/ (accessed 8 June 2017).

DETR (Department of the Environment, Transport and the Regions) (2000) *Quality and Choice: A Decent Home for All* (London: DETR).

Deutsch, K.W. (1966) *The Nerves of Government: Models of Political Communication and Control* (New York, NY: Free Press).

Dicey, A.V. (1915) *The Law of the Constitution* (8th edn) (London: Macmillan).

Dixon, R.M. and Jones, J.A. (2017) 'Mapping mutations in legislation: a bioinformatics approach', paper presented at the Political Studies Association, Glasgow.

Dowding, K., Wispelaere, J.D. and White, S. (eds) (2003) *The Ethics of Stakeholding* (Basingstoke: Palgrave Macmillan).

Dunleavy, P. (1991) *Democracy, Bureaucracy and Public Choice* (Hemel Hempstead: Harvester Wheatsheaf).

Dworkin, R. (1977) *Taking Rights Seriously* (Cambridge, MA: Harvard University Press).

Dworkin, R. (1986) *Law's Empire* (London: Fontana).

Dyevre, A. (2005) 'The constitutionalisation of the European Union: discourse, present, future and facts', *European Law Review*, 30:2, 165–89.

Dyevre, A. (2010) 'Unifying the field of comparative judicial politics: towards a general theory of judicial behaviour', *European Political Science Review*, 2:2, 297–327.

Easton, D. (1965) *A Framework for Political Analysis* (Englewood Cliffs, NJ: Prentice-Hall).

Edelman, L.B. (1992) 'Legal ambiguity and symbolic structures: organizational mediation of civil rights law', *The American Journal of Sociology*, 97:6, 1531–76.

Edwards, H.T. (1984) 'Public misperceptions concerning the politics of judging: dispelling some myths about the DC Circuit', *University of Colorado Law Review*, 4:2, 619–46.

Edwards, R.A. (2002) 'Judicial deference under the Human Rights Act', *The Modern Law Review*, 65:6, 859–82.

Elliott, M. (2000) 'The ultra vires doctrine in a constitutional setting: still the central principle of administrative law', in Forsyth, C. (ed) *Judicial Review and the Constitution* (London: Hart Publishing).

Elster, J. (1995) 'Forces and mechanisms in the constitution-making process', *Duke Law Journal*, 45:2, 364–96.

Elton, G.R. (1953) 'An early Tudor Poor Law', *The Economic History Review*, 6:1, 55–67.

Empson, W. (1953) *Seven Types of Ambiguity* (London: Chatto and Windus).

Endicott, T. (2011) 'The value of vagueness', in Marmor, A. and Soames, S. (eds) *Philosophical Foundations of Language in the Law* (Oxford: Oxford University Press), pp 14–30.

Epstein, D. and O'Halloran, S. (1999) *Delegating Powers: A Transaction Cost Politics Approach to Policy-Making Under Separate Powers* (Cambridge: Cambridge University Press).

Epstein, L. and Knight, J. (1998) *The Choices Justices Make* (Washington, DC: CQ Press).

Eskridge, W.N., Jr and Ferejohn, J. (1992) 'Making the deal stick: enforcing the original constitutional structure of law-making in the modern regulatory state', *Journal of Law, Economics and Development*, 8:1, 165–89.

Evans, M., McIntosh, W., Lin, J. and Cates, C. (2007) 'Recounting the courts? Applying automated content analysis to enhance empirical legal research', *Journal of Empirical Legal Studies*, 4:4, 1007–39.

Evans, P.B., Rueschemeyer, D. and Skocpol, T. (1985) *Bringing the State Back In* (Cambridge: Cambridge University Press).

Ewing, K.D. (1999) 'The Human Rights Act and parliamentary democracy', *Modern Law Review*, 62:1, 79–100.

Fahey, T. and Norris, M. (2010) 'Housing', in Castles, F.G., Leibfried, S., Lewis, J., Obinger, H. and Pierson, C. (eds) *The Oxford Handbook of the Welfare State* (Oxford: Oxford University Press), pp 479–93.

Falconer, C. (2006) 'Review of the implementation of the Human Rights Act'. Available at: www.dca.gov.uk/peoples-rights/human-rights/pdf/exec_summ_intro.pdf (accessed on 20 November 2011).

Feldman, D. (2004) *English Public Law* (Oxford: Oxford University Press).

Fenwick, H. (2011) 'The Conservative anti-ECHR stance and a British Bill of Rights: rhetoric and reality', UK Constitutional Law Group Blog. Available at: http://ukconstitutionallaw.org/blog/page/2/ (accessed 20 November 2011).

Ferejohn, J. and Weingast, B. (1991) 'Limitation of statutes: strategic statutory interpretation', *Georgia Law Review*, 80:4, 565–82.

Fitzpatrick, S. and Jones, A. (2005) 'Pursuing social justice or social cohesion? Coercion in street homelessness policies in England', *Journal of Social Policy*, 34:3, 389–406.

Fitzpatrick, S. and Stephens, M. (1999) 'Homelessness, need and desert in the allocation of housing', *Housing Studies*, 14:4, 413–31.

Flanagan, B. (2010) 'Revisiting the contribution of literal meaning to legal meaning', *Oxford Journal of Legal Studies*, 30:2, 255–71.

Flinders, M. (2008) *Delegated Governance and the British State: Walking Without Order* (Oxford: Oxford University Press).

Foster, C.D. (2005) *British Government in Crisis, or, the Third English Revolution* (Oxford: Hart Publishing).

Foster, C.D. and Plowden, F.J. (1996) *The State Under Stress* (Buckingham: Open University Press).

Foucault, M. (1988) *Politics, Philosophy, Culture: Interviews and Other Writings, 1977–1984* (London: Routledge).

Freeden, M. (1996) *Ideologies and Political Theory* (Oxford: Clarendon Press).

Freeman, G.P. (1995) 'Modes of immigration politics in liberal democratic states', *International Migration Review*, 29:4, 881–902.

Freeman, M.D.A. (2008) *Lloyd's Introduction to Jurisprudence* (London: Sweet & Maxwell).

Freeman, R. (2008) 'Learning in public policy', in Moran, M., Rein, M. and Goodin, R.E. (eds) *Oxford Handbook of Public Policy* (Oxford: Oxford University Press), pp 367–88.

Freund, E. (1920) 'Use of indefinite terms in statutes', *Yale Law Review*, 30:5, 437–55.

Gamble, A. (1981) *Britain in Decline: Economic Policy, Political Strategy and the British State* (London: Macmillan).

Gamble, A. (1988) *The Free Economy and the Strong State: The Politics of Thatcherism* (Basingstoke: Macmillan).

Garrett, G., Keleman, R.D. and Schulz, H. (1998) 'The European Court of Justice, national governments, and legal integration in the European Union', *International Organization*, 52:1, 149–76.

Geddes, B. (2003) *Paradigms and Sand Castles: Theory Building and Research Design in Comparative Politics* (Ann Arbor, MI: University of Michigan Press).

Gibson, J.L. (1978) 'Judges' role orientations, attitudes and decisions: An interactive model', *American Political Science Review*, 72:3, 911–24.

Goertz, G. (2006) *Social Science Concepts: A User's Guide* (Oxford: Princeton University Press).

Goldsworthy, J. (2004) *The Sovereignty of Parliament* (Oxford: Oxford University Press).

Griffith, J.A.G. (1977) *The Politics of the Judiciary* (Manchester: Manchester University Press).

Gustafsson, M. (1975) *Some Syntactic Properties of English Law Language* (Turku, Finland: University of Turku).

Habermas, J. and Luhmann, N. (1971) *Theorie der Gesellschaft oder Sozialtechnologie* (Frankfurt: Suhrkamp).

Hall, P.A. (1993) 'Policy paradigms, social learning and the state: the case of economic policymaking in Britain', *Comparative Politics*, 25:3, 275–96.

Hall, P.A. and Taylor, R.C. (1996) 'Political science and the three new institutionalisms', *Political Studies*, 44:5, 936–57.

Hanretty, C. (2013) 'The decisions and ideal points of British Law Lords', *British Journal of Political Science*, 43:3, 703–16.

Hansen, R. (2009) 'Immigration and citizenship', in Flinders, M. (ed) *The Oxford Handbook of British Politics* (Oxford: Oxford University Press).

Hart, H.L.A. (1958) 'Positivism and the separation of law and morals', *Harvard Law Review*, 71:4, 593–629.

Hart, H.L.A. (1961) *The Concept of the Law* (Oxford: Clarendon).

Hay, C. (2008) 'Constructivist institutionalism', in Rockman, B.A., Binder, S.A. and Rhodes, R.A.W. (eds) *The Oxford Handbook of Political Institutions* (Oxford: Oxford University Press), pp 56–74.

Heclo, H. (1974) *Modern Social Politics in Britain and Sweden: From Relief to Income Maintenance* (New Haven, CT: Yale University Press).

Hennessy, P. (1998) *The Hidden Wiring: Unearthing the British Constitution* (London: Indigo).

Hiltunen, R. (2012) 'The grammar and structure of legal texts', in Solan, L.M. and Tiersma, P.M. (eds) *The Oxford Handbook of Language and Law* (Oxford: Oxford University Press).

Hirschl, R. (2004) *Towards Juristocracy: The Origins and Consequences of the New Constitutionalism* (Cambridge, MA: Harvard University Press).

Hirschl, R. (2006) 'The new constitutionalism and the judicialization of pure politics worldwide', *Fordham Law Review*, 75:2, 721–53.

Hirschl, R. (2008) 'The judicialization of mega-politics and the rise of political courts', *Annual Review of Political Science*, 11, 93–118.

Ho, D.E., Imai, K., King, G. and Stuart, E.A. (2011) 'MatchIt: nonparametric preprocessing for parametric causal inference', *Journal of Statistical Software*, 42:8, 1–28.

Holmwood, L. and Fitzsimmons, C. (2008) 'Max Mosley wins £60,000 in privacy case', *The Guardian*. Available at: http://www.guardian.co.uk/uk/2008/jul/24/mosley.privacy (accessed 31 November 2011).

Hönnige, C. (2011) 'Beyond judicialization: why we need more comparative research about constitutional courts', *European Political Science*, 10, 346–58.

Hood, C. (1991) 'A public management for all seasons?', *Public Administration*, 69:1, 3–19.

Hood, C. and Dixon, R.M. (2015) *A Government that Worked Better and Cost Less?* (Oxford: Oxford University Press).

House of Lords Select Committee on the Constitution (2016) 'Delegated legislation and Parliament: a response to the Strathclyde Review', 9th Report of Session 2015–16, HL 116.

Huber, J.D. and Shipan, C.R. (2002) *Deliberate Discretion? The Institutional Foundations of Bureaucratic Autonomy* (Cambridge: Cambridge University Press).

JCHR (Joint Committee on Human Rights) (2015) 'Declarations of incompatibility by UK courts', *Human Rights Judgments: Seventh Report of Session 2014–15* (House of Lords, House of Commons), pp 17-20.

Jefferson, T. (1774) 'A summary view of the rights of British America'. Available at: http://www.history.org/almanack/life/politics/sumview.cfm (accessed 28 April 2017).

Jowell, J. (1994) 'Is equality a constitutional principle?', *Current Legal Problems*, 47:2, 1–18.

Kavanagh, A. (2009) *Constitutional Review Under the UK Human Rights Act* (Cambridge: Cambridge University Press).

Kettl, D.F. (1980) *Managing Community Development in the New Federalism* (New York, NY: Praeger).

King, A. (1975) 'Overload: problems of governing in the 1970s', *Political Studies*, 23:2/3, 284–96.

King, G., Keohane, R. and Verba, S. (1994) *Designing Social Inquiry: Scientific Inference in Qualitative Research* (Princeton, NJ: Princeton University Press).

Kingdon, J. (1995) *Agendas, Alternatives, and Public Politics* (2nd edn) (New York, NY: Harper Collins).

Koch, I.E. (2005) 'Dichotomies, trichotomies, or waves of duties', *Human Rights Law Review*, 5:1, 81–103.

Krippendorff, K. (1980) *Content Analysis: An Introduction to its Methodology* (London: Sage Publications).

Kurzon, D. (1986) *Pragmatics and Beyond VII* (Amsterdam: John Benjamins Publishing Co).

Labov, W. (1972) *Sociolinguistic Patterns* (Philadelphia, PA: University of Pennsylvania Press).

Laitin, D.D. (2002) 'Comparative politics: the state of the subdiscipline', in Katznelson, I. and Milner, H.V. (eds) *Political Science: The State of the Discipline* (New York, NY: New York University Press).

Lasswell, H.D. (1936) *Politics: Who Gets What, When, How* (New York, NY: Whittlesey House).

Laurie, E. (2004) 'The Homelessness Act 2002 and housing allocations: all change or business as usual?', *The Modern Law Review*, 67:1, 48–68.

Laver, M., Benoit, K. and Garry, J. (2003) 'Extracting policy positions from political texts using words as data', *American Political Science Review*, 97:2, 311–31.

Lee, H.P. (1992) '"Manner and form": an imbroglio in Victoria', *University of New South Wales Law Journal*, 15:2, 516–39.

Lester, R. and Piore, M. (2004) *Innovation: The Missing Dimension* (Cambridge, MA.: Harvard University Press).

Levi, E. H. (1948) 'An introduction to legal reasoning', *The University of Chicago Law Review*, 15, 501-574.

Levitsky, S. and Way, L.A. (2006) 'Linkage versus leverage. Rethinking the international dimension of regime change', *Comparative Politics*, 38:4, 379–400.

Lijphart, A. (2012) *Patterns of Democracy: Government Forms and Performance in Thirty-Six Countries* (New Haven, CT: Yale University Press).

Lindblom, C.E. (1959) 'The science of "muddling through"', *Public Administration Review*, 19:2, 79–88.

Loughran, T. and McDonald, B. (2011) 'When is a liability not a liability? Textual analysis, dictionaries, and 10-Ks', *The Journal of Finance*, 66:1, 35–65.

Loveland, I. (2006) *Constitutional Law, Administrative Law and Human Rights: A Critical Introduction* (4th edn) (Oxford: Oxford University Press).

Lowi, T. (1972) 'Four systems of policy, politics, and choice', *Public Administration Review*, 32:4, 298–310.

Luba, J. and Davies, L. (2010) *Housing Allocation and Homelessness: Law and Practice* (Bristol: Jordans).

Lukes, S. (1974) *Power: A Radical View* (London: Macmillan Press).

Lyotard, J.-F., Crome, K. and Williams, J. (2006) *The Lyotard Reader and Guide* (Edinburgh: Edinburgh University Press).

MacCormick, N. (2005) *Rhetoric and the Rule of Law: A Theory of Legal Reasoning* (Oxford: Oxford University Press).

Maine, H.S. (1861) *Ancient Law: Its Connection with the Early History of Society and Its Relation to Modern Ideas* (London: John Murray).

Mancini, S. (2010) 'Supreme Court of the United Kingdom – to be or not to be Jewish: the Supreme Court answers the question', *European Constitutional Law Review*, 6:3, 481–502.

March, J.G. and Olsen, J.P. (1989) *Rediscovering Institutions: The Organisational Basis of Politics* (New York, NY: The Free Press).

Martin, L.W. and Vanberg, G. (2008) 'A robust procedure for interpreting political text', *Political Analysis*, 16, 93–100.

Mayhew, D.R. (1991) *Divided We Govern: Party Control, Lawmaking, and Investigations, 1946–1990* (New Haven, CT: Yale University Press).

Mayo, M. (2003) *Rethinking the Reasonable Person: An Egalitarian Reconstruction of the Objective Standard* (Oxford: Oxford University Press).

McCubbins, M.D., Noll, R.G. and Weingast, B.R. (1987) 'Administrative procedures as instruments of political control', *Journal of Law, Economics, and Organization*, 3:2, 243–77.

Melton, J., Elkins, Z., Ginsburg, T. and Leetaru, K. (2013) 'On the interpretability of law: lessons from the decoding of national constitutions', *British Journal of Political Science*, 43:2, 399–423.

Merryman, J.H. (1981) 'On the convergence (and divergence) of the civil law and the common law', *Stanford Journal of International Law*, 17:2, 357–88.

Mettler, S. (2011) *The Submerged State: How Invisible Government Policies Undermine American Democracy* (Chicago, IL: University of Chicago Press).

Mitchell, H. (2009) 'Reform of the immigration appeals system', Migration Watch UK, 13 August. Available at: https://www.migrationwatchuk.org/briefing-paper/159

Moretti, F. (2013) *Distant Reading* (London: Verso).

Morris, C.W. (1946) *Signs, Language, and Behaviour* (New York, NY: G. Braziller).

Morris, N. (2008) 'More than 3,600 new offences under Labour'. Available at: http://www.independent.co.uk/news/uk/home-news/more-than-3600-new-offences-under-labour-918053.html (accessed 28 April 2015).

Nicol, D. (2001) *EC Membership and the Judicialization of British Politics* (Oxford: Oxford University Press).

North, D. and Weingast, B. (1989) 'Constitutions and commitment: the evolution of institutions governing public choice in seventeenth-century England', *Journal of Economic History*, 49:4, 803–32.

O'Barr, J.F. and O'Barr, W.M. (1976) *Language and Politics* (The Hague: Mouton).

Ormerod, D.C. and Laird, K. (2015) *Smith and Hogan's Criminal Law* (Oxford: Oxford University Press).

Pang, B. and Lee, L. (2008) 'Opinion mining and sentiment analysis', *Foundations and Trends® in Information Retrieval*, 2:1, 1–135.

Peirce, C.S. (1992) 'How to make our ideas clear', in Houser, N. and Kloesel, C. (eds) *The Essential Peirce, Vol 1* (Bloomington, IN: Indiana University Press), pp 124–41.

Persson, T. and Tabellini, G. (2003) *The Economic Effects of Constitutions* (Cambridge, MA: MIT Press).

Phillipson, G. (2011) 'Constitutional principles and the Human Rights Act: moving beyond one-way street approaches', UK Constitutional Law Group Blog. Available at: http://ukconstitutionallaw.org/blog/page/4/ (accessed 30 October 2011).

Pierson, P. and Skocpol, T. (2002) 'Historical institutionalism in contemporary political science', in Katznelson, I. and Milner, H.V. (eds) *Political Science: State of the Discipline* (New York, NY: W.W. Norton), pp 693–721.

Pimlott, B., Kavanagh, D. and Morris, P. (1989) 'Is the "postwar consensus" a myth?', *Contemporary Record*, 2:6, 12–15.

Poguntke, T. and Webb, P. (2005) *The Presidentialization of Politics: A Comparative Study of Modern Democracies* (Oxford: Oxford University Press).

Pollitt, C. and Bouckaert, G. (2004) *Public Management Reform: A Comparative Analysis* (2nd edn) (Oxford: Oxford University Press).

Poscher, R. (2012) 'Ambiguity and vagueness in legal interpretation', in Solan, L.M. and Tiersma, P.M. (eds) *The Oxford Handbook of Language and Law* (Oxford: Oxford University Press).

Posner, R.A. (2003) *How Judges Think* (London: Harvard University Press).

Post, R.C. (1994) 'Reconceptualizing vagueness: legal rules and social orders', *California Law Review*, 82:3, 491–508.

Rainey, H.G. and Jung, C.S. (2015) 'A conceptual framework for analysis of goal ambiguity in public organizations', *Journal of Public Administration Research and Theory*, 75:1, 71–99.

Rhodes, R.A.W. (1994) 'The hollowing out of the state: the changing nature of the public service in Britain', *Political Quarterly*, 65:2, 138–51.

Rhodes, R.A.W. (1996) 'The new governance: governing without government', *Political Studies*, 44:4, 652–67.

Rhodes, R.A.W. (1997) *Understanding Governance: Policy Networks, Governance, Reflexivity and Accountability* (Buckingham: Open University Press).

Rhodes, R.A.W. and Dunleavy, P. (1995) *Prime Minister, Cabinet and Core Executive* (Basingstoke: St Martin's Press).

Richards, D. (2008) *New Labour and the Civil Service* (London: Palgrave Macmillan).

Robertson, D. (1998) *Judicial Discretion in the House of Lords* (Oxford: Clarendon Press).

Robertson, D. (2010) *The Judge as Political Theorist: Contemporary Constitutional Review* (Princeton, NJ: Princeton University Press).

Roche, M. (2004) 'Complicated problems, complicated solutions? Homelessness and joined-up policy responses', *Social Policy and Administration*, 38:7, 758–74.

Rodrik, D. (2000) 'How far will international economic integration go?', *Journal of Economic Perspectives*, 14:1, 177–86.

Roosevelt, K. (2006) *The Myth of Judicial Activism: Making Sense of Supreme Court Decisions* (New Haven, CT: Yale University Press).

Schiek, D. and Chege, V. (2009) *European Union Non-Discrimination Law: Comparative Perspectives on Multidimensional Equality Law* (London: Routledge).

Schmidt, V.A. (2008) 'Discursive institutionalism: the explanatory power of ideas and discourse', *The Annual Review of Political Science*, 11, 303–26.

Schmidt, V.A. (2010) 'Taking ideas and discourse seriously: explaining change through discursive institutionalism as the fourth "new institutionalism"', *European Political Science Review*, 2, 1–25.

Schotter, A. (1981) *The Economic Theory of Social Institutions* (Cambridge: Cambridge University Press).

Schubert, G. (1965) *The Judicial Mind* (Evanston, IL: Northwestern University Press).

Segal, J.A. and Spaeth, H.J. (2002) *The Supreme Court and the Attitudinal Model Revisited* (Cambridge: Cambridge University Press).

Shepsle, K.A. and Bonchek, M.S. (1997) *Analyzing Politics: Rationality, Behavior, and Institutions* (London: W.W. Norton).

Sisk, G.C., Heise, M. and Morriss, A.P. (1998) 'Charting the influences on the judicial mind: an empirical study of judicial reasoning', *New York University Law Review*, 73:5, 1377–500.

Slaughter, M.J. (2001) 'Trade liberalization and per capita income convergence: a difference-in-differences analysis', *Journal of International Economics*, 55:1, 203–28.

Sprat, T. (1722 [1667]) *The History of the Royal Society of London* (3rd edn) (London: Samuel Chapman).

Staton, J.K. and Vanberg, G. (2008) 'The value of vagueness: delegation, defiance and judicial opinions', *American Journal of Political Science*, 52:3, 504–19.

Stolcke, V. (1995) 'New rhetorics of exclusion in Europe', *Current Anthropology*, 36:1, 1–24.

Stone Sweet, A. (2000) *Governing with Judges: Constitutional Politics in Europe* (Oxford: Oxford University Press).

Strøm, K. (1990) 'A behavioral theory of competitive political parties', *American Journal of Political Science*, 34:2, 565–98.

Strøm, K., Müller, W.C. and Bergman, T. (2003) *Delegation and Accountability in Parliamentary Democracies* (Oxford: Oxford University Press).

Tate, C.N. and Vallinder, T. (1995) *The Global Expansion of Judicial Power* (New York, NY: New York University Press).

Taylor, G.D.S. (1976) 'Judicial review of improper purposes and irrelevant considerations', *The Cambridge Law Journal*, 35:2, 272–91.

Thring, H. (1902) *Practical Legislation: The Composition of Acts of Parliament and Business Documents* (London: John Murray).

Tsebelis, G. (2002) *Veto Players: How Political Institutions Work* (Princeton, NJ: Princeton University Press).

Tsebelis, G. and Nardi, D.J. (2016) 'A long constitution is a (positively) bad constitution: evidence from OECD countries', *British Journal of Political Science*, 46:2, 457–78.

Vallance, C. (2010) 'Wikileaks and Iceland MPs propose "journalism haven"', *BBC News*, 12 February. Available at: http://news.bbc.co.uk/1/hi/technology/8504972.stm (accessed 19 July 2016).

Van Gog, R. and Van Engers, T.M. (2001) 'Modelling legislation using natural language processing', paper presented at the IEEE International Conference on Systems, Man, and Cybernetics.

Voigt, S. (2009) 'Explaining constitutional garrulity', *International Review of Law and Economics*, 29:4, 290–303.

Wade, H.W.R. (1955) 'The basis of legal sovereignty', *The Cambridge Law Journal*, 13:2, 172–97.

Wade, H.W.R. (1969) 'Constitutional and administrative aspects of the Anisminic case', *Law Quarterly Review*, 85, 198–212.

Webster, T.L. (1917) *A Treatise on the Law, Privileges, Proceedings and Usage of Parliament* (12th edn) (London: Butterworth).

Whitefield, S. (2006) 'Mind the representation gap: explaining differences in public views of representation in postcommunist democracies', *Comparative Political Studies*, 39:6, 733–58.

Wickham-Jones, M. (1998) *Economic Strategy and the Labour Party: Politics and Policy- Making, 1970–1983* (Basingstoke: Macmillan).

Widner, M. (2016) 'Text-mining the Middle Ages'. Available at: https://people.stanford.edu/widner/content/text-mining-middle-ages (accessed 24 April 2017).

Williams, M. (2016) 'Indeterminate sovereignty and the rule of law', *British Politics*, 11:1, 26–48.

Williams, M. (2017a) 'Legislative language and judicial politics: the effects of changing parliamentary language on UK immigration disputes', *British Journal of Politics and International Relations*, 19:3, 592–608.

Williams, M. (2017b) 'The grammar of politics: a brief history of legislative language in Britain', *Political Quarterly*, 88:2, 248–57.

Woodhouse, J. and Dempsey, N. (2016) 'Briefing paper: domestic violence in England and Wales'. Available at: www.parliament.uk/briefing-papers/sn06337.pdf (accessed 9 March 2016).

Woolf, H. (1995) 'Droit public – English style', *Public Law*, 72, 56–71.

Woolf, H., Jowell, J. and Le Sueur, A. (2007) *De Smith's Judicial Review* (6th edn) (London: Sweet and Maxwell).

Index

Note: Page numbers followed by an n indicate footnotes.

S

T

U

W

Y